ptics Digest

Optics Digest

by

Clair Rees

with contributions by
John Barsness
Craig Boddington
Mark Mazour
Bill McRae

SAFARI PRESS INC.

Rees, Clair

First edition

Safari Press Inc.

2005, Long Beach, California

ISBN 1-57157-317-8

Library of Congress Catalog Card Number: 2004094421

10 9 8 7 6 5 4 3 2 1

Readers wishing to receive the Safari Press catalog, featuring many fine books on big-game hunting, wingshooting, and sporting firearms, should write to Safari Press Inc., P.O. Box 3095, Long Beach, CA 90803, USA. Tel: (714) 894-9080 or visit our Web site at www.safaripress.com.

This book is dedicated to my wife, Dixie, with thanks for her patience, and to my sons, Richard, James, and John, who made writing necessary.

Table of Contents

Chapter 1

Introduction

I have been a serious hunter for more than forty years, but I still have a lot to learn about my favorite sport. One lesson I *have* learned in a lifetime afield is how important optics are to success. As a dirt-poor teenager, I could usually pony up just enough cash to gas up the car and buy a few groceries for camp. My deer rifle was a bare-bones economy model. Because I couldn't afford them, I never even considered a scope sight or binocular.

In those days I wanted venison. Any dry doe would do. Deer were plentiful in my neck of the woods, and I often managed to score before the season ended. In time, my preference shifted to bucks—the bigger and "hornier" the better. Eventually, I was able to buy a new rifle and a 4X scope, and then, a few years later, I purchased my first binocular. The more I hunted, the greater I came to appreciate the invaluable aid a really good binocular with clear, sharp optics provides. The same holds true for scope sights, and today nearly all my rifles wear a good scope sight.

People are surprised when I tell them that if I had to choose between carrying a binocular or a riflescope, the binocular would win almost every time. My eyes are getting older, but I can still shoot pretty well with aperture sights out to two hundred

This buck was discovered as Rees examined a brush-covered hillside with his 10X Kahles binocular, then shot with the help of a 2–7X variable Kahles scope. Savvy hunters always use both kinds of optics.

Good binoculars let you locate distant game before it sees you.

Binoculars—never riflescopes—are used to glass for game. The scope comes into play only when it's time to shoot.

fifty or maybe even three hundred yards. Except under exceptional circumstances, those distances are about as far as I care to shoot, even when my rifle wears a high-powered scope.

However, I have *always* had trouble spotting game in the distance without a binocular. This is due less to fading eyesight than to the fact that *no* human hunter, regardless of age, can see as well as many animals can. Pronghorn supposedly have vision equivalent to what you see through a good 8X binocular. For sure, they can see you coming from a l-o-n-g way off. The eyesight of some other prey species is nearly as acute. Because their lives depend on it, these animals are *always* alert for movement. If you don't use a binocular to spot them from cover *before* they see you moving along a hillside, you will have little chance of a successful stalk.

In addition to finding animals at long ranges that you would likely miss with your naked eye, a good 7X, 8X, or 10X binocular lets you see into deep shadows that can hold hidden game. This characteristic of a binocular affords the hunter a huge advantage. Quality lenses bring game into focus, giving you a brighter, sharper image than you would otherwise see. This is particularly true in the early morning or evening when the light is dim.

Only misguided hunters try to use their riflescopes to glass for game. In the first place, it's dangerous to point your scoped rifle at anything you don't intend to shoot. This emphatically includes other hunters sitting on a distant hillside. If you think rifles *do not* accidentally fire, you haven't been shooting very long. I can count a half dozen times that a firearm I was holding discharged before I intended it to. Thankfully, my father long ago drilled the Ten Commandments of Gun Safety into me. I always keep the muzzle pointed in a safe direction until I am ready to shoot.

An even better reason to *never* use your scope in place of a binocular is that riflescopes are lousy choices for the job. A binocular lets you see with both eyes, providing three-dimensional viewing. Using both eyes greatly reduces eyestrain and fatigue so you can spend more time *seriously*

Brown bear hunters in Alaska demand top-quality, high-resolution binoculars like this 7X50 Swarovski.

looking for game. I stress the word *seriously* because very few hunters actually find game by looking through a riflescope. They usually spot the animal with their naked eye, then throw their rifle up for a closer look. Invariably, the animal will have seen you first—and will be eyeing you in return as it plans its escape route. Use a binocular properly, and you are much more likely to see game before it sees you.

What all this boils down to is: Riflescopes are designed for *aiming*, which means they allow you to see the target clearly and place your shot as precisely as possible. Binoculars, on the other hand, are specifically designed for extended long-range *viewing*, which means they allow you to *look* for game. A good binocular (and I stress *good)* lets you spend twenty or thirty minutes at a stretch with your eyes glued to the eyepieces—*without* straining the muscles in your eye or arm or without giving you a pounding headache. Quality binoculars also deliver a much brighter, sharper image than riflescopes can.

Binoculars are not exclusively long-range tools. They also come in handy for hunting in brushy draws or dense timber. Before passing up thick cover, I slowly pick it apart with my binocular. I have spotted legs, parts of antlers, and twitching ears that I would never have seen without the use of magnifying optics. I have carefully searched for game at distances of just fifteen or twenty yards. A quality binocular is not a luxury—it is a vital hunting tool.

If you are interested in bringing a braggin' trophy home, you need a spotting scope, too. You hunt for game with a binocular, but there is no substitute for a spotting scope when it comes to evaluating antlers from a quarter mile or more away. A binocular will help find the game, but a spotting scope will give you a much closer look at the animal. This saves time and energy you might otherwise waste stalking something you don't really want to shoot. A spotting scope will also save unnecessary steps at the rifle range by allowing you to see where your bullet hit the paper target.

As I have already mentioned, I have not always enjoyed the benefit of quality optical gear. The first time I hunted deer, I was barely old enough to buy a Utah hunting license, a purchase that used up most of my hunting budget. I didn't own a rifle, let alone a scope sight or binocular. I went hunting that year only because my favorite uncle took me under his wing and loaned me a battered Arisaka rifle he had liberated during World War II.

I remember that my uncle and I camped high on a sagebrush-covered hillside. It was still dark the next morning when he guided me to a point overlooking a well-used deer trail. "Lie there," he said as he swung the rifle's built-in monopod down and locked it in place. "The deer should be moving soon. If one comes up that trail, wait until it's right below you before you shoot. Remember to stay calm, and aim just behind the shoulder."

A half hour later five does appeared, walking single-file along the trail. When the deer were forty yards away, I placed the barleycorn front sight behind the biggest animal's shoulder and remembered to *s-q-u-e-e-z-e,* not pull the trigger. The rifle barked, belched an orange flame, and the doe went down. I had killed my first deer over open sights, and they had done their job well.

Later, I saved enough money to buy a 1903-A3 Springfield and add a mail-order stock from Herter's. Adjustable aperture sights were a big improvement over the crude military sights on the Arisaka. I hunted with the Springfield for a single deer season, and the following year I purchased my first, brand-new, store-bought hunting rifle. I went all out and mounted a 4X Weaver scope on the .308 Savage 110. I thought I was about as well equipped as a deer hunter could hope to be.

My hunting style was simple and straightforward. I seldom bothered scouting an area in advance. Instead, I would drive to a wooded hillside and park my car. After hiking a hundred yards or so, I would begin looking around for deer. Not surprisingly, these tactics seldom paid off. On the other hand, however, deer were more plentiful then, so I sometimes got lucky.

After taking several mule deer with that rifle and scope, I went hunting with a friend who had a binocular and knew how to use it. Instead of walking through the woods, alert for the flash of a fleeing deer, he called a halt every few minutes to sit and painstakingly scan ahead. I was anxious to get on with our hunting, but the binocular soon revealed game I would have never seen with my eyes alone.

When he finally spotted a nice four-point buck hidden in distant shadows, he used the binocular to identify terrain that would hide us as we stalked. To make a long story short, the half-hour stalk was successful, and I shot the buck.

As soon as I returned home, I began shopping for a hunting binocular of my own. I finally settled on Bushnell's 6X26 Custom Compact—a neat, little porro-prism binocular that weighed only twelve ounces and tucked handily away inside my shirt pocket. I still had not figured out how important a full-size binocular could be, so I avoided having extra weight hanging from my neck.

The little Custom Compact had excellent optics, and I carried it on many hunts. It found deer I would not have seen without the help of the binocular's 6X lenses. It often proved its worth as I still-hunted thick stands of cedar and aspen, and it came in equally handy for examining hillsides five hundred or six hundred yards away. After doing without a binocular for so many years, I found the Custom Compact made a big difference in my hunting success.

I was so pleased with the lightweight handiness of that shirt-pocket-size binocular that it took me awhile to admit it wasn't suitable for some hunting conditions. I was forced to face this fact during a trip to Alaska. We were out hunting for brown bear, and my guide spotted one across Gravina Bay, but

Nothing beats a spotting scope for getting a detailed look at distant game.

These British Columbia guides use binoculars to prospect for game during lunch.

the distance and dim light overpowered my 6X26 Bushnell. When I looked through my guide's 10X42 binocular, however, I could clearly see the bruin.

A few weeks later, I broke down and bought a fine Zeiss 10X40 roof-prism binocular. The 6X26 Bushnell was relegated to hunting upland game and waterfowl. While the 6X model has since been discontinued, I continue to tuck a 7X26 Custom Compact in my shirt pocket whenever I go on a hike, backpack, or hunt small game. Anytime I spend a few hours outdoors, I feel naked without a binocular.

I didn't own a spotting scope until another guide used one atop British Columbia's Skeena range to locate a double-shovel mountain caribou. The bull was napping in the snow nearly two miles away. I had examined the same spot through my binocular, but it took the spotting scope's 25X lens to detect the twin antlers of the bull jutting skyward.

During that same hunt, the spotting scope found a rutting bull moose on the far bank of Lake Kluyaz.

It would have been impossible to see the animal with binoculars. The bull was so far away that it took a half hour to motorboat across the lake, but the guide soon grunted the animal to within easy shooting range.

Finally convinced of how useful a spotting scope could be, I bought one when I returned home. After regularly using a spotting scope for the past few decades, I cannot imagine how I ever got along without one. A spotting scope is bulkier than a binocular, which means that you will need to carry it in a backpack while hanging a binocular from your neck. It is well worth the effort to be able to locate and examine game beyond the reach of an 8- or 10-power binocular.

Back in the Jurassic Period of hunting (the 1940s and 1950s), only a handful of binoculars and riflescopes was offered by relatively few manufacturers. Most people who mounted a scope on their rifles chose a fixed-power 2.5X or 4X model.

Still in their infancy, variable-magnification scopes were widely mistrusted. The number of spotting scopes available was even more limited. Hunting optics simply did not enjoy the widespread use and acceptance they do today.

How times have changed! Today's outdoorsman has a dizzying selection of riflescopes to choose from, along with a similarly dazzling array of binoculars. Spotting scope numbers have also multiplied.

Today hunters no longer ask, "*Should* I buy a riflescope or binocular," but instead they say, "*Which* scope or binocular should I choose?" With the huge number of models now available, it is easy to get confused. How much magnification do you need in a hunting scope? Should you buy a scope with fixed-power or variable power? How can you test optical quality before you leave the store? Should you select a 7X, 8X, or 10X binocular? Should you go for a porro prism or roof prism? Do you need a full-size model with large objective lenses, or are you better off with a midsize or compact binocular that will be easier to carry? How much should you expect to pay for decent optical quality and dependable service? This book answers all your questions.

You will find a listing of nearly every rifle, pistol, and shotgun scope on the market, along with virtually every binocular and spotting scope now available. In true digest form, this book puts comparative information, including magnification, objective lens diameter, field of view, exit pupil size, weight, and price, at your fingertips.

Both riflescope and binoculars are vital tools for deer hunters.

I should point out this digest does NOT include models with a retail list price of less than $100. Some cut-rate retailers offer bargain-basement optics for $39, $49, or $59 to tempt budget-minded hunters. While some good low-priced values are available, my experience has been that most binoculars, riflescopes, or spotting scopes with a price tag under $100 aren't worth carrying afield. Many are outright junk. Others may seem OK at first, but they quickly fall apart when subjected to serious use. Attempting to include all the "el-cheapo" optics that manufacturers offer would be a waste of space.

Red-dot sights and laser rangefinders are also covered here. Red-dot sights—along with Bushnell's Holosight—are very useful optical aids in aiming handguns, shotguns, and rifles. Laser rangefinders have become increasingly popular and affordable, allowing hunters to measure distance quickly and with uncanny accuracy. Today's laser rangefinders are incorporated into monoculars and binoculars with magnifying optics, so they qualify for treatment here.

In addition to providing data to help you decide which model to buy, this book also tells you what it takes to produce top-quality optics that deliver the best performance while out hunting. It discusses the importance of coated lenses and helps you

Scopes with large objective lenses make for bright viewing, but add bulk and heft. They must also be mounted higher above the bore.

understand what "coated," "multi coated," and "p-coated" really means. You will learn how to evaluate optical brightness, clarity, manufacturing quality, and other important factors, and you will learn how to compare riflescopes, binoculars, or spotting scopes before leaving the store.

While scope sights, binoculars, and spotting scopes are different in design, certain useful terms apply to all three, so a brief discussion of the terms is relevant to understanding the text. The objective lens is the large lens at the front of the instrument. All other things being equal (lens quality, coating, internal construction), the larger the objective lens, the brighter the picture. However, choosing a scope or binocular with a large objective lens is a two-edged sword. While a large objective offers a real optical advantage, it adds unwelcome weight. That is why American hunters seldom pack the big, bulky 8X56 binoculars that Germans are so fond of. When I hunted in Germany, I learned why hunters there insist on binoculars and riflescopes sporting 56mm objectives.

European sportsmen often hunt well into the night, long after most American hunters have eaten dinner and headed for the sleeping bag. Europeans look for game in nearly pitch-black conditions, so they need all the optical help they can get. Americans do not—and legally cannot—hunt after dark; consequently, American hunters, logically, prefer scopes and binoculars with considerably less heft.

If you want the bright viewing picture a large objective lens on your riflescope provides, you will

Rees's first binocular (left) was a 6X26mm Bausch & Lomb Custom compact (later replaced by a 7X26mm model). While shirt-pocket binoculars are light, handy, and compact, they can't give the kind of performance a full-size binocular like this 10X50mm Swarovski (right) delivers.

run into other problems. The larger the front lens, the higher you will need to mount the scope to prevent the lens housing from impinging on the barrel. Tall-mounted scopes are more vulnerable to damage and require you to raise your head to see through them.

Exit pupil is another useful optical term. Exit pupil size determines the amount of light available to your eye when you look through a scope sight, binocular, or spotting scope. Exit pupil size can be calculated by dividing the diameter of the objective lens (measured in millimeters) by the instrument's magnification. Thus, an 8X32 binocular has an exit pupil 4mm in diameter. You can physically measure the exit pupil by pointing the instrument's objective lens toward a source of light, then measuring the small dot of light visible in the rear eyepiece with a metric ruler or caliper.

The larger the exit pupil, the more light your eye can see . . . up to a point. For normal daylight viewing, anything much larger than a 4mm exit pupil is superfluous. In full daylight, the pupil in your eye automatically contracts to approximately that 4mm size. As night falls, the pupil in your eye expands to a maximum of 7mm. That means 7mm is the largest exit pupil diameter your eye can accommodate. For low-light viewing, the 8X56 binocular mentioned earlier—and the 7mm exit pupil it offers—is the absolute optimum.

In his book, *Optics for the Hunter* (available from Safari Press), my friend John Barsness notes that as we become older, the maximum size of our pupils gradually shrinks. Once we enter our forties, a 6mm pupil is the largest our eyes can muster. At age sixty or so, this is further reduced to around 4mm. That makes large objective lenses and 7mm exit pupils less useful by the time we begin cashing Social Security checks.

Yet another useful measurement to keep in mind when choosing a binocular or riflescope is eye relief. For some reason, in the United States eye relief is typically expressed in inches when discussing rifle and handgun scopes, and millimeters when discussing binoculars. In essence, eye relief tells you

Rees sits with a tree bracing his back as he hunts for game with his binocular.

the distance your eye must be positioned behind the rear lens to see the maximum field of view.

If you wear prescription eyeglasses, you will need a binocular with reasonably long eye relief; otherwise, you will be able to see only a limited field of view. Eye relief has a different importance when it comes to riflescopes. If a scope sight has moderate to relatively short eye relief (let's say less than 3½ inches), mounting it on a hard-kicking rifle may prove hazardous to your health. Place your eye too close to the eyepiece, and I guarantee that when that .375 H&H or .416 Rigby fires, you will be left with a bloody (and painful) eyebrow. Scopes designed for handgun use have extended eye relief, allowing you to see through the reticle when the handgun is held at arms' length.

As I said at the start of this chapter, I am still learning about hunting and hunting optics. That said, I have close to a half century of hunting and viewing experience behind me, and I am happy to share what I have learned thus far.

Varmint hunter aims at distant prairie dog, while another hunter with a binocular serves as a spotter.

It is my hope that the *Optics Digest* will clear up some common misconceptions about hunting optics as well as being an aid to sportsmen (and sportswomen) in choosing the optical equipment that best suits their needs. This book shows how to compare competing products before making a purchase. You will learn how to predict in advance how a particular riflescope, binocular, or spotting scope is likely to perform afield . . . and how to be sure you are getting the best value for your money.

Chapter 2
The Basics: Optical Terms Explained
by Mark Mazour*

One of the handiest things to have in the outdoors is a quality binocular. Whether you are hiking, viewing wildlife, hunting, or attending a sporting event, a binocular can bring the outdoors a little closer to you. A binocular comes in handy to survey the terrain ahead, scout for and view wildlife without spooking them, or just enjoy a piece of nature up close that you may have otherwise missed. Selecting the right binocular is crucial to your enjoyment of the outdoors.

A binocular performs two basic functions for you. It increases the size of the image you are viewing, and it lets in more light than your eyes can, making images appear brighter in low-light conditions. When you first start looking for a binocular, it can be confusing comparing one model to another; therefore, let us start off this discussion by reviewing some of the basic properties of any binocular. Once you understand the terminology, it is easier to compare binocular brands and models.

Power, Field of View, and Exit Pupil

Power: The first main comparison used in binoculars is power. Binocular powers are expressed as two numbers such as 8X42. The first number, 8 in this example, is the magnification. It expresses the magnification as a factor compared to the naked

This photo shows the difference in size between a full-size binocular (left) and a compact one. While the compact binocular is much lighter to carry, it will not be as versatile as a full-size binocular.

*Mark Mazour wrote this and the following articles for the Cabela's Web site.

eye. So, 8 power magnifies the objects in view up to 8 times. An object would appear to be 8 times closer than it would with the naked eye. Therefore, a higher number has a greater magnification.

The second number, 42 in this example, is the diameter of the objective lens in millimeters. So a 42 designation means that the outer lens is 42mm in diameter. A larger number indicates a larger lens. Large lenses are more bulky, but they also let in more light, making your image clearer—especially in low-light conditions.

Field of View (1,000 yards): FOV, the second most used comparison with binoculars, stands for Field of View. The FOV is how wide an area (in feet) that you can view through your binocular at 1,000 yards. A higher number indicates a wider area, while a smaller number indicates a narrower area. The focal length of the objective lenses and the eyepiece design have the most impact on the actual FOV. The power of the binocular also has an inverse relationship with the FOV. As the magnification increases, a smaller FOV results.

Your choice of FOV depends on your intended use of the binocular. If you want to use a binocular in a wide-open area to scan for mule deer, a narrower field of view is not a big deal. However, if you are scanning a dense forest for hidden black-tailed deer at ranges at or around one hundred yards, you will want to select a model that has a wider field of view.

Exit Pupil: Exit pupil is related to the power of the binocular and the size of the objective lens. If you hold a binocular away from your face, you will see a small circle of bright light in the eyepiece. This is the exit pupil, the size of the beam of light that leaves the binocular. The exit-pupil diameter can easily be calculated (in millimeters) by dividing the diameter of the objective lens by the power. Therefore, an 8X42 binocular has an exit pupil of 5.25mm. On a bright day, the human pupil will vary from 2mm at noon to 4mm later in the day. When your eyes become adapted to dark conditions, the pupil will vary from around 5mm to a maximum of 7mm.

In daylight, having a binocular with a larger exit pupil will have little effect. The only difference you may notice is that you will be able to move a binocular with a larger exit pupil and still maintain the image, which is extremely helpful if you are in an unstable situation such as in a boat. The main difference occurs in low-light conditions. If you plan on using your binocular near dawn or dusk, which is a time when many hunters depend on their optics, it is recommended that you select an exit pupil greater than 4mm so as to fully take advantage of the amount of light your eyes can let in. An exit pupil larger than your pupil's diameter at the time does not result in a brighter image. Your eye can only handle so much.

You can see from the exit-pupil calculation that if you choose a higher-power binocular, you will also need to increase the size of the objective to maintain the same diameter of light leaving the binocular.

Prisms

As light passes through a binocular, the image becomes inverted. Erecting a prism within the binocular corrects this problem. The two main types you will find in binoculars are roof and porro prisms.

A **roof-prism** design reflects the light five times, and the resultant light comes out on the same line that it came in on. This straight-through design lends itself to slimmer dimensions, a more compact body, and, usually, lighter weight since the objective lens is in a direct line with the eyepiece. In general, roof prisms cost more because they are more difficult to manufacture.

A **porro prism** binocular requires a bit larger body than a roof prism because the light, reflected only four times, comes out on a different line from where it enters the objective lens. From a side view, the objective lens is usually a small distance above the eyepiece.

Many people debate about which design is better, and it actually depends more on the glass quality, manufacturing tolerances, and individual design as to which delivers the best image. Within

Most hunts consist of a great deal of glassing, so buy the best binocular you can afford!

porro prisms, two different types of glass are used: BK-7 and BAK-4.

BK-7 utilizes boro-silicate glass, while BAK-4 uses barium crown glass. The BAK-4 is a finer glass (higher density) that eliminates internal light scattering, therefore producing sharper images than the BK-7 glass. The finer glass in a BAK-4 prism comes at a higher price than ones using BK-7 prisms.

Optical Coatings

The largest limitation to the transmission of light in binoculars is reflected light. Anytime light strikes a glass surface, up to 5 percent of the light can be reflected back. In a binocular, light can pass through at least ten glass surfaces. If you do the math, you can see that it is easy to lose 50 percent of the ambient light. Moreover, much of this reflected light remains inside the binocular causing glare and poor contrast.

However, if a thin chemical film (a common one being magnesium fluoride) is used to coat the surface of the glass, much of the reflection can be eliminated. The coating reduces light loss and glare, increases light transmission, and results in brighter, clearer images. By coating a surface with multiple films, the effect of the coating is increased, at times limiting the amount of reflected light to between 0.25 percent and 0.5 percent per glass surface.

The coating must be applied correctly and uniformly, or the effect is lost. You may also notice that certain coatings exhibit different colors. Contrary to popular belief, this does not have a direct effect on the quality. Depending on the chemicals used and number of coatings, colors can vary from violet to blue, to even red, yellow, or green.

While any coating will usually increase the performance of a binocular, you need to understand several more definitions to make a full comparison or to justify the expense of a certain model.

Coated Optics: This generally means that one or more glass surfaces on at least one lens has received an anti-reflective optical coating.

Fully Coated: This generally means that all glass surfaces have been coated with an antireflective optical coating.

Multi-Coated: This generally means that one or more glass surfaces on at least one lens has received multiple antireflective optical coatings.

Fully Multi-Coated: This means that all glass surfaces have received multiple antireflective optical coatings.

Phase Shift Coating: A phase-shift coating is used on the roof prism of many newer models to correct for light loss on the horizontal image plane. As light waves come through a roof prism, up to 70 percent of the waves reflected off one roof surface will be one-half a wavelength shifted from those coming off the other roof surface.

OK, what does that mean? What can happen is that the phase difference between the horizontal and vertical light in a noncoated roof prism can cause a loss of contrast. A phase-shift coating in upper-end roof prism models corrects this, increasing contrast and image quality, putting them on equal playing fields with high-end porro prism models.

While phase-coated prisms will provide more contrast than a nonphase-coated pair, the small phase error on nonphase-coated roof prisms can only be detected if all other manufacturing tolerance errors are minimized. In other words, phase coating

a cheap pair of roof prism binoculars does little to improve the image.

Eye Relief

Eye relief is the comfortable distance that a binocular can be held from the eye while still allowing the viewer to see the entire image. A long eye relief allows for comfortable viewing and is a must for viewing with eyeglasses or sunglasses. Another option to look for is extendable eyepieces or fold-down rubber eyecups. These features will allow you to obtain a larger field of view while still keeping your glasses on.

Other Considerations: Size, Weight, Exterior Coating, and Waterproofing

The size and weight are also important considerations in choosing a binocular. While a high-power, full-size 10X42 binocular may give you some serious range and let in a lot of light, it can weigh almost two pounds or more. The weight will vary with the amount and type of glass used within the binocular, but, in general, as power and the size of the objective lens increases, the weight does as well.

Weight is a serious consideration because a big pair of binoculars can weigh heavily on your neck or in your pack. Most compact binoculars weigh under a pound and can fit in a shirt pocket, but they do not let in as much light and can be a bit more straining to the eye.

If you are active in the outdoors, two final characteristics to look for are **rubber coating and waterproofing**. Not only does the coating make your binoculars nonslip, even when wet, but it softens the blows of hard use and protects your binocular for the long haul. An added bonus for hunters is that rubber coating also makes your binocular quiet and nonreflective for that stealthy approach.

Another big concern, if you count on your binocular in all kinds of conditions, is waterproofing. Some less expensive models are not waterproof, and that will be a concern if you are using them in wet weather. Other models are fully sealed and charged with nitrogen gas to keep them fully waterproof . . . just in case you take an occasional dunking into the lake.

Cost

Cost is probably the largest differential factor in purchasing a binocular. This book attests to the fact that there are many models of and many price ranges for binoculars. There is no substitute for high-quality glass in providing high-quality images, and good glass and good coatings cost good money . . . period. More expensive models are usually constructed to tighter tolerances and have better glass with more coatings.

However, that does not mean that you must spend $900 to have a decent binocular. How much you spend should also depend on how often you use your binocular. Some professional guides, whose success depends on glassing for animals, spend much of their day looking through their binoculars, and they opt for the highest-quality optics to make their job easier and avoid eyestrain; consequently, it makes sense for them to pay more to get the very best. Before you buy, determine how often you will use your binocular and under what conditions and then do some comparison shopping to get exactly what you need. Remember, however, there is no substitute for quality optics.

Chapter 3
The Basics of Telescopic Sights
by Mark Mazour

Telescopic sights have been around since before the Civil War, but only in the years after World War II did manufacturers continue to make improvements to scopes that offered hunters reliable equipment—equipment that would soon become a standard on modern hunting rifles.

What Does a Scope Do for You?

One of the main uses of a riflescope is that it magnifies your target, giving you a clearer picture than you would get with the naked eye. This not only allows you to shoot more accurately at a greater distance, but it also increases safety since you can better see the target and what lies behind it.

A scope can also give you more hunting time since it allows you to hunt early and late in the day, which are two prime times for big game to be moving to and from their bedding areas. With iron sights, however, often there is not enough ambient light available to make an ethical shot either late in the day or early in the morning. Riflescopes accentuate available light and make it possible for you to shoot accurately in low-light conditions.

A riflescope also allows a higher level of precision than traditional iron sights do. At one hundred yards, an iron ramp sight will cover up to six inches of the target. Precise bullet placement is limited by the large amount of the target that is covered. Riflescopes, however, use various reticles

Butler Creek scope covers keep dust and rain off your lenses.

More and more scopes now show greater ranges in magnification. The one above is in the 4.5–14 range, with a 44-mm objective lens.

(commonly called cross hairs) that in fine target models only cover an eighth of an inch at one hundred yards. This qualifies as the ultimate in precision because it allows you to place a shot exactly where you want every time—even in the same hole as the previous one.

Finally, a riflescope allows you to take full advantage of the modern cartridges and rifles available today. New calibers and rifles shoot flatter, farther, and have more energy than turn-of-the-century models. With a correctly mounted and sighted-in riflescope and with a little practice, hunters can now make precise shots on game at longer distances then before thought possible.

The Numbers and What They Mean

When you first look at scopes, you will be amazed at the number of models available. Manufacturers typically use a series of numbers to identify each scope. In order for you to make a comparison, you need to know what these numbers mean. The following is a synopsis of the meaning of the numbers used to identify the various scopes.

Power: Commonly a riflescope will be expressed in a series of numbers such as 3.5–10X50 or 4X32. The first number(s), in this case 3.5-10 or 4, is the power. Power expresses the magnification as a factor compared to the naked eye. So in a **fixed power** scope, such as the 4X32, the object in view is magnified 4 times. An object would appear to be 4 times closer than it would with the naked eye. Therefore, the higher the number the higher the magnification. Most scopes sold today have **variable power**, such as the 3.5-10 mentioned above. This allows greater versatility, since in this case, the shooter can vary the magnification from 3.5 to up to 10, with infinite values in between.

The power that you select depends upon the kind of hunting you will be doing. If you are planning on hunting in close cover, you will want either a low power fixed scope such as a 4X or a variable that goes down to 3.5X or even lower. This will give you a wider field of view and allow you to focus on a target quickly in close cover. On the other hand, if long-range varmint or target shooting is your goal, you might want a scope that goes as high as 16X or even 20X. Magnification at these levels will allow you to see small prairie dogs or the 10-ring clearly at 400 yards. For all-round hunting, a range of 3.5–10 or 4–12 will allow some serious range variation, while still dialing down for close shots.

Objective: The second number listed for a scope, such as the 50 in a 3.5–10X50, is the diameter of the objective lens in millimeters. A 50 designation means that the outer lens is 50mm in diameter. The larger the number the larger the lens. Large lenses are more bulky, but they also offer a bit larger field of view. They also let in more light, which makes your image clearer, especially in low-light conditions.

The low-light performance is due to the maximum exit pupil offered by a larger objective. Exit pupil is the size of the beam of light that leaves the scope. The exit pupil can easily be calculated (in millimeters) by dividing the diameter of the objective lens by the power. Therefore, a 4X32 scope has an exit pupil of 8mm. On a bright day, the human pupil will vary from 2mm at noon to 4mm later in the day. When your eyes become adapted to dark conditions, such as predawn and after sunset, which is when big game move about, the pupil will vary from 5mm to a maximum of 7mm.

On a bright day, having a scope with a larger exit pupil will have little effect. The only difference you may notice is that you will be able to move the scope and still maintain the image. In low light, the exit pupil is the biggest factor in getting as much light as possible to your eye.

Adjustable Objective: On some scopes, the objective lenses are adjustable, which will have markings on them that allow you to adjust the focus for specific ranges. This enables you to focus at distances over 100 yards away and still adjust for a condition called parallax. Parallax, the condition of the reticle appearing to shift or move, occurs

when viewing distant targets. This can happen when the image in the scope is in one focal plane and the reticle is in another. Most scopes without adjustable objectives are factory set to compensate for parallax; these focus at an optimum distance of 100 or 150 yards. Parallax is usually only an issue at magnification over 10 power. When looking at a scope that will be used for distant targets in higher power, an adjustable objective is a good choice.

Reticle: The reticle is the aiming point within the scope. It is more commonly known as the "cross hairs" of the scope because of the standard arrangement of two thin wires that cross. Reticles, or cross hairs, are also available in different combinations that include pointed posts, dots, multiple dots, and bars. One of the more common reticles is a duplex or multiplex design where the main cross hairs are thicker for easier viewing (especially in low light), and as they near the center where they cross, the cross hairs become very fine, allowing for precise target placement. You will want to choose a reticle that best suits your style of shooting. For example, a heavy duplex reticle would be best for a shotgun scope used in heavy brush, where fine reticles would be difficult to see.

Eye Relief: Eye relief is the comfortable distance that a scope can be held from the eye while still allowing the shooter to see the entire image. It is literally the distance of your shooting eye to the eyepiece. It will usually be stated as a range, since in a variable power scope the eye relief will vary with the power. Lateral adjustment can be made while mounting the scope to give the individual shooter the optimum eye relief. On a rifle, the more generous the eye relief the better. This will allow you to acquire the target more quickly, which is a must for running shots. Three to four inches is a good number that will fit most hunters. On large, magnum rifles, you want a maximum of relief, so when the rifle recoils, the scope does not come back and hit you in the forehead.

When mounting a scope on a handgun, you will need a special pistol scope that has an eye relief of 12 to 24 inches. This will allow you to hold your handgun in a comfortable shooting stance and still see the full image through the scope.

FOV at 100 yards: FOV stands for field of view. The FOV is how wide an area (in feet) that you can view through your binocular at 100 yards. A higher number indicates a wider area, while a smaller number indicates a narrower area. The focal length of the objective lenses and the eyepiece design has the most impact on the actual FOV. The power of the scope has an inverse relationship with FOV. As the magnification increases, a smaller FOV results. If you are looking for a scope that will focus quickly on a target in close cover, your will need a wider field of view and, therefore, a smaller power.

Minute of Angle: Minute of Angle (MOA) is a term to designate variances on a target at 100 yards distant. Most commonly, it is used to describe the adjustment on a scope. If a scope's adjustments are listed at ¼" MOA, then for every click of the adjustment knob, the bullet's point of impact will move ¼" at 100 yards.

Windage: Windage is the term used for the horizontal adjustment of your scope.

Elevation: Elevation is the term used for the vertical adjustment of your scope.

Tube Diameter: The majority of the scopes on the market come with the main tube that has a one-inch diameter. Several European models and now a few others also come with a 30mm tube diameter. Contrary to popular belief, the larger tube does not allow more light to reach your eye. The exit pupil mentioned above controls this. However, a larger tube diameter adds strength and

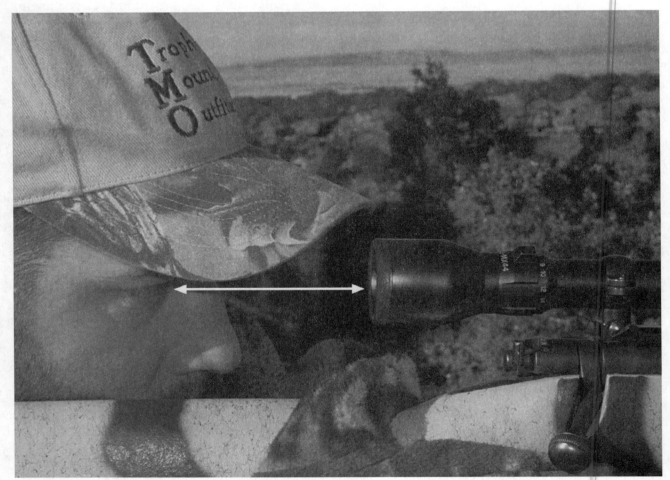

Eye relief is critical, especially when shooting heavier calibers.

Long shots are the moment when a perfect mount and riflescope pay off.

rigidity because of the greater cross-sectional area and larger rings and mounts. A larger tube diameter also increases the range of adjustment for both windage and elevation.

Optical Coatings: The largest limitation of light transmission in riflescopes is reflected light. Any time that light strikes a glass surface, up to 5 percent of the light can be reflected back. However, if a thin chemical film (commonly magnesium fluoride) is used to coat the surface of the glass, much of the reflection can be eliminated. The coating reduces the loss of light and glare, thus increasing light transmission that results in brighter, clearer images. By coating a surface with multiple films, the effect of the coating is increased, at times limiting the amount of reflected light to 0.25 percent to 0.5 percent per glass surface.

Airgun Scopes: The unique recoil pattern of spring-piston airguns requires the purchase of a special airgun scope. Unlike centerfire and rimfire rifles that recoil only in one direction, airguns recoil both rearward and forward. This double recoil action can damage scopes that are not designed to handle it.

Length and Weight: When carrying your rifle for a long time, every extra ounce can weigh you down. Larger objectives and variable power have their benefits, but they come with extra weight, and the extra ounces quickly add up for all these features. If you are looking to minimize the weight of a rifle that you will be carrying a lot, consider a compact, fixed-power scope with a medium-size objective. It will provide a large exit pupil with a bright image and weigh a lot less than a variable power scope.

Chapter 4

The Follies and Fallacies of Long-Range Shooting
by Bill McRae

Recently, while I was representing an optics manufacturer at a sportsman's show, a gentleman eyeballed the riflescope selection and asked, "Which scope would you recommend for shooting elk at a thousand yards?"

Trying to maintain my composure, I politely asked, "A thousand yards is more than half a mile. Why on earth would you want to shoot elk at such distances?"

"Because there's a ridge about that far from my back porch where bull elk routinely come out to feed, and I'd like to knock 'em off from there. I'll also need one of them rangefinder gizmos for figuring bullet drop."

I would like to believe that such thinking is rare, but, sadly, it is not. Later, another guy came by and bragged about how much fun he and his buddies had been having shooting mule deer at ranges in excess of seven hundred yards.

Where do people get such misguided ideas? There are many places to lay blame, but I will start at home with today's shooting and hunting

Many shooters erroneously believe that a rifle that shoots 1-inch groups from a benchrest at 100 yards will do likewise at any distance. Not so!

Though shooting-range conditions, replete with benchrests, don't exist in the field, improvised rests should be used whenever possible.

magazines, which occasionally publish articles condoning, if not actually encouraging, such ultra-long-range shooting. Adding tacit encouragement are the gun and ammunition manufacturers that keep trying to defy the law of gravity by producing ever flatter-shooting rifles and cartridges. And, not without blame are the optics companies with their increasingly powerful riflescopes, rangefinding reticles, and longer-range laser rangefinders. In fairness, it must be noted that all such products can, and usually do, serve the legitimate purpose of helping hunters make humane kills within reasonable shooting distances.

For starters, I will tell you what I consider to be reasonable shooting distances—based on my experience of having hunted in the wide-open spaces of Montana's prairies and mountains. It depends, of course, on the marksmanship skills of the individual shooter. Many people have a hard

time making clean kills at distances less than a hundred yards. But, even for experienced long-range shooters, it is very hard to justify shooting at big-game animals much beyond three hundred yards or, at the very most, four hundred yards.

That aside, the two questions that I want to address are: 1) Given today's best rifles and optics, what kind of accuracy do you have a right to expect at ranges from, say, five hundred to one thousand yards? 2) Given those accuracy limitations, as well as the small remaining energy of even the most powerful cartridges at extremely long ranges, can such shooting be ethically justified?

Rifle Accuracy

Many shooters erroneously believe that a rifle that shoots 1-inch groups at 100 yards should be capable of doing likewise at any distance. On the

Long-range shooting is contingent on open terrain, where, over a distance of 500 yards, the wind might be blowing in twenty different directions, including straight up and down.

contrary, mathematics tells us that a 1-inch group at 100 yards will have opened up to 5 inches at 500 yards and 10 inches at 1,000 yards. The error, I believe, stems from confusing groups measured in inches, which are linear measurements, with groups measured in minutes of angle (MOA), which are angular measurements. Adding to the confusion is the coincidence that 1 MOA (which is 1⁄60 of a degree) happens to subtend 1-inch (1.047 inches) at a distance of 100 yards, which is the only distance where they are synonymous. At distances closer than 100 yards, 1 MOA equals a fraction of an inch, such as ½ inch at 50 yards; whereas, at distances greater than 100 yards, 1 MOA equals multiple inches, such as 2 inches at 200 yards, 3 inches at 300 yards and so forth. For consistency's sake, hereafter in this article we will speak of group sizes and deviations for the point of aim in linear terms, i.e., either inches or feet at specific distances. For our ballistic machinations we have chosen the archetypical .300 Weatherby Magnum as loaded by Remington with their 180-grain Pointed Soft Point Core-Lokt bullets at a muzzle velocity of 3,120 fps and sighted-in at 250 yards. (See the accompanying ballistics table.)

Getting back to the accuracy that can be expected from modern hunting rifles, the average 100-yard group size is probably about 2 inches, which theoretically translates to 10 inches at 500 yards and 20 inches at 1,000 yards. Such theoretical groups are unlikely, however, because, in the real world where game is taken, a band of ballistic gremlins is continually conspiring to degrade your long-range shooting accuracy.

First off, those wondrous 1-inch groups and more typical 2-inch groups are usually fired from benchrests located at shooting ranges. Unfortunately, benchrests are seldom found in game country. Improvised rests, however, should be used whenever possible.

Ballistics Table

.300 Weatherby Magnum With 180-Grain Bullets* at 3,120 fps
(250-yard zero, 20-mph crosswind and 10-mph target speed)

Range:	0	100	200	300	400	500	600	700	800	900	1,000	yds
Path (LOS):	- 1.5	2.3	1.9	-3.5	-15.1	-33.9	-61.3	-100.8	-152.7	-223.0	-314.8	in
Velocity:	3,120	2,866	2,627	2,399	2,184	1,979	1,786	1,609	1,446	1,305	1,184	fps
Energy:	3,890	3,283	2,758	2,301	1,906	1,565	1,275	1,035	835	680	562	ft-lb
Time of Flt.:	0.00	0.10	0.21	0.33	0.46	0.60	0.76	0.94	1.14	1.36	1.60	sec
Drop (bore):	0.0	-1.9	-8.0	-19.2	-36.4	-61.0	-94.3	-139.3	-197.3	-273.4	-370.4	in
Target Lead:	0.0	1.5	3.1	4.8	6.8	8.9	11.2	13.8	16.7	19.9	23.4	ft
Wind Drift:	0.0	1.4	6.1	14.2	26.6	43.6	65.7	94.6	129.6	173.0	224.1	in

Remington Pointed Soft Point Core-Lokt® bullets with a ballistic coefficient of 0.383

Gravity: The Immutable Force

Gravity sucks, but, if it didn't, we would fall off the earth, which wouldn't matter because without gravity the universe would not exist. Gravity causes unsupported objects, including bullets, to fall toward the center of the earth. Remember the famous physics question: "If a bullet is dropped from the same height and at the same moment as an identical bullet is fired horizontally from a gun, which bullet will hit the ground first?" The answer is that both bullets will reach the ground at the same time because they will fall at the same rate. The horizontal velocity of the fired bullet has no effect on its vertical motion. (Nitpickers may argue with that, citing aerodynamic effects, but it is still fundamentally true.) In other words, a bullet's drop from the line of bore or departure (which is different from the line of sight) is a function of time. Bullets with greater velocities shoot flatter only because they travel farther in specified periods of time.

Does this mean that your trajectory will be helped by upping the velocity with an even-hotter magnum round? Yes, but not nearly as much as you might think. The spoiler here is the infamous law of diminishing returns, which in this case involves two adverse factors. The first is the lopsided deceleration of fast-moving objects due to air resistance: When you double the velocity of a bullet, you quadruple the air resistance. This explains why bullets that start faster shed their initial velocity faster. As the ballistics table shows, the 180-grain bullet lost 254 fps in 0.10 of a second while going the first 100 yards, but lost only 121 fps in 0.24 of a second while going from 900 to 1,000 yards.

The second factor is the acceleration of gravity, which in a vacuum causes freely falling objects to accelerate at a rate of "32 feet per second." In which case any object, regardless of its mass or shape, will have fallen 193 inches (16 feet) during the first second and 772 inches (64 feet) by the end of the second second. The results are only slightly less astounding for bullets falling in the earth's atmosphere, which explains why a 180-grain bullet is able to drop 370.4 inches (30.4 feet) in just 1.6 seconds. Interestingly, unlike deceleration due to air resistance, where the greatest velocity loss occurs during the first 100 yards of bullet travel, the situation is reversed regarding the affects of gravity. In this instance, a bullet drops a mere 1.9 inches in the first 100 yards but 97 inches while going from 900 to 1,000 yards. The point is that, regardless of their initial velocities, all bullets fall like proverbial rocks at distances beyond about 400 yards.

Remaining Energy

Kinetic energy, stated in foot pounds, is invariably included on ballistic tables, because it, more than any other factor, represents the bullets capacity to do lethal damage, i.e., kill game. How much energy does it take to ensure humane kills on, say, elk? Without wading into this swamp, where every would-be ballistician seems to have a different opinion, I will quote Jim Zumbo, who is America's most widely recognized expert on elk hunting. In his book *Hunt Elk,* he says, "Foot pounds (of energy) is the all-important factor, which must be sufficient out to the point where the elk is standing or running, not at the muzzle or in between. I'd be wary of any firearm that doesn't deliver at least 1,800 foot-pounds at the point of impact." If you disagree, blame Zumbo or, better yet, buy the book and read for yourself what he has to say.

Interestingly, the remaining energy of our .300 Weatherby Magnum 180-grain round reaches that point at roughly 430 yards. By 700 yards, its remaining energy is down to 1035 ft/lbs, which is only slightly better than a 170-grain .30-30 Winchester bullet at 200 yards. By 1,000 yards the energy is a piddling 562 ft/lbs, which is less than what a 110-grain .30 carbine bullet has at 100 yards.

Wind: The Shooter's Worst Nemesis

As if bullet drop and energy loss were not sufficiently troubling, take a gander at the bullet's deflection caused by a 20-mph crosswind, which I computed using Speer's PC Bullet ballistic software. If 20-mph winds seem unduly high, remember that seeing game at great distances necessitate vast open spaces such as the prairies, plains, and alpine terrain of western North America where the local folk are inclined to think of 20-mph winds as gentle breezes. As the ballistics table shows, from about 200 yards to slightly past 700 yards, the bullet deflection caused by the wind is even greater than that caused by the bullet drop. And, though it is eventually surpassed by bullet drop, the wind drift at 1,000 yards is still an astounding 224.1 inches (18.7 ft).

The wind's worst characteristic, in comparison to gravity, is its total unpredictability, particularly in rough terrain where its vectors (velocities and directions) change almost yard by yard. On the front ranges of the Rocky Mountains where I do much of my big-game and varmint shooting, a bullet might be buffeted from twenty different directions, including straight up and straight down, on its way to a five-hundred-yard target. In short, wind doping, which has become an art form for target shooters, is virtually impossible in game country.

Target Lead

The only basic advantage of long-range shooting is that the target is less apt to be disturbed and, therefore, more apt to be standing still . . . at least until after the first shot is fired. I would much rather shoot at a standing animal at 300 yards than at one running all-out at 50 yards. Here the target-lead ballistics (computed in feet (not inches) for a target speed of 10 mph) show that such a relatively slow-moving animal would require a lead of 3.1 feet at 200 yards; 8.9 feet at 500 yards; and 23.4 feet at 1,000 yards.

Other Uncertainties

Until now we have talked about ballistics tables as though they were sent down from heaven by Sir Isaac Newton and are, therefore, infallible. The problem is not that the math is wrong but that there are so many variables, any of which can greatly skew the results. These include:

Inconsistent velocities: Even with the best factory or hand-loaded ammo, fired from the same rifle under identical conditions, it is common to have extreme spreads in velocity ranging from 50 to 100 fps. Moreover, cartridges from the same lot are apt to show even greater velocity deviations when fired from different rifles.

Bullet irregularities and improper stabilization: Not all bullets of a prescribed weight, such as 180 grains, weigh exactly what they are supposed to, and not all bullets are perfectly balanced concentrically. Furthermore, bullets of different weights and length must have proper rates of rotation so as to remain stable in flight. The negative scenarios can range anywhere from minor changes in points of impact to bullets wobbling so badly that they begin tumbling end over end.

Atmospheric effects: As if air resistance and wind drift were not problematic enough, both are further complicated by changes in barometric pressure and altitude. Bullets hit lower at higher barometric pressures and higher at higher elevations.

Powder temperatures: *The NRA Firearms Fact Book* says, "For the IMR powders, each change in temperature of one degree F. changes the muzzle velocity by 1.7 fps in the same direction." Suppose, for example, that you sighted-in your rifle on a 90-degree August day, during which the cartridges were allowed to sit in direct sunlight for several minutes before being loaded into the rifle's already hot chamber. Then, in late November you find yourself shooting long-range at a bull elk when it is 20 below zero—in which case the bullet could be moving anywhere from 150 to 200 fps slower than when you sighted-in.

Barrel conditions: Bullets fly slower from shorter rifle barrels by between 20 and 30 fps per inch of barrel length. Squeaky-clean and well-oiled barrels shoot differently from barrels that have been

Elk, Dall sheep, grizzly bear, and pronghorn antelope habituate terrain where one is tempted to take exceptionally long shots.

fouled. And, hot barrels shoot differently than do cold barrels.

Considering all of the above, the responsibility for determining reasonable shooting distances still rests with the individual shooter, who before pulling the trigger should pause to consider that the future of sport hunting depends greatly on his or her ability to make humane kills. Nothing is more damaging to the hunter's image than the sight of an otherwise beautiful game animal struggling to survive with a leg shot off. Think about it!

Chapter 5

Shooting: Up, Down, and On the Level
by Bill McRae

Ballistics is a favorite topic around hunting camps. Take, for example, the erudite discussion that took place one evening in a camp located in the Cassiar Mountains of northern British Columbia. At the center of the dialogue was a hunter—known to be a good marksman—who had missed several shots at a mountain goat that was standing roughly 300 yards uphill on a 60-degree slope.

"I had a rock-solid rest and carefully squeezed off each shot, but I never touched a hair," the hunter moaned. "I thought the rifle was off, but, later when I checked it, it was dead-on."

Various explanations were offered, such as flinching, poor range estimation, or poor ammo, but the hunter would not buy them. Finally, someone suggested that the steep angle at which the shot was fired might have affected the bullet's trajectory. That led to the following debate.

"When shooting uphill you need to hold high, and when shooting downhill you need to hold low," one hunter said.

"It's the other way around," another argued. "When shooting uphill you must hold low, and when shooting downhill you must hold high."

Shots at Rocky Mountain goats, as with other alpine species, are apt to be taken at very steep angles.

"You're both wrong," a third hunter said, who was an avid gun nut. "When shooting, either uphill or downhill, you should hold low. But, since you don't know how low to hold, a good trick is to estimate the horizontal distance to an imaginary vertical line running through the target and then hold for that range. I know that's right because I read it in Jack O'Connor's *Complete Book of Rifles and Shotguns*." (For those too young to remember, the late Jack O'Connor was one of the greatest gunwriters of all time.)

"I'm no ballistics expert," said the guide, who had been listening quietly. "But, I've seen hundreds of animals killed in the mountains, and experience has taught me that when an animal is taken from above, the bullet hole tends to be high on its body. Whereas, if it is taken from below, the bullet hole tends to be low."

Who was right? They were all about half right, or half wrong, depending on how you look at it. We will get back to some of their ideas later, but first the facts: When fired either uphill or downhill, a bullet will have a flatter trajectory and, consequently, will strike higher than if fired at the same range on the level. Therefore, when shooting, either uphill or down, you must compensate by holding lower. The steeper the angle, the lower you must hold. Though insignificant differences exist, caused by air density and gravity, the effect is the same, either uphill or down.

To appreciate why the above is true, one must understand the laws of gravity and motion as they relate to bullet flight as well as having some understanding of ballistic terms. Hence, I offer the following.

1. Gravity begins to pull a bullet down the instant it leaves the muzzle of a firearm. The pull of gravity is always straight downward—that is, toward the center of the earth. Ballisticians call this effect of gravity on a bullet "drop" (see glossary for a definition of this and other terms) although a bullet with an upward direction of travel might not actually be dropping.

2. Drop is measured (in inches) straight downward from the bullet's "line of departure."

Note that this measurement is taken at a right angle only when the line of departure is level; otherwise, it is taken at an acute or obtuse angle.

3. Amount of drop is determined by the bullet's time of flight. Therefore, time of flight and velocity being equal, drop at a given distance is the same, regardless of the angle of fire.

To make sense of this, with regards to uphill and downhill shooting, we now turn our attention to the accompanying ballistic table, which was compiled for a 150gr Speer BT bullet at a velocity of 2,900 fps, using figures generated by Speer's PC Bullet Computer Program. Here we learn that at

When shooting either uphill or downhill you must hold lower than you otherwise would. The effect on trajectory is the same both uphill and downhill. Real trouble begins at angles greater than 20 degrees, and in some of these photos, the hunter is shooting at about a 50-degree angle, which will cause major trajectory problems.

Ballistics Table

TRAJECTORY 30-06 150gr Speer BT at 2,900 (fps)

Range (yds)	Muzzle	100	200	300	400	500	600	700
0° angle	-1.5	4.1	4.9	0.0	-11.7	-31.2	-60.8	-102.1
15° angle	-1.5	4.2	5.2	0.7	-10.3	-28.8	-57.2	-96.8
30° angle	-1.5	4.4	6.1	2.9	-6.2	-22.0	-46.6	-81.3
45° angle	-1.5	4.8	7.6	6.4	0.4	-11.1	-29.7	-56.7
60° angle	-1.5	5.2	9.5	11.0	9.0	3.2	-7.7	-24.5
75° angle	-1.5	5.7	11.7	16.3	19.0	19.8	17.9	13.0
Drop (in)	0.0	2.2	9.2	21.9	41.5	68.7	106.1	155.6
Time (sec)	0.0	0.11	0.22	0.35	0.49	0.64	0.80	0.99

This table, for a .30-06 150gr. Speer Boattail bullet at 2,900 fps, shows bullet path when the round is fired at various degrees either uphill or downhill. Also shown are drop from the line of sight and time of flight, both of which remain constant at all angles. The figures used were generated using the Speer/RCBS PC Bullet Program.

300 yards this bullet has a drop of 21.9 inches from the line of departure in .35 seconds. To reemphasize a point made earlier, note that both the drop and the time figures are the same for this round at this range, regardless of the angle of fire. This seems to contradict the trajectory or "path" figures, which change from 0.0 inches at a 0-degree angle to 16.3 inches high at a 75-degree angle. The difference is that, while drop is measured straight down from the line of departure (as explained above), the path figure is measured at a right angle from the "line of sight."

Line of sight is important, but let's forget it for now and do a simple experiment that will give us a better mental picture of how drop relates to a bullet's path. Get a fishing pole, pull out about 22 inches of line, and attach a small sinker (or other weight) to the end of line. The pole (which should be assumed to be perfectly straight, whether it is or not) represents a bullet's line of departure. The 22 inches of line represents the drop at 300 yards for the above cartridge, and the sinker represents a bullet.

Now, holding the pole by its handle, tip it slowly from a horizontal position to a vertical position.

Notice how that, though the length of the line (representing drop) remains the same, the sinker's right-angle distance from the pole decreases from 22 inches on the level until it touches the pole at 90 degrees. Next, tip the pole downward from level to vertical and see how a similar thing happens.

If in raising and lowering the pole, you noticed that the sinker got progressively closer to your hand as you tilted the pole upward and progressively farther from your hand as you tilted it downward, you discovered the only real difference between uphill and downhill shooting. Specifically, that gravity slows an upward-bound bullet a slight bit, shortening its travel distance in a given time of flight. Conversely, gravity accelerates a downward-bound bullet a slight bit, increasing its travel distance. Although the experiment might suggest otherwise, this difference in travel distance is totally insignificant at any reasonable shooting range, because, for the 22-inch drop represented by line's length to be realistic, the pole would need to be 300 yards long. The point is that nothing is either gained or lost in the few microseconds it takes a bullet to go 22 inches more or less.

GLOSSARY OF BALLISTIC TERMS

BALLISTICS: The science of projectiles in motion. Interior ballistics pertains to what happens inside the gun. Exterior ballistics deals with the motion of projectiles after they leave the gun.

BORE: The inside of a firearm's barrel.

DROP: The distance a bullet falls due to gravity, measured or calculated straight down from the bullet's line of departure.

LINE OF DEPARTURE: Also called bore line, this is a projection of the axis of the bore from which a bullet is fired. The bullet immediately falls away from this imaginary line.

LINE OF SIGHT: A straight line through the sight (or sights) of a firearm to the point of aim.

PATH: The bullet's vertical component of travel, measured from the line of sight. This is the same as the trajectory.

POINT OF AIM: The point with which a firearm's sight is aligned.

POINT OF IMPACT: The point at which a bullet strikes.

POINT-BLANK RANGE: The maximum range throughout which a bullet aimed directly at the center of a target will hit within the specified target radius before dropping below the target.

TIME OF FLIGHT: The elapsed time, in seconds, that it takes a bullet to cover a given distance. The longer the time of flight, the greater the drop.

TRAJECTORY: The path of the bullet in flight.

ZERO: The sight setting at which the point of impact and the point of aim coincide at a given range.

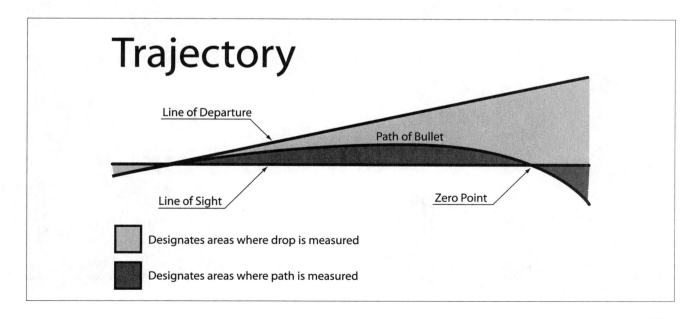

Shooting at a steep downhill angle can cause the bullet to strike high if the horizontal distance to the target isn't considered.

Lobbing the Bullet

If you were a cave man throwing a rock at a rabbit, you would not throw the rock directly at the animal. Instead, you would keep your eye on the rabbit while instinctively lobbing the rock upward to counteract the force of gravity. Similarly, when zeroing a firearm for a specific distance, we adjust the sight so that the barrel points slightly upward, thereby lobbing the bullet in an arching path toward the target.

The most efficient way to zero a firearm is to lob the bullet just enough above the line of sight to get the longest possible "point-blank range" with a center hold on a target of a given size. For deer-size game, an ideal target is deemed to measure about twelve inches vertically, which roughly corresponds to the depth of the animal's vital zone.

Turning again to the ballistics table, we find that our 150gr Speer BT bullet will stay within such a 12-inch zone out to a point-blank range of about 350 yards. Ergo, it will not rise or fall more than 6 inches. The spoiler is that this is true only when the angle of fire is less than 20 degrees. Whereas, at angles steeper than 20 degrees, the midrange path of the bullet rises more than 6 inches above the line of sight and thereafter we have a ballistic condition that can lead to overshooting of game, or worse, wounding.

It was, no doubt, such a midrange bullet rise that caused the aforementioned hunter to miss the mountain goat that was 300 yards above him on a 60-degree slope. Assuming his rifle had a trajectory similar to the one in the ballistics table (most modern big-game rifles do) the bullet would have been 11 inches (at a right angle) above the line of sight at 300 yards. If perchance, the angle was even steeper, say 75 degrees, it would have been 16.3 inches high. Obviously, he shot over!

Debunking a Myth

Now, we will consider the opinion of the well-read hunter, who used Jack O'Connor as his authority. I hate to say this, since O'Connor was my hero, but he was wrong regarding the notion that when shooting either uphill or down, one should hold for the horizontal range, instead of the greater slant range. It sounds good, but it simply does not work mathematically, which we will prove by once more turning to the ballistic table.

Suppose, for example, that you have spotted a deer at 700 yards on a 45-degree uphill slope. The horizontal distance to the spot directly below the deer (if you were smart enough to figure it in your head) would be 495 (approximately 500) yards. Using O'Connor's theory (which probably did not originate with him), you would use the path figure for 500 yards on the level, which is 31.2 inches, and thus you would hold 31.2 inches high. Would the bullet smack the deer right in the engine room? No, indeed! Instead, as the table shows, at 700 yards and with a 45-degree angle, the bullet would hit 56.7 inches low, which means that you would undershoot the deer by roughly two feet.

Incidentally, I do not claim to be smarter than O'Connor was. It is just that I have access to computerized ballistics programs, like Speer's PC Bullet and Oehler's Ballistic Explorer, which he lacked.

Vindicating the Guide

What about the guide's assertion that, in his experience, animals shot from above tended to be hit high in the body, while those shot from below tended to be hit low? It is hard to argue with experience, and I won't because the guide was right. We will give Jack O'Connor a chance to redeem himself by letting him explain this one in his own words.

"When shooting at an animal below you, you aim at the top of his body because that is what you see. If you miss, your shot is usually over. When shooting at an animal above you, you aim at the lower part of the body. In this case, hits are in the lower part of the body and misses generally are low."

Though this may seem to contradict what has been said thus far, it doesn't really because we are dealing with two totally different phenomena. The first involves how gravity affects bullets fired at various angles. The second is a simple matter of hitting the part of the animal that you are shooting at. And, as such, it has nothing to do with bullet drop. However, the two phenomena do tend to nullify each other in certain instances.

It should also be noted that, whatever the shooting angle, most big game is taken at ranges less than 100 yards, where bullet rise or fall is of little consequence. For example, the ballistics table tells us that, even at a 75-degree angle, the bullet hits only 1.6 inches higher at 100 yards than at the same distance on the level. In such a case, one would think that the bullet hit exactly where it should have.

What does it all mean? It means that shooting uphill and down is a very complicated matter that does not lend itself to easy answers, particularly in the field. The broad rule is that, when shooting at steep angles, particularly, at a distance much beyond 100 yards, you must hold considerably lower than you otherwise would. Better yet, if you have access to a personal computer with a ballistics program, you should create a trajectory table for the ammo you are using and you should carry a printout with you. (Such programs are relatively inexpensive and easy to install and use.) Finally, if it is practical, get out in the mountains and practice shooting at various angles and distances.

Chapter 6
Twilight Factor: Fact or Fallacy
by Bill McRae

With just minutes of legal hunting time left, I was about to climb down from my tree stand when the shadowy figure of a white-tailed deer caught my eye. Thinking the deer might be a buck, I looked through my 2–7X32mm riflescope, which was set on 2X. This slightly enlarged view allowed me to see that the deer had antlers of some sort. Then, after zooming to 7X, I could count the antler points on what amounted to a mediocre 4x4 rack. Taking him would have been a cinch, but, hoping for something larger, I let him go.

That incident lends credence to the popular mathematical formula called "twilight factor," which numerically predicts how well optical instruments (such as binoculars, scope sights, and spotting scopes) will perform in low light. The higher the twilight factor number, the more image detail will be visible under twilight conditions. To calculate twilight factor, you multiply the diameter of the instrument's objective lens in millimeters by its magnification and then extract the square root of the product. It is an easy thing to do with a pocket calculator having a square-root function key.

The search for a workable mathematical formula was begun by a German named A. Kuehl

When the sun is blood red and going down, the pertinent question is, "How long will your hunting optics keep on working?"

The author with his low-light-resolution target. Though the lines are easy to see in bright sunlight, when viewed at 100 yards under twilight conditions, at some point, the individual lines are no longer resolvable and the target appears uniformly gray.

who studied the subject from 1929 through 1949 and formulated a rather complicated theory for the performance of telescopes under different light levels. Then, in 1959, two Carl Zeiss employees, A. Koehler and R. Leinhos, published the currently used equation and coined the expressions "Twilight Factor" and "Twilight Performance."

By making magnification an important part of the equation, the twilight factor formula differs from the older and now sadly neglected relative brightness formula (which is the square of the diameter of the instrument's exit pupil). The underlying principle is that larger (i.e., magnified) objects are easier to see in low light, which is not surprising since the same is true in bright light. The low-light situation is different because, to be visible at all, the image of a viewed object must be spread over a much larger area of the eye's retina.

An example of how twilight factor works can be seen by comparing a 10X40 binocular having a twilight factor of 20 with an 8X40 glass having a twilight factor of 17.9. The 10X40 will show the same amount of image detail at 200 yards as the 8X40 will show at 179 yards. This is taken to mean that, under identical light conditions, a deer hunter using a 10X40 binocular will be able to count antler points at a proportionately greater distance than with an 8X40 glass. It also means that, in varying light conditions, a hunter using a 10x40 binocular will be able to count antler points at specific distances, such as 100 yards, when it is proportionately darker.

My field tests (see Tables 1 and 2) showed that the twilight factor formula works as predicted, provided instruments of equal optical quality are used. However, for the full story on low-light performance, we must also consider "relative brightness" as it relates to the human vision and "light transmission" as it relates to optical quality.

Relative Brightness

Relative brightness, also called the "geometrical luminosity factor," is the traditional guide for comparing image brightness between optical instruments of different magnifications and objective lens diameters. Specifically, it predicts image brightness based on the square (i.e., area) of the optical system's exit pupil. The exit pupil, for those unfamiliar with the term, is the small circle of light that can be seen at the eyepiece when an instrument is held at arm's length and pointed toward a bright background. This window, through which light passes when exiting the instrument, is not located within the eyepiece as it appears to be, but in space at the point where the eye must be held to see the full field of view of the instrument.

To calculate relative brightness, find the diameter of the exit pupil by dividing the diameter, in millimeters, of the objective lens by the magnification and then square the results. Accordingly, an 8X binocular with a 40mm object lenses has 5mm exit pupils ($40 \div 8 = 5$) and a relative brightness of 25 (5^2); whereas a 10X binocular with 40mm objectives has 4mm exit pupils ($40 \div 10 = 4$) and a relative brightness of 16 (4^2). Relative brightness numbers reflect the optical truth that larger exit pupils, all other factors being equal, can transmit more light than smaller exit pupils. This is analogous to more light passing through larger windows than through smaller windows.

The limiting factor regarding larger exit pupils is the diameter of the viewer's eye pupil under the existing light conditions. Eye pupil diameters vary in young adults from about 1mm in very bright light to slightly larger than 7mm in total darkness—with 4mm to 5mm being the maximum diameters for middle-age and older adults. Accordingly, whenever the exit pupil is larger than the eye pupil,

as often happens in bright light, the eye cannot receive all the light that is available.

This explains why an 8X20 binocular with its tiny 2.5mm exit pupils and an 8X56 glass with its huge 7mm exit pupils may seem equally bright at high noon. The 8X56 glass, however, will produce a much brighter image at dawn or dusk after eye pupils have become significantly larger than 2.5mm. Conversely, whenever the exit pupils are smaller than the eye pupils, as happens with compact binoculars in low light, the eyes are not getting all the available light that they could otherwise use. Accordingly, when choosing instruments for use in low light, there is no advantage to having an exit pupil larger than 7mm or a relative brightness greater than 49. Similarly, the exit pupils should not be smaller than 4mm nor the relative brightness less than 16.

Some argue that calculating relative brightness is an unnecessary step since you can learn all that you need to know by comparing exit-pupil diameters. That might apply to those who are mathematically astute, but it is not true for most of us. For example, most people do not realize that the 5mm exit pupils of an 8X40 binocular contain four times more light than the 2.5mm exit pupils of an 8X20 glass. Whereas, the respective relative brightness of 25 and 6.25 make that abundantly clear. Unfortunately, not all optical companies still include relative brightness on their spec sheets.

Conflicting Results

When taken individually, both twilight factor and relative brightness seem to make perfect sense. When compared side by side, however, the results are at best confusing. Sometimes, as with the binoculars in Table 1, the relative brightness numbers remain static while the twilight factors improve dramatically as a result of larger objective lenses and higher magnifications. Other times, as with the variable-power riflescopes in Table 2, we find that when magnifications change and the objective diameter remains constant the results are

LOW-LIGHT PERFORMANCE SPECIFICATIONS

Magnification Objective Dia.	Exit Pupil Diameter	Relative Brightness	Twilight Factor
7X21	3.0mm	9	12.1
7X35	5.0mm	25	15.7
7X42	6.0mm	36	17.1
7X50	7.1mm	51	18.7
8X20	2.5mm	6.3	12.6
8X30	3.8mm	14.1	15.5
8X32	4.0mm	16	16
8X40	5.0mm	25	17.9
8X42	5.3mm	27.6	18.3
8X50	6.3mm	39	20
8X56	7.0mm	49	21.2
9X63	7.0mm	49	23.8
10X25	2.5mm	6.3	15.8
10X40	4.0mm	16	20
10X42	4.2mm	17.6	20.5
10X50	5.0mm	25	22.4
10X56	5.6mm	31.4	23.7
10X70	7.0mm	49	26.5
12X25	2.1mm	4.3	17.3
12X50	4.2mm	17.4	24.5
12X56	4.7mm	21.7	26
15X60	4.0mm	16	30
20X60	3.0mm	9	34.6
15–45X60	4–1.3mm	16–1.8	30–52
20–60X80	4–1.3mm	16–1.8	40–69
20–60X85	4.3–1.4mm	18–2	41–71

diametrically opposite. Note that when zooming from 2.5X to 24X, the relative brightness decreased from a superfluously high 256 to a dismally low 2.8, while the twilight factor increased from a barely sufficient 10 to an unusably high 31. The ultimate absurdity is a 60X60mm spotting scope, which has a 1mm exit pupil, a relative brightness of 1, and a twilight factor of 60.

What accounts for such discrepancies? As previously shown, neither formula is reliable when carried to extremes. Beyond that, however, they deal with two very different facets of low-light performance. With relative brightness, you see better because the image is brighter as a result of the eye receiving more light, whereas, with twilight factor you see better primarily because the image is larger.

Light Transmission

A serious shortcoming of both relative brightness and twilight factor is that, being purely mathematical, neither addresses the important subject of "light transmission," which denotes the percentage of light that makes it all the way through the optical system relative to the amount that entered. Light that does not get through the system

Optics to be used in low light must have reasonably large objective (front) lenses, like the 50mm objectives of this 7X50 binocular shown here.

is either absorbed by the optical glass or is reflected off the various optical surfaces—which number anywhere from 12 to 16. Light transmission can vary from as little as 50 percent for instruments with uncoated optics to about 95 percent for those having high-quality, fully multicoated optics. Unfortunately, light transmission also has its limitation, because even the best optical systems cannot transmit all of the available light. Unfortunately, optics companies seldom disclose the light transmission percentages for their various products, especially if they are unfavorable.

Twilight Factor Tested

Having had misgivings about the twilight factor formula, I devised a means whereby it could be tested under field conditions with the criterion being the ability to count the antler points on a buck deer at various low-light levels. However, since the local deer would not stand still long enough to complete the test, I designed a 10-inch circular target covered transversely with alternate half-inch, black-and-white lines. The target was then placed in woodland shade and viewed at a distance of 100 yards, where each set of lines (one black and one white) subtended one minute of angle. The purpose of the tests, which were conducted in the evening, was to determine the number of minutes after sunset that the lines could be distinguished as separate entities. After that time the target appeared uniformly gray.

Given the high-contrast between the white and black lines, the target was roughly similar to seeing a buck's antlers against a snow or bright-sky background. Seeing antlers against a homogeneous brush background would be much harder. To keep the

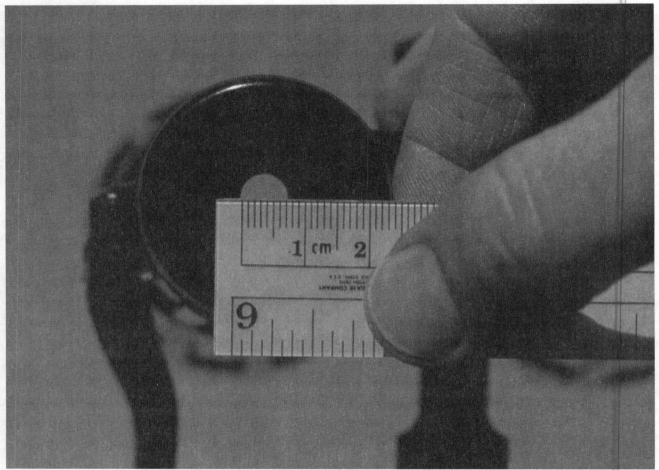

Here we see one of the 7.1mm exit pupils of the above 7X50 binocular. Exit pupils are the optical windows through which light exiting an optical instrument enters the user's eye. Its diameter in millimeters is calculated by dividing the diameter of the objective lens by the magnification; accordingly a 7X50 binocular has 7.1 mm exit pupils (50 ÷ 7 = 7.1).

viewer's eyes honest, the target was rotated every minute to change the orientation of the lines. Weatherwise, the sky was clear overhead, while a band of clouds hung lazily over the mountains to the west.

Moreover, to make the tests the most meaningful with regard to twilight factors, the optics were carefully chosen from specific product lines, thereby minimizing differences in optical quality and, especially, antireflection coatings. Instruments of similar optical quality from other manufacturers would, no doubt, have shown similar results.

Binocular Test

Of the four binoculars tested, three—the 8X32, 10X42, and 12X50 models—were from Nikon's Superior E Series. These porro prism glasses are so similar that the only differences I can detect are in the diameters and focal lengths of their objective lenses, which account for the differences in magnification. The fourth binocular was the recently reintroduced Zeiss 15X60 B/GA, which also has porro prism lenses and fully multi-coated optics. This test was especially interesting regarding the affect of magnification on low-light performance in that the exit-pupil diameters and, subsequent, relative brightness of the binoculars were nearly identical. A 7X binocular was not used because I could not find a fully multicoated porro prism model that fit the 4mm exit-pupil niche. In eight powers, equally good 8X42, 8X50, and 8X56 models would have outperformed the 8X32 by progressively larger margins, and in 10 powers, 10X50 and 10X56 models would have outperformed the 10X42.

Riflescope Test

With riflescopes, just two optically similar models—the Bausch & Lomb Elite 4200 2.5-10X40mm and 6–24X40mm—allowed me to cover the magnification range of from 2.5X to 24X with 40mm objective lenses. Unlike the binocular test, where the exit-pupil diameters remained constant, here the exit pupils became smaller as the magnifications were zoomed upward. Therefore, I was able to see where the darkening effects of progressively smaller exit pupils nullified the detail-revealing effects of higher magnifications. For my old eyes, that happened at 12X with a 3.3mm exit pupil. From there through 20X, though I could distinguish the white lines for a few minutes longer, the overall image was so dark that I could not tell where the target ended and background began. Shooting at game under such conditions would have been stupid.

Do not read too much into the fact that at 2.5X the lines on the test target were not resolvable nine minutes before sunset. The explanations are, first, that the test was done near the eastern slopes of the Rockies where the sun invariably slips behind the mountains before the official time of sunset; i.e., it was already getting dark. Second, that at 2.5X the target pattern was very near the 1 minute-of-angle resolution limit of the human eye, which deteriorates quickly in lowering light. And, third, though I could not resolve the lines, the target and the surrounding area was still bright enough that I could easily have taken game. The slightly better performance of 6–24X40mm over the 2.5–10X40mm was, I believe, due to my having fine-tuned the focus on the test target by using the scope's adjustable objective, which the 2.5–10X40mm lacked. Quality being equal, scopes with 50mm objectives lenses, no doubt, would have performed better at the higher magnifications. Beyond that the test results speak for themselves.

Chapter 7

Optics for Dangerous Game
by Craig Boddington

Whether you're talking about rifles, cartridges, or optics, the big difference with dangerous game is just that: *Danger!* Even so, the actual risk factor in hunting animals that can turn the tables is probably best stated as "potentially hazardous to your health." I firmly believe that it's very unusual to get into serious trouble with unwounded, unmolested animals, even in the case of legendary troublemakers like lions, grizzlies, and Cape buffalo. There's always the potential of getting between a mamma bear and her cub or stumbling a bit too close to a sleeping lion (or anything else) in thick bush, but under normal hunting conditions genuine unprovoked charges are extremely rare. Most of the time accidents with animals—even the most potentially dangerous animals—result from human error. The error may be poor shot placement, overconfidence, or lack of caution. Whatever the cause, the best way to avoid turning potential danger into reality is to use plenty of caution and common sense . . . and to place that first shot with absolute precision.

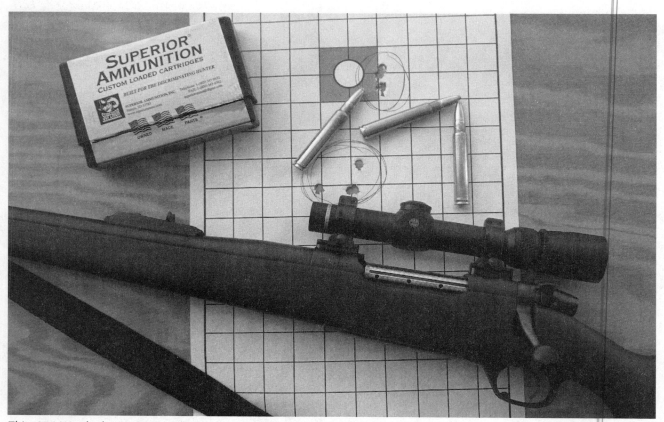

This .375 Weatherby Magnum with 1.5–5X Leupold uses detachable Talley mounts. This is an ideal setup for dangerous game, and, as much as I love the open-sighted big bores, I firmly believe more and better trophies will be taken with a setup like this.

The banteng is a small wild ox that lives in heavy cover and has a reputation for being bad-tempered. Note that both my professional hunter and I used rifles with scopes despite the thick jungle!

This is where riflescopes come into play. The situation is no different with dangerous game than with anything else: You shoot better if you can see better. A good, clear riflescope allows you to see better as well as faster and in poorer light, thus enabling better shot placement. That said, there are some differences between riflescopes for dangerous game and riflescopes for all other types of hunting.

The most obvious is that, literally, you are putting your life and the lives of your hunting party on the line. Absolute reliability is a must, so riflescopes for dangerous game should be of the highest quality. This requirement is jeopardized by the recoil factor. With the exception of leopard, all the animals we think of as dangerous are fairly

large and require rifles of significant power. The more powerful the rifle the more recoil. Recoil is the riflescope's greatest enemy, and the best way to mitigate this problem is also through the use of high-quality, name brand scopes.

There is also some simplicity in choosing scopes for hunting dangerous game because long shots are simply out of the question! In Africa a shot beyond one hundred yards is very unusual on any member of the Big Five. On big bears it is sometimes necessary to reach out a couple hundred yards, maybe a bit more, or go home empty-handed. This is still not long range with a modern rifle, and the target size is such that high magnification is not necessary. So, to my thinking, ideal scopes for dangerous game rifles are limited to fixed power scopes of 4X and below, and to variable scopes with a high-end magnification of no more than 6X or 7X.

This fits well with the third primary requirement of a scope for hunting dangerous game: If Murphy's Law applies and things go from bad to worse, it may be necessary to stop a charge at point-blank range. Stopping a charge implies the use of adequate cartridges and good bullets. That's a different subject, and for our current discussion not even very important. In my experience it doesn't make much difference how big a cannon you're using. Raw power helps, but in a serious charge only *shot placement* will save you. Whether or not a scope should be used will be discussed later, but if a scope is used it must be of extremely low power with a wide field of view. You can't afford the tunnel vision of higher magnification, and for darn sure you can't afford to see just a blur of hair through the scope before the animal hits you!

So, ideal scopes for hunting dangerous game must be absolutely reliable, incredibly rugged, and of relatively low magnification. These criteria apply across the spectrum of dangerous game, but different situations suggest some variances. In a little bit I will discuss scopes specifically suited for thick-skinned dangerous game, lion, leopard, and the big bears. We will conclude with a brief discussion of other optics recommended for these types of hunting. But first there are a couple of basic questions that should be answered.

TO SCOPE OR NOT TO SCOPE?

For most hunting situations, there is simply no argument: You'll do better with a scope than you will with iron sights. The two clear exceptions are when it's raining or when hunting with hounds. The former is obvious. Even with the best scope covers, a serious downpour can obscure your lenses before you can get off a shot. In hound hunting there are two issues that make scope use

questionable. First, the shots are usually so close that a scope simply isn't needed. Second, and more important, if the animal (whether bear, boar, mountain lion, or leopard) is bayed on the ground then the shot must be taken while the dogs are darting in and out. Even the slightest restriction on peripheral vision caused by focusing through a scope's lens increases the risk of danger to the dogs. A lot of houndsmen simply won't allow scopes to be used, which is a pretty good call.

A lot of old-timers, especially African professional hunters, will argue that iron sights are also best for dangerous game, and especially for following up dangerous game that has been wounded. There are a few circumstances where this may be correct, but it is definitely not true all the time. Again, you see better with a scope. This means that you can place your shot with more precision, thus precluding the necessity for following a wounded, dangerous animal. These days most of us grew up shooting with scopes, so we're more accustomed to them than to iron sights, and, thus we shoot better with them. Most of us are also able to align a cross hair faster and thus shoot faster than we can with iron sights. This happens because a scope works on just one focal plane; thus, all the eye has to do is align the cross hairs on the animal. With open sights, the eye must attempt to shift back and forth between three focal planes: rear sight, front sight, target. This is difficult enough for young eyes, and at some point past forty years of age it becomes impossible for most of us. Aperture or "peep" sights are better because the eye naturally centers the front sight in the aperture, but there are still two focal planes to worry about: the front sight and the target.

The late Finn Aagaard was one of very few African professional hunters I have known who believed in low-powered scopes for dangerous game in thick cover. To prove his theory, he ran stopwatch tests on well-placed shots at animal silhouettes at various ranges. He compared the times, from the word "go," using scopes, open sights, and aperture sights. Everybody he tested, including me, shot more quickly and more accurately with a low-powered scope!

That said, in the final instants of a charge, when there's only one last chance to stop the animal, a scope may not be the right answer. Come to think of it, iron sights may not be, either. At that moment, sights of any kind are superfluous. What matters are cool nerves, confidence, gun fit, and knowledge of animal anatomy. We're talking a matter of a few feet or yards, where the rifle must be pointed like a shotgun, not aimed like a rifle. If the gun fits, and if you shoot with both eyes open, you can make such a shot despite the scope (rather than because of it). If you must shoot a rifle with one eye closed, however, under such an extremity you are far better off with iron sights—

and you should ignore them and rely on gun fit to get your barrel to point in the right direction.

WHAT ABOUT THE "SCOUT" SCOPE?

The so-called "scout scope" is a long eye relief scope mounted forward on the barrel rather than over the action. It's a concept that seems to come and go in popularity, but it does have a small and loyal following. I am not among them, but I concede there are a couple of advantages. On rifles with extremely heavy recoil, it is very difficult to keep a conventionally mounted scope off your forehead all the time. The scout scope eliminates any possibility of scope cuts, so they have some genuine value for rifles chambered to huge

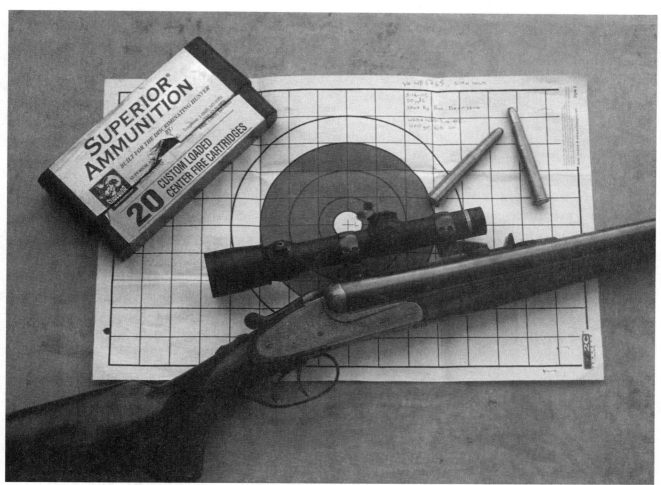

This new John Rigby .450-400 sidelock is double mounted and has a low-powered scope. Traditionally, double rifles have open sights, but a low-power variable extends their capabilities considerably.

cartridges like .500 Jeffery and .505 Gibbs. Another common argument is that they leave the breech of a bolt-action rifle exposed for quicker reloading. This is absolutely true, but when hunting dangerous game you've already made several mistakes if you need to pause in midcharge to stuff shells in the magazine.

The major argument for the scout scope, however, is that it is supposed to be faster to use. If that is the case for you, that's fine, but I don't buy it. Fast scope use is a matter of gun fit: As the rifle touches your shoulder and your cheek touches the stock, the rifle should fit so that when it comes up your eye instantly achieves a full field of view. If this is the case then I don't think it matters where the scope is mounted.

The final consideration, however, depends on whether you shoot with both eyes open or must keep one eye closed. I shoot left-handed and my left eye is strongly dominant. I keep both eyes open when shooting with a scope; my left eye takes over and my right eye fuzzes out—but I keep my peripheral vision. This is especially important for close-range shooting with a scope. In that regard I'm fortunate, and a scout scope offers me no advantage whatsoever. But that's my particular situation. If you shoot right-handed but are left-eye dominant, or vice versa, or if you simply cannot train yourself to shoot a scope with both eyes open, then a scout scope might well be a good choice for close-in work on dangerous game.

THICK-SKINNED DANGEROUS GAME

I don't believe a scope—or the lack thereof—is particularly important on either elephant or rhino. I have hunted elephants with scoped bolt actions and with open-sighted doubles, and the difference isn't significant. This is not because the target is so huge. Elephant are certainly huge, but pinpoint shot placement is essential, and the actual vital zone isn't all that large—especially if you're going for the tricky brain shot. The thing is that ranges are generally very, very short. Most elephants today are hunted in

very thick cover, where forty yards is a long shot and most shots will be closer to twenty-five yards. Under those circumstances it really doesn't make much difference whether you're shooting with a scope or with open sights. In open country, rare in elephant hunting today, a rifle with a low-powered scope gets the nod. With a scoped .375 or .416 (and thorough understanding of where to place the cross hairs!) you can make a brain shot at 60 or 70 yards. Most of us shouldn't attempt a shot this tricky and this precise with open sights.

It's pretty much the same with rhino. Although their sense of smell is excellent, their eyesight is very poor. If you keep the wind right, your shot will be close enough so that choice of sighting equipment isn't important.

Buffalo are a different story. Here, of course, I'm talking about true buffalo, the African and Asian varieties. American (and I suppose European) bison are big enough to be dangerous, but you have to mess up really badly to make them so. It isn't so much that they are more docile by nature—any rancher who raises bison will argue that point! Rather, it's that they live in much more open country. If the American bison lived in thick bush or forest, he might have an altogether different reputation!

I've hunted Africa's buffalo a great deal, and I have hunted water buffalo in Asia and banteng in northern Australia. Water buffalo are bigger than Cape buffalo, but I am convinced they are less aggressive. Banteng are much smaller, but can be downright nasty. Cape buffalo have a fearsome reputation that I'm not sure they deserve. Wounded, a Cape buffalo can show incredible stamina, determination, and courage—but unprovoked charges are extremely rare. Whatever, the concept in hunting buffalo is to locate the best bull you can find and take him as cleanly and efficiently as you can. The classic choice is an open-sighted big bore, either a bolt action or a double. But I am absolutely convinced that you will take more buffalo and bigger buffalo and expend fewer cartridges with a scoped rifle!

The obvious reason is shot placement, which for most of us will be more consistent with a scope. This is compounded by two factors. First, buffalo are herd animals. The idea is to get in as close as you can, but all too often the bull you want will be on the far side of the herd, with too many keen noses, eyes, and ears to allow a closer approach. No, you don't want to take a long shot, but with a scoped rifle of any adequate caliber you can take a shot at 100 or 125 yards. With open sights this is pushing the envelope for most of us.

The second factor is the nature of buffalo. Once in a while you'll catch them grazing in the open. Then a scoped rifle is clearly superior, because you cannot sneak up on buffalo on open ground. More often you will find tracks in the early morning and follow the herd until you catch them resting in the midday hours. They will have found shade—often in some of the thickest bush around. So now you're crawling from bush to bush, studying buffalo and looking at black animals in black shadow. Once a suitable bull is located, it can be very difficult to pick out the correct aiming point with open sights, but it's very easy with a scope.

Which scope to use is pretty simple. A fixed 2.5X or 3X is plenty, and low powered enough that there isn't any reason to remove it during the followup. More common today is the low-range variable, from 1–4X on up to 1.5–6X. These are just great: In open country the higher setting may be useful, and you can turn them down all the way in thick stuff. Reticles need to be very bold and very visible. A bold dot with cross hairs, rare today, is very good. The more common "plex"-type reticle with thick outer wires and a thin center is also good. Even better are the newer, more specialized reticles such as Swarovski's "dangerous game" reticle, combining a bold "plex" with a circle around the center. For general use I think this reticle covers up a bit too much of the animal, but it's wonderful for dangerous game in thick cover.

LION

In lion hunting a scoped rifle is the correct choice. Period. The animal (and its vital zone) is much smaller than any breed of buffalo, but if things go wrong buffalo are a whole lot more dangerous. Long shots are out of the question, but opportunities do occur at 100 or even 150 yards. While buffalo hunting is complicated by looking at black animals in black shadow, lion hunting is complicated even more by looking at tawny animals in yellow grass. And one thing more: Baiting is a common technique for hunting lion. Most shots over bait will be taken at dawn, but occasionally lions will come to bait in the evening. Either way, the shot is likely to come in very poor light!

My first lion came on the last day of a hunt in Zambia twenty-odd years ago. The previous day, while stalking to the blind in predawn blackness, we heard lion snarling and squabbling over the bait. It was still dark when we reached the blind, but through the shooting port I was sure I could make out tawny forms around the reeking hippo that served as our bait. They were gone by the time it was light enough to shoot, and there was nothing to be done about it. The next morning, the last morning, it was quiet as we walked to the bait. When the light came up, there was nothing there, so, with nothing to lose, we approached the bait carefully. There, just beyond the hippo, was a male lion. I shot him very carefully from perhaps seven yards. The rifle was a .375, scoped with a Leupold 1.75–5X. This type of scope is the classic dangerous game scope: Had a lion been on the bait in the first gray of dawn, I would have been able to take the shot; moreover, because its magnification was low enough I could also take the close-range shot that I needed.

LEOPARD

The classic method for hunting leopard is over bait. Once in a while, in truly undisturbed country, a leopard will come to bait in the late afternoon.

I used a .338 Winchester Magnum with fixed 4X Swarovski scope to take this leopard in Botswana in very poor light. A scope like this will gather more light than any low-range variable.

Too, some cats are morning feeders. Most of the time, however, the best you can hope for is that the leopard will come to the bait in the last few moments of shooting light. Many leopards are purely nocturnal feeders, and in many jurisdictions it is perfectly legal to hunt leopards at night.

The leopard is not a big animal. A nice tom might weigh 150 pounds, and a 200-pound leopard is extremely rare. But if a wounded leopard gets to you, he will seem very large indeed! There is rarely an opportunity for more than one shot. It must be placed very carefully, and you can expect that this must be done in very poor light. Magnification is not important. I have never seen a blind placed more than 100 yards from a bait, with 60 to 70 yards much more likely. The ability of a scope to gather plenty of light is critical.

This is one of very few applications in dangerous game hunting where the better light-gathering capabilities of a top-quality scope with 30mm tube have a clear advantage. It is also one of very few applications in dangerous game hunting where the standard "dangerous game" low-range variable with objective lens the same size as the scope tube may not be the best choice. You do not need a huge scope with a massive objective lens; however, a standard riflescope, like a fixed 4X with a 40mm tube, will gather more light than a 1–75-5X scope with a straight (32mm) objective lens.

A bold reticle that you can see in the very worst light is also essential. This is one of very few applications in hunting where I see a clear advantage to a lighted reticle. In fading (or almost no) light, it is very difficult to pick up the proper aiming point on a leopard. Hell, it can be difficult to be sure you're focused on the center of the field of view! A reticle with a lighted dot in the center, now offered by almost all scope manufacturers, is definitely a huge plus in leopard hunting.

THE BIG BEARS

In the context of "dangerous game," we're generally thinking about coastal brown bears, interior grizzly bears, and polar bears—all of which are found in both the Old World and the new. Where you hunt them doesn't matter much, so long as you give them plenty of respect. Grizzly bears are bigger and tougher than African lions, and both brown and polar bears can be bigger than Cape buffalo and just as tough! It's also worth mentioning that black bears, while generally (not always!) smaller than grizzlies, are also potentially dangerous. Black bear hunting varies depending on technique, with most wild boar hunting paralleling the methods used for black bear.

Under most conditions, coastal bears are taken at closer ranges and in heavier cover than grizzlies. Grizzly hunting is also less successful than brown bear hunting, so it's important to be able to take any reasonable shot. This applies in spades with polar bear, and the shots run the gamut. A fair number of polar bears are taken when they wander into camp to eat the dogs—but there's also the possibility for a shot at some distance to prevent a bear getting across an open lead or into a pressure ridge where he cannot be followed. So the standard "Cape buffalo" scope, a low-range variable or fixed-power scope of minimal magnification, is just fine for brown bear. For grizzly and polar bear, you might want a bit more magnification just in case a shot past two hundred yards is required—but you

also need very low magnification for a close encounter (and that's where the power ring should stay unless and until you actually need more magnification!). The older 2–7X variables are good choices, and the newer 1.5–6X variables are also very good.

Black bear hunting methods vary depending on the technique, with most wild boar being hunted using many of the same techniques. As discussed earlier, if hounds are used, the shots are very close and telescopic sights may not be the best choice. When hunting over bait, you can figure the shot will come at 100 yards or less, and you can also expect low-light conditions, since black bears (especially the larger, older bears) are most likely to approach the bait at dusk. High magnification is not needed, but light-gathering potential is important. This is, thus, another place where the best 30mm scopes are appropriate—and since you'll be trying to find an aiming point on a dark animal in dark shadows, lighted reticles are also excellent. While spot-and-stalk hunting for both black bear and wild boar can require somewhat longer shots, it is important to understand that genuine long-range shooting is not appropriate for any potentially dangerous animal. Even so, it might be necessary and quite practical to reach out to 300 yards or so. With that in mind, the midrange variable scopes ranging from 2–7X on up to 3.5–10 (including the most universal 3–9X) are good choices.

A WORD ABOUT MOUNTS

The choice of a scope mount is actually just as important as the choice of a scope. This is not only because absolute reliability is essential, but also because the recoil of powerful cartridges for dangerous game is just as hard on mounts as it is on scopes. The most popular mount is probably the Redfield-type mount with opposing screws on the rear and a dovetail on the front. This mount is not strong enough for recoil much above the .338 Winchester Magnum or .375 H&H levels and should be avoided. The old Weaver-type mount is

This cow elephant had killed a villager the day before, so this was a very serious hunt. Scopes are definitely not needed for most elephant hunting, but a low-powered scope is a great asset if you wish to make a tricky brain shot.

wonderfully strong, while my personal favorites include the newer Leupold dual-dovetail and the good old Conetrol mounts. Integral mounts from Sako and Ruger are also very good.

An important question to be answered is whether you want detachable mounts or not. There are some very good ones today, including Leupold, Warne, and, of course, the excellent Talley mounts. Obviously a detachable must be just as rugged as a fixed in order to be practical, but to me the decision rests upon whether, under any circumstances, you would actually remove the scope and use the irons. If the answer is yes, then you should go the detachable route. Most of my African rifles wear detachables because,

in the heaviest cover, I just might take the scope off so I can better use the rifle like a shotgun. Although less frequently considered, I submit that detachables with good iron sights are excellent for much bear hunting simply because it rains an awful lot in much of what is considered good bear country!

If you go the detachable route, then it's essential that you spend some time with the iron sights, not only making sure they are properly zeroed, but also practicing with them until you are as comfortable with them as you are with the scope. If you don't do these things, you might as well leave the barrel plain, mount the scope with a rugged nondetachable mount, and plan on using the scope for all of your shooting (which is not a bad plan at all!).

OTHER OPTICS

For most dangerous game hunting, other requirements are very simple. You *always* need a good binocular. While the "mini" binoculars are light and handy, I prefer full-size binoculars because of their superior light-gathering capabilities, and because they are much easier to hold steady when you're tired or out of breath. In close cover, high magnification is overkill and hard to use. For hunting in thornbush or forest for buffalo, elephant, or even lion, I prefer a good, bright 7X or 8X binocular. For years I carried a porro prism 7X42 Swarovski, but today the more compact 8X30s and 8X32s are simply wonderful for this kind of hunting.

This also applies to bear hunting in close-cover situations, but in open country where serious glassing is required there is no substitute for a full-size 10X40 or 10X42 glass. Depending on the circumstances, you might want to back up your binocular with a spotting scope. Glassing for bears in big country isn't much different from glassing for sheep or anything else, except that bears are relatively easy to spot—but size is very difficult to judge at long range.

Rangefinders are rarely necessary. If you need a rangefinder when hunting dangerous game with a centerfire rifle, it's likely you just need to get closer! The primary exception to this is spot-and-stalk bear hunting. In any case, I almost always have a small Nikon, Leica, or Bushnell rangefinder in my daypack. In Africa, you are often hunting multiple species simultaneously, and with bear hunting you just never know!

OTHER OPTIONS

Although I have mentioned lighted reticles, until now I have ignored the relatively new "lighted sights," such as the Aimpoint, and the projected image or hologram sights offered by Bushnell and others. In general I don't believe these sights are as precise as traditional telescopic sights and certainly not when shooting at objects when the distances extend beyond one hundred yards.

On the other hand, they are very, very fast and exceptionally visible, which make them ideal for short-range use, and equally ideal in low light. They are definitely a sound option for hunting dangerous game in close cover. They are also lighter and present a smaller profile (thus making it easier to snake through brush) than any scope, yet they are infinitely faster and more visible than any iron sights. Just the other day I saw a classic .500-450 double by Holland & Holland that had been cleverly fitted with a hologram sight. Its owner stated that he couldn't see mounting a scope on such a rifle, but he was no longer able to see open sights well enough to rely on them. (He's about my age!) He found a very good solution, and that's the key to choosing sights for hunting dangerous game. Whatever system you choose must work for *you*, and you must not only have the skill to use it well, but also with total confidence. Your life may depend on it!

Chapter 8

Optics for Turkey Hunting

by John Barsness

Turkey hunting is a very curious pastime. To shoot at any other game bird on the ground is considered highly unethical, and it is illegal to hunt other birds during the spring mating season, yet ground-sluicing a lust-addled gobbler with a load of number 6's is regarded as one of the pinnacles of sporting achievement.

How did this come to be? The best guess is that "traditional" turkey hunting evolved in the South from a time when many folks could only afford one hunting gun. The most versatile firearm was a shotgun for the game available. With fine shot it killed quail and squirrels, with slightly larger shot it took gobblers or groundhogs, and with buck or ball it sufficed for big game at close range.

A scope has become increasingly popular for turkey hunting.

Squinty-eyed mountain folk learned that wild turkeys could only be reliably killed by shots in the head and neck, so they found several ways to get close enough to hit the target. Some tactics have fallen in disrepute—roost shooting, for instance, or the cost-effective trench. With the latter method, a shallow, narrow trench was baited with corn. The shooter sat hidden a few yards away, looking directly down the trench. When a flock of turkeys waddled up and started feeding, heads all in a row, one 12-gauge shell could harvest a pile of fine eating. Roost and trench shooting turned out to be so effective, however, that wild turkeys almost disappeared. Another method, calling in spring gobblers, however, did not really affect the population, so it was allowed—after the turkey population rebounded.

An old-time turkey hunter would probably find a lot of modern turkey hunting laughable. Dozens of fancy calls, camouflage clothing to match every kind of tree in seventeen states, face-paint, and jackets with pillows attached are just some of the paraphernalia available today. Just what is the world coming to? But the most amusing aspect of modern turkey hunting to our old-timer would be a scoped shotgun. Why, he might ask, is the point of putting a scope on a shotgun when the whole idea of a scattergun is a spray of shot? All you need to do, he would add, is just point the shotgun at a turkey's head and let the spray do its job. After all, aiming is for rifles, not shotguns.

The trouble is that the modern turkey shotgun has evolved into a specialized hunting arm, rather than the all-purpose scattergun of the Old South. Its single job is to put as many pellets in a gobbler's head and neck from as far away as possible. At ranges under thirty yards, today's turkey-chokes can make shotguns shoot almost like rifles. They may kill a gobbler cleanly at forty-five yards, but they can also miss one completely at twenty, especially if the shooter points the thing like a quail gun. This is the reason that more and more of today's super-magnum, camouflage-designed, sling-equipped turkey guns end up with some sort of aiming arrangement, including optical sights.

Here I must admit to some ambivalence about the use of turkey sights, even though my first turkey fell to a scoped firearm. This was not even a scattergun, but a Remington 700 BDL in .243 Winchester, which I carried into the ponderosa pine hills above Montana's Tongue River in October 1975. It wore a 3–9X Tasco, my very first variable, and the magazine was full of handloads using the 105-grain Speer spitzer. With such equipment, I had high hopes of reducing a mule deer to possession.

But I also had a two-dollar turkey tag in my pocket, since the piney hills also held a sizable flock of Merriam's birds. At dawn I parked along a dirt road in a deer-filled canyon, then hiked up the nearest ridge. While cresting the top, I heard a sound I had never heard before: the sound of a wild turkey. Using my Sears, Roebuck 7X35 binocular, I scanned the other hillside, finding what appeared to be a herd of porcupines grazing along. Then one raised its head. Turkeys! I sat down, guessed the range at close to three hundred yards, and held the cross hairs just above one of the biggest birds. At the shot, the turkeys scattered, but none fell. This time I held right on the backline, and at the shot my turkey flopped to the side, while the rest ran over the ridge.

The range turned out to be around two hundred yards (distances appear longer across canyons in the dim light of early morning), and my bird turned out to be a mature hen. Until then my total knowledge of turkey hunting consisted of a few articles in outdoor magazines. These made taking a wild turkey seem as difficult a feat as climbing

Because of very tight turkey shotgun chokes, accurate aim is even more important. Here scopes help.

Mount Everest while doing quantum physics in your head. But my hunt had not been so tough.

Over the next twenty-five years I hunted turkeys from California to Florida, eventually taking the four varieties native to the United States. After a while it did not seem so simple. Along the way I also learned that optics can help the turkey hunter considerably, even if a given turkey hunter does not believe in rifle hunting or putting sights on a shotgun.

It still amazes me how many turkey hunters do not carry binoculars. Yes, calling a gobbler to a shotgun ends up as a short-range affair, even with today's tight chokes and big shells. But a binocular comes in handy quite often. For one thing, a good glass makes the sport safer. We can tell whether that bird on the other side of the meadow is a real hen or somebody's decoy or whether that dark movement down in the draw is a gobbler or a hunter.

I took my first eastern bird in Alabama, at the well-known White Oak Plantation, hunting with the legendary Mr. Bo Pitman himself. We found what eventually became my bird about noon, after having

Optics Digest

listened to him gobbling for an hour from an oak draw in the middle of a hayfield. We kept to the edge of the hayfield and finally worked around to an angle where we could see both the gobbler and three or four hens through the trees. He paraded up and down like a general reviewing his troops, but the hens were lazy in the midday heat and did not want to play.

Bo whispered in my ear. "I believe if we can get to the edge of that draw without spooking those turkeys, we can kill him when they come out to feed later. He will follow those hens."

And that is what we did, crawling along the ground for almost an hour. Bo had correctly guessed the direction they would go to feed, and I killed the gobbler from a distance of eighteen yards. Many people frown upon the tactic of sneaking up on turkeys because of the danger of shooting other hunters. But this adventure took place on the strictly private land of White Oak, and because of our binoculars we were absolutely sure that a real live gobbler was strutting in that draw.

My old friend Jim Conley of Orlando, Florida, is one of the best Osceola turkey guides, partly because he has been doing it for decades. Osceolas typically live in swampy terrain, so they are often killed at very short range. Even so, Jim feels naked without a binocular because so much Osceola country is decidedly dim. With a good binocular he can spot the red of a gobbler's head two hundred yards back in the cypress and palmettos as the bird sneaks its incredibly cautious way toward Jim's calls. Osceolas have a reputation as the most "shut-mouth" of turkeys, so it helps to see them before they arrive.

I killed my lone Osceola while hunting by myself on one of Jim's leases, but I do most of my turkey hunting in the wide-open West. Out in the ponderosa breaks you can hear a turkey gobble for a true mile, and the sound is sometimes difficult to pinpoint as it echoes off the twisted coulees. It helps to be able to spot the bird from a distance. Very often they will strut on an open ridgetop, so the gobbler's red head will be distinctly visible with

good glass. Then you work your way onto the same ridge and give him a few clucks . . . and, with luck, a load of number 5 shot.

Despite the vast differences between Jim Conley's swamps and my pine ridges, we have both come to a similar conclusion about binoculars for hunting turkeys. While any glass is better than none, we both prefer full-size binoculars rather than the compacts so often seen hanging around a turkey-hunter's neck. The reason? Bigger glasses gather more light and provide better definition. Both factors come into play in turkey country, whether in the Florida swamps or the Montana breaks.

This does not mean we handicap ourselves with the giant goggles big-game hunters favor. Probably the best choice is an 8X30 or 8X32. These generally weigh around 20-24 ounces and provide a clear enough look for turkey hunting in any part of North America. They also double nicely as woods binoculars for big game, whether tree stand whitetails or lodge-pole elk.

For the tradition-minded gobbler hunter the best turkey sights are fiber-optic open sights like those provided on the turkey version of the Browning Gold. These can be sighted-in precisely to the center of the pattern, yet they do not get in the way if you decide to hunt other birds with your turkey gun. A couple of years ago in Alabama I hunted gobblers in the morning with the Mossy Oak boys and then quail in the afternoon, all with the same shotgun. Fiber-optics pick up the slightest amount of light, making it possible to aim even at first and last light on cloudy days, deep in a southern swamp.

But some other sights also work well, especially if you are not too traditional. One of the finest all-round shotgun sights I have ever used is the Bushnell Holosight. This not only can be sighted-in precisely, but it works very well for wingshooting. Purists hate the idea, but there is nothing more effective for long-range goose shooting than a Holosight on a tightly choked, 12-gauge magnum turkey gun.

Scopes also work on turkey shotguns, and dedicated turkey scopes help us make sure a gobbler

This tom was shot with a scoped rifle, where legal rifles with scopes make sense for turkey hunting.

is in range. They come equipped with a range-finding reticle designed to encircle the average gobbler's body at forty yards. Unlike a laser rangefinder, they do not require any movement of our hands. I have used the Simmons 4X more than any other, partly because it doubles quite well as a deer scope in shotgun-only areas. With a change of choke tubes from tight-turkey to rifled, my old Remington 870 changes from a forty-yard turkey getter to a hundred-yard deer rifle.

While variable scopes are almost standard on big-game rifles anymore, a fixed scope is better for rangefinding, because the reticle does not change size relative to the bird. The exception would be variables with the reticle in the first focal plane, the so-called European system. Swarovski makes a variable scope (1.25–4X) with a turkey reticle in the first focal plane, which works very well indeed, if at a somewhat higher price than my 4X Simmons.

Of course, rifles are still legal for turkeys in some areas, especially in autumn. Here in Montana we finally outlawed them during the spring, but can still use them in the fall season. And I do, mostly because I am not about to pass up a fall turkey just because I am carrying a .270 rather than a 12-gauge.

A 2½X or 4X on a light .22 Magnum or .22 Hornet would be ideal, but most of my fall turkeys come during "mixed-bag" hunts for deer and even elk. It is just as tough to get a clean shot at a big fall gobbler as it is at a buck or bull. This is especially true if you want to punch a small entrance hole in his breast, letting the Nosler expand only on backbone. When using big-game rifles on fall gobblers, such precise bullet placement makes all the difference at Thanksgiving, which is why my rifles usually wear a fixed 6X, or a variable topping out at no more than 9X.

On a recent Montana whitetail hunt, my wife Eillen took advantage of the concurrent turkey season by taking a big hen at 75 yards with one precise shot through the base of the neck. The rifle was a New Ultra Light Arms Model 20 in .257 Roberts and the scope a 3–9X Pentax Whitetails Unlimited, cranked all the way up. This turkey graced our Thanksgiving table, without any annoying number 5 shot in the upper beast. Some of you will, no doubt, shake your heads at such barbarism. I guess that makes me a barbarian . . . but one who really loves to eat wild turkeys, whether ground-sluiced in spring or precisely center-punched in fall.

Chapter 9
Telescopic Sights

As a teenager, I couldn't afford a riflescope; consequently, I hunted everything from rabbits and ground squirrels to deer and black bear with iron sights. I didn't feel particularly handicapped since most of my hunting buddies were similarly equipped. More often than not, we brought game home for the freezer. Iron sights (particularly aperture "peep" sights) work as well as they did a half century ago, but magnifying scope sights are now ubiquitous. These days the first thing a hunter does after buying a new rifle is to have a scope mounted on it, which is a smart move.

Scope sights are by far the most popular optical accessories hunters buy—and for good reason.

While iron sights are still useful, a good scope offers many worthwhile advantages. First and foremost, a scope shows your target more clearly, particularly in dim morning or evening light. A scope presents a much brighter, sharper image than you can see with your naked eye. Viewing an animal through a magnifying 9X, 6X, or even 2X lens shows detail your unaided eye will miss. In addition to giving you a better look at the size of those antlers, a scope can confirm that you are about to shoot a deer or elk . . . *not* some idiot hunter in brown clothing!

Looking at a sharp, magnified image helps you to place your shot with greater precision. At any distance beyond point-blank range, an iron front

Visual examination allows you to compare the brightness and resolution of different riflescopes, but this examination is best done in dim indoor light.

Leupold's Vari-X II (and the new VX-1) series scopes have single-coated lenses and are fully waterproof. Leupold's higher-priced Vari-X III models feature fully multicoated lenses, and are noticeably brighter.

sight obscures part of the target. An open, semibuckhorn rear sight may hide the entire lower half of the animal from view. The greater the range, the less target you will see. Nestling the top of the front-sight blade or bead behind an animal's shoulder shows only *approximately* where the bullet will go. A scope's cross-hair reticle (particularly of the Leupold Duplex style that is thin near the center) will not block your view, and it precisely defines your aiming point.

Scope sights are a big help in hunting pronghorn, deer, elk, or any other large and possibly distant game. Scope sights are absolutely vital for sharpshooting prairie dogs standing three hundred, four hundred, or even farther away. You need a good 10X scope to see these Coke-bottle-size critters clearly at such extended ranges. Again, a fine cross hair aids in placing the bullet precisely.

Almost all hunters put scopes on their rifles, and many handgunners install models with long eye relief on their hunting pistols or revolvers. Other scopes are designed for turkey-shooting shotguns or slug guns for the deer woods. Riflescopes are offered in dizzying variety—big scopes, compact scopes, fixed-power scopes, variable scopes, scopes for long- and short-range shooting, varmint scopes—the list is almost endless. If you are a hunter, therefore, you will almost certainly be in the market for another scope soon. The question is, *which* scope to buy?

Buying the Right Scope

Riflescopes come in several sizes and a wide range of magnifications. I will discuss the best size and magnification for different types of hunting later in this chapter. No matter what configuration you choose, you should compare several brands and models before you buy. Not all scopes are created equal, and you want to get the best bang for your buck.

It doesn't take an optics expert to buy a riflescope that will perform well and provide dependable service. All it takes is a little knowhow to help you make the right choice. It is relatively easy to separate good equipment from the junk you may be offered. While price is not the only criterion, you generally get what you pay for. It isn't always necessary to cough up top dollar to get quality optics, but bargain-basement $49.95 scopes are usually worthless. They may show a bright image when you look through them at the store, but they almost always come up short under actual hunting conditions. Simply put, you cannot get quality, multicoated lenses or durable construction for that kind of money. Sure, some low-priced manufacturers offer no-cost replacement warranties, but how much good will that do you when you are stranded in the middle of a hunt with a useless sight?

That is why you won't see any really cheap scopes listed in this book. If a scope carries a recommended retail price of under $100—and probably sells for even less—it won't be included here. Only the good-to-excellent quality scopes on the market deserve your consideration. Buying cheap is false economy. Instead of getting a new replacement scope every season, you are far better off paying a few more bucks for something that will last. Optical equipment should be regarded as a lifetime investment. If $600 seems like a lot to pay for a scope, that amortizes out to just $60 per year over ten years. Scope quality is so important that I would far rather put a costly scope on a budget-priced rifle than the other way around.

You need to do a bit of research before buying a scope. In chapter 1, I pointed out some of the advantages—and disadvantages—of a large objective lens. A large objective can deliver a

Scopes with large objective lenses offer a bright viewing picture, but must be mounted higher to clear the barrel.

brighter image. Remember that exit pupil size, which determines the amount of light available to your eye, is calculated by dividing objective lens diameter by magnification. A 9X36 scope offers a 4mm-exit pupil, while a 9X50 scope sports an exit pupil measuring 5.5mm across. An 8X56 scope gives you an exit pupil 7mm in diameter, which provides all the light your eye can accommodate. Anything larger than 7mm is wasted potential.

The objective lens and the exit pupil size are not the only variables determining image brightness on dark, dingy days or when the sun sinks below the horizon. Twilight factor offers another measure of comparison. A scope's twilight factor can be determined by multiplying magnification by objective lens diameter, then calculating the square root of this product. The higher the twilight factor, the brighter the image.

Magnification plays a big part here. The closer you get to an animal or object, the brighter it looks. This is true in spite of exit pupil size. For instance, a 3–9X40 variable scope set on 3X has a huge 13.3 exit pupil and a twilight factor of 10.9. Set the same scope at 9X and exit pupil diameter shrinks to 4.4mm, but the twilight factor jumps to 19.

While large objective lenses offer optical advantages, the downsides are extra weight and the need to mount the scope higher above the receiver. Scopes with large objectives also may be more expensive. Lens quality is another factor. Premium

Scopes with 30mm tubes are bulkier, heavier, and usually more expensive than 1-inch models. They offer an optical advantage only if they house 30-mm internal optics and more windage and elevation adjustment (like this Swarovski variable does).

optical glass is expensive, and it is yet another reason top scopes cost more than budget models do.

Coated Lenses

Lens coatings are another important consideration. Zeiss developed coated lenses three-quarters of a century ago. Zeiss engineers knew that when light rays strike a glass surface, half the rays were reflected back into the atmosphere, while the other half passed through the glass. They discovered that applying a thin layer of magnesium fluoride to the surface of a lens greatly reduced light lost by reflection, producing a brighter image. Instead of allowing light rays to bounce off the surface of the glass, the magnesium fluoride coating redirected them into the instrument and toward your eye. This made a huge difference. While an uncoated lens transmits some 50 percent of the available light, a coated lens transmits 85 or 90 percent.

Then another discovery was made. Light is made up of several different wavelengths, and applying additional coatings of other compounds allowed more wavelengths to pass through. While single-coated lenses were 85 to 90 percent efficient in transmitting light, a lens with multiple coatings transmitted 95 to 99 percent of the light striking its surface.

Scopes should be sized to the rifle you're using. This Nikon variable is properly proportioned for the ultralight Ruger it's mounted on.

Specialized scopes like this 6–24X Bausch & Lomb are specifically designed for long-range varmint shooting.

You want coated lenses in any scope you buy. Some scopes like Leupold's Vari-X II series have single-coated lenses. For the past dozen years I have had 1–4X20 Vari-X IIs mounted on two magnum bear rifles. These scopes are light (9 ounces), compact, offer plenty of eye relief, and at 1X (actually 1.6X) provide a generous 75-foot field of view at 100 yards. They are also fully waterproof. While I have been very satisfied with these moderately priced workhorse scopes, Leupold's higher-priced Vari-X III models featuring fully multicoated lenses are noticeably brighter. Leupold has since replaced the old Vari-X II series with a line of VX-11 scopes featuring multicoated lenses. Leupold's new VX-1 scopes have single-coated lenses.

A multicoated lens typically has from three to as many as seven coats, and all top-quality scopes feature multicoated lenses throughout. Manufacturers of lesser-quality scopes may multicoat only one lens and single-coat the others.

All scopes have at least three lenses: the large front objective, the ocular (rear eyepiece) lens, and the erector lens that turns the target image right side up (without this lens you would see the image upside down). Because of their complexity, variable-magnification scopes contain more lenses than fixed-power scopes typically do. Each lens in the system reduces the amount of light transmitted, which is why fixed-power models are often brighter than variables. To increase light-transmitting efficiency, good scopes typically have their interiors treated with antireflective paint. Performance suffers in cheap scopes lacking this feature.

Comparing Competing Models

You don't need an optical laboratory to compare scope brightness. The most practical way to choose the brightest scope among three or four models is to hold a pair of the scopes side-by-side, then look through each one in turn. Don't test in bright sunlight because all scopes look great in bright light. Instead, look at an object up in the rafters or in the darkest corner of the store. If the store's interior is too bright, ask to visit the storeroom and make the comparison there. If you are buying a variable, be sure each scope is set to the same magnification.

Speaking of variables, another easy test of quality is seeing how hard the power ring turns. This is not a definitive test, but it takes some effort to change magnification on a first-class scope. If the power ring turns too easily, that should be a possible flag.

You need to test for more than just brightness. A scope's optics should be sharp, too. When you are comparing scopes, aim them at the lettering on a sign or some other image a few blocks away. But before you discard a particular model because it isn't delivering a crisp, sharp image, check to see that it is properly focused for your eye. Some people are not aware that scopes *can* be focused. There is a locking ring on the eyepiece of most American-style scopes. Unscrew this ring a couple of turns,

Note the level mounted on this Bausch & Lomb. It helps you keep the rifle plumb, which is good for small targets.

then turn the eyepiece itself as you look at a distant object through the lens. Several turns may be needed, but once the object appears in sharp focus, screw the locking ring back to its locked position. European-style scopes feature a focus ring at the very rear of the eyepiece. This typically requires less than one full turn to focus the scope.

Other tests cannot be performed in the store, but they should be done once you have purchased the scope and brought it home. Not all scopes are waterproof. You won't need a waterproof scope for 80 percent of the hunting you are likely to do, but that other 20 percent is the rub. I live in a dry, desert state, but I have hunted in nearby mountains in almost continual sleet or snow. Anyone who carries anything but a 100 percent waterproof scope in Alaska is just asking for trouble. If a scope leaks water, it is sure to fog when the temperature drops, and a fogged scope is worse than useless. For these and other reasons, all the scopes I have mounted on my rifles are waterproof—*not* "weather resistant." Most high-quality scopes *are* waterproof . . . at least that is what it says on the box.

The only way to be 100 percent sure the scope you just bought *is* waterproof is to immerse it in warm water, then watch for bubbles. If a stream of bubbles appear, the scope fails the test and should promptly be returned to the store. Before or a few hours after you perform this underwater test, it is a good idea to put the scope in your freezer for forty or fifty minutes. If it fogs up inside, it means that the manufacturer failed to purge all the moisture from the scope after assembly. Again, this scope should go back to the store. Don't make the mistake of taking the scope immediately from the warm-water dunk test and immediately freezing it. Any scope will fog under those conditions. Be sure the scope is dry and at room temperature before placing it in the freezer.

You should also test the accuracy—and repeatability—of the windage and elevation adjustments. This is best done at a shooting range with the help of a solid rest and sandbags. Mount the scope on a rifle you know is accurate, then fire a few rounds at 25 yards until the scope is zeroed. Now move the target to 100 yards and verify the zero. Next, fire a three-shot group, then dial in 32 or so clicks of right windage. (This assumes the scope has ¼-minute adjustment clicks; otherwise, use just enough windage to move the point of impact 7 or 8 inches to the right.) Fire another three-shot group, then dial up 8 inches of elevation and shoot again. Add 8 inches of left windage and fire another three-shot group. Finally, move the cross hairs down the same amount and shoot again. If the windage and elevation adjustments are accurate, the final 3-shot group will be superimposed over the first. The other groups will describe a more-or-less perfect square. The square need not be perfect, but if you are left with a wildly irregular rhomboid the adjustments are out of whack. If so, return the scope.

If you know the rifle is accurate, but it sprays bullets all over the place when used with the new scope, that is a sign of other problems. One possibility is bad parallax. Parallax means the target appears to shift as you move your head to either side while looking through the lens. A certain amount of parallax is present in all riflescopes, but if the target shows noticeable movement when you move your head from side to side, that is unacceptable.

There are other things to consider when buying a scope. Do you want a one-inch or 30mm tube? The only reason you have two diameters to choose from is that Europe long ago adopted the 30mm

The Zeiss 3–9X variable is a top choice for hunting deer and elk.

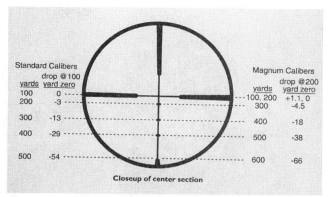

Standard Calibers drop @100		Magnum Calibers drop @200	
yards	yard zero	yards	yard zero
100	0	100, 200	+1.1, 0
200	-3	300	-4.5
300	-13	400	-18
400	-29	500	-38
500	-54	600	-66

Closeup of center section

Rangefinding reticles help shooters determine the holdover needed to connect on distant targets.

tube as standard, while Americans opted for a smaller 1-inch tube. Extra space inside a 30mm scope tube allows a wider range of elevation and windage adjustments, but, contrary to popular belief, one tube size offers no optical advantage over the other *unless* the 30mm tube actually houses 30mm internal optics. Larger lens systems can deliver brighter images, but there are 30-mm scopes that house the same, old 1-inch internal systems. Scopes with 30mm tubes are bulkier, heavier, and usually more expensive than 1-inch scopes, which is why shooters on this side of the pond continue to prefer the smaller tube size. At one time, 26mm, ⅞ inch, and other tube sizes were available, but those are pretty much part of the past—and good riddance!

While different reticles are available, the vast majority of scopes on retailer shelves wear one of two basic reticle types: the standard cross hair or the Duplex-type reticle with cross hairs that are wide at the perimeter and narrower at the center of the viewing field. While I am a fan of the Duplex reticle, simple cross-hair reticles work well, too. You cannot go far wrong with either choice unless you have special needs. Different rangefinding reticles are being marketed, including reticles with mil-dot reference points for making windage and elevation adjustments, reticles with stadia wires for bracketing the target animal, and even more specialized reticles cluttered with several smaller, individual aiming points for shooting at different ranges.

The Leupold 1–4X variable offers a wide field of view, which is needed for dangerous game. Set at 1X, it allows you to aim with both eyes open.

One problem with most rangefinding reticles is they are predicated on finding and targeting an animal measuring a uniform eighteen inches from back to brisket. Deer, elk, and pronghorn are obviously of different size, and no two animals are exactly alike. The animal must also patiently pose while you bracket its body in the reticle. While rangefinding reticles can be useful, you will get more accurate results by simply tucking a laser rangefinder in your pocket.

Hunting Scopes

For several years now, the most popular riflescope on the market has been the 3–9X variable. For hunting deer, elk, and similar game, this remains an excellent choice. If you are expecting a running shot at close range, cranking the magnification down to 3X gives you a wide field of view. Conversely, 9X is all the magnification you need to place your bullets precisely at 300 yards or more.

Today, hunters seem increasingly concerned with long-range shooting. As a result, higher-powered 3.5–10X and even 4.5–14X variables seem to be giving 3–9X models a run for their money. Too, the 40mm objective lenses that 3–9X scopes typically wear are giving way to larger, brighter 50mm objectives. The inevitable result is extra bulk and heft. For hunting deer, my money remains on the smaller, lighter 3–9X variable. It is still a great choice.

Personally, I have always been fond of 1–4X and 1.5–5X variables. That puts me in the minority, but there is a lot to be said for low-power variables. When you hunt brown bears and other large, dangerous game, the wide field of view 1X or 1.5X provides is surely comforting. You can (and should) use these scopes with both eyes open, providing almost unlimited binocular vision. For shooting a toothy critter that is already close—and rapidly getting closer—only the old-fashioned peep sight is faster.

Even if Alaska and Africa are not in your hunting plans, the 1.5–5X variable still makes a lot of sense. I like light, compact deer rifles; consequently, the light, compact low-power variables seem the perfect choice for mounting on these quick-handling firearms.

High-powered scopes have their place. They are exactly what you need for gunning pint-size prairie dogs at 300 or 400 yards. Under these conditions, at least 10X magnification is required for precise shot placement, and there is no need for a wide field of view. You are usually shooting from sandbags or a bipod rest, and there is no real hurry to fire.

I once surprised a young buck napping beside the trail I was sauntering along on my way back to camp for lunch. Bolting from practically underfoot, the deer scared me half to death. Acting on adrenaline-powered reflex, I threw my rifle up. At that range I saw nothing but hair in the 9X reticle. Delay saved the little buck's life. By the time he had put some distance between us, my heart had stopped ricocheting around my rib cage. I was looking for a bigger trophy, so I decided not to shoot.

How much magnification do you really need to shoot a deer? I was carrying a .308 Sako rifle with its 1.5–4.5X Bushnell variable set at 1.5X when I killed my first really big mule deer. I was sitting quietly in the snow, waiting for a flurry to pass. When the miniblizzard ended, I took a fast look around. I was surprised to see three bucks bedding down just over 200 yards away. The largest spotted me as I was bringing my rifle to bear on him. He lurched to his feet as I triggered a shot, and he collapsed on the spot. When I glanced at my scope, it was still set at 1.5X. There had not been time to increase the magnification, but 1.5X had proven no handicap.

I will cover long-range scopes in a minute, but for hunting deer a 1.5–5X scope offers plenty of magnification. So does a fixed-power 4X or 6X scope. When it comes right down to it, the 3–9X variable mentioned earlier covers all the bases, which is why it is *still* the most popular all-round hunting scope on the market. But if you are using a 3–9X variable, it is a good idea to keep it set at its lowest magnification while you move through the woods.

Eye relief is an important consideration, particularly when the scope is mounted on a hard-kicking rifle. Any scope you intend to use on a rifle that chambers a big-game caliber like the .338, .375, .416, or .458 magnums should have a minimum eye relief of 3½ inches. Four inches is even better.

Assuming that the scopes are of similar quality, the larger the objective lens, the brighter the image. Larger objectives do add bulk and heft, and usually add to the scope's price.

If eye relief is insufficient, you are practically guaranteed to wind up with a painful "shooter's eyebrow"—the bloody half-moon mark left by the scope's eyepiece as it slams into your forehead. Long eye relief may mean a slightly smaller field of view, but this is an inconsequential sacrifice.

If you are shooting a standard caliber like the 7mm-08, .270, or .30-06, then 3 inches of eye relief is sufficient. For light-recoiling numbers like the .22 centerfires, eye relief is less important. At the same time, I want at least 3½ inches between the scope and my eyebrow when I am using a 7mm or .30-caliber magnum.

Some scopes are intended for use on shotguns. For obvious reasons (high recoil), these scopes feature relatively long eye relief—typically 4 or 5 inches. A few scopes with intermediate eye relief (around 10 inches or so) are designed to be positioned *not* directly above a rifle's receiver, but mounted just *ahead* of it. The typically short, light carbines that sport this configuration are called *Scout rifles*.

Scopes for Long-Range Shooting

Years ago, 4X was considered plenty of magnification for distant shots at deer. Today, "beanfield" rifles are increasingly popular and long-range shooting is no longer frowned on.

Today I own a growing battery of accurate, flat-shooting varmint rifles. Each wears a scope designed specifically for long-range shooting. Hitting pint-size pests at four hundred yards or more demands top-grade optics. High-quality scopes provide a crisp, clear image with enough resolving power for precise shot placement.

Shooting prairie dogs calls for very specialized equipment. Firing is done from a solid rest a few steps from your truck. There is no need to tote gear more than a couple of yards, which is a good thing because rifles used for long-range varminting are heavy, bull-barreled affairs designed to deliver tack-driving accuracy. Varmint scopes are typically heavy, long-tube affairs featuring high magnification and removable sunshades.

One varmint scope I have had excellent luck with is Bushnell's Elite 4200 8–32X40 model with adjustable parallax. It measures a full 18 inches in length and weighs 22 ounces. The other is a Burris 8–32X44 Signature Series model with tall target knobs. These were my first serious scopes for varmint shooting, and they still see a lot of use. While they can be cranked up to 32X magnification, I have never used them at that setting. Extreme magnification amplifies both rifle movement and heat shimmer. It also produces an extremely dim, tiny field of view, making target acquisition a time-consuming affair. Depth of field—the front-to-back section of the viewing field that stays in sharp focus—also decreases with greater magnification.

I seldom bother using more than 12X, even at 400 yards. I can see a prairie dog fine at that magnification, and can quickly find it again after I shoot. For varminting, I also like fixed-power, target scopes like the venerable Weaver T10; it did an excellent job on varmints. The T10 has been dropped from Weaver's T-series lineup, but I understand it may return soon. Because fixed-power scopes have fewer moving parts, they tend to be trouble-free. Another excellent fixed-power scope for varmint hunting is Leupold's M8 12X40 model with parallax-adjustable objective lens.

Variables do offer great versatility. I have used Leupold's Vari-X III 3.5–10X40 scope with target-style turrets and the LPS 3.5–14X50 scope on both varmint and big-game rifles. The 3.5–10X Vari-X III sports Leupold's Mil-Dot reticle. Dots spaced one millradian apart on the vertical and horizontal cross hairs can be used to estimate range.

Most riflescopes designed for the military use Mil-Dot reticles. Tactical scopes made by Springfield Armory, Nightforce, BSA, and others take their Mil-Dot reticles to even higher levels. Springfield Armory Professional Optics scopes can be ordered with a proprietary, patented reticle designed for counter-sniping. The lower half of this reticle is cluttered with multiple tiny cross hairs and

Rees took this 14-point Texas whitetail with a Thompson/Center Contender mounting variable-power Thompson/Center pistol scope.

graduated horizontal lines. With practice, these various markings can be used to estimate the range quickly. An internal bubble level visible at the bottom of the viewing field helps avoid canting.

A similar device, the Scoplevel, can be mounted on ether 1-inch or 30mm scope tubes. These inexpensive, bubble-type levels can be seen at an upward glance while looking through the scope.

Even slight canting can result in a miss when you are targeting small pests 300 or more yards away.

Shepherd Enterprises offers rangefinding scopes in different models and calibrated for specific trajectories. The Model 310-P3 Shepherd scope can be used with more than a dozen factory loads, ranging from 55-grain, .222 Remington ammo to 150-grain, .308, and .30-06 fodder. The same scope

Long eye-relief scopes are needed for handguns. Note the level device mounted on the scope. This helps prevent canting.

can be used on .375 H&H Magnums throwing 270-grain bullets.

Shepherd reticles display a series of descending-size circles overlaying the cross hair's lower leg. Circles representing a 24-inch-deep target can be used to find the range of elk, and deer hunters can choose a reticle that subtends 18 inches at 100 yards. These circles represent the brisket area on elk and mule deer, respectively.

I had never used a .22 rimfire suitable for long-range shooting until I mounted a Shepherd's scope designed specifically for Long-Rifle ammo on a target-barrel Ruger 10/22. Prairie-dog-size aiming circles indicated ranges out to 500 yards. At that distance, a 40-grain high-velocity LR bullet in .22 caliber drops a full 41 feet when the scope is zeroed at 50 yards. You don't hit prairie dogs with every shot at 300 yards, but I have learned you *can* score with surprising regularity.

Some high-power scopes are designed for long-range deer hunting. I pride myself on stalking as close as possible before firing, but sometimes long-range shooting is the only option available. I have no quarrel with those who have the necessary skills to shoot deer at four hundred yards or more, but

too many inexperienced hunters believe that a magnum rifle with a high-power scope will compensate for poor marksmanship.

A slew of 3.5–10X, 4–14X, and 6–20X variables are now available to long-range deer hunters. Nearly all these scopes have adjustable objectives, and many sport target-style windage and elevation knobs. Oversized 50mm and 56mm objective lenses deliver optimum brightness, even in dim light. These scopes and the beanfield rifles they are mounted on are too big and heavy to lug long distances. But for extreme-range shooting from a Texas tower, they are hard to beat.

A few years ago, a good friend and I rode horses into the Nevada high country looking for trophy deer. The steep terrain and sparse cover made for difficult stalking, but we were both prepared for long-range shooting. My .300 Weatherby Magnum was paired with a 3–12X Zeiss scope. The sight was extremely bright and sharp as well as offering plenty of magnification, but it lacked the heft typical of beanfield scopes.

Randy Brooks, a good friend of mine and the co-owner (with his wife Coni) of Barnes Bullets, is the best rifle marksman I know. Hunting in the old

Russian Federation of Tajikistan, he recently took a fine Marco Polo ram at a distance, measured by laser, of 540 yards. Terrain made stalking any closer impossible, and Randy had the knowledge, skill, and equipment to get the job done. His custom .300 Weatherby Magnum rifle was fitted with a Burris 3–12X50 Black Diamond scope with a combination Plex/Mil-Dot reticle.

Some scopes are available with illuminated reticles. These battery-powered cross hairs are easy to see in low (or almost no) light, and many hunters swear by them. On the other hand, scopes with illuminated reticles are slightly heavier and require batteries. Maybe it is a generational thing, but so far illuminated reticles hold little appeal for me. Personally, I prefer the European solution of a dark, heavy cross hair when hunting in dim light.

Parallax

Most serious scopes designed for long-range shooting feature adjustable parallax. Parallax describes the apparent shift in aiming point when your eye moves to either side of center as you sight through the scope. Most fixed-power hunting scopes are parallax adjusted for a specific distance—usually 100 or 150 yards. At shorter or longer ranges, some parallax appears.

Parallax is most noticeable in high magnification scopes that have a shallow depth of field. If not corrected, parallax can cause misses at extended ranges. Parallax happens when the scope is out of focus. Scopes with parallax-adjustable objective lenses can be quickly refocused, which allows the scope to remain in sharp focus and parallax free regardless of the distance to the target.

Handgun Scopes

Scopes designed specifically for handgun use feature very long eye relief, allowing the guns they are mounted on to be held two feet or more in front of the shooter. Extended eye relief is necessary for this specialized application, but the downside is a tiny, relatively dim viewing field. Only seven manufacturers currently offer handgun scopes. They include Burris, Bushnell, Leupold, Nikon, Sightron, Thompson/Center, and Nikon. Fixed-power models range from 1X to 10X in magnification, while several variable scopes are offered, including everything from 1.5–4X through 9–12X models.

How to Read the Tables

We have divided the tables into the following main categories: (1) telescopic sights (commonly known as "scopes") (2) binoculars (3) spotting scopes (4) rangefinders (5) holographic sights and red-dot sights. In addition there are many subcategories for the various uses: varmint, target, handgun, and long eye-relief scopes; large to extreme range binoculars; and so on.

Note that the tables start with the lowest magnification and end with the highest magnification within each subcategory* We ranked two items of equal magnification value by the size of the objective lens, again starting with the lowest and working up to the highest. If two items had the same magnification and the same size objective lens, we ranked the items alphabetically according to the name of the manufacturer.

We sorted laser rangefinders by the maximum distance the device can read. We sorted holographic sights and red-dot sights alphabetically by manufacturer. We listed eye relief in inches for the telescopic sights and in millimeters for the other optical devices.

Keep in mind that we did not include any item in the tables that were made for nonhunting/game viewing purposes such as binoculars to view operas. In addition, we have excluded optics that have a recommended retail price of below $100.

Spotting scopes needed a special treatment. Many spotting scopes come with individual eyepieces that are sold separately from the spotting-scope body. For instance, Leica's model Televid 62 can be bought with 16X or 32X fixed eyepieces as well as a 16–48X variable eyepiece. In cases such as these, we have listed the data for the entire unit (body and eyepiece) as many times as there are combinations. The retail price listed is the combined price for the body and the eyepiece.

The great value of this book lies in the fact that we list multiple measurements such as weight, field of view, eye relief, and so on in as uniform a manner as possible. This makes it very easy to comparison shop for optics. In some cases the manufacturer would not or could not make the data available to us, despite our best efforts. We have indicated this by using an NA for not available. Depending on the data made available by the manufacturers, we have listed eye relief either as a fixed value or as a range. Also note that some manufacturers gave one field-of-view value even though the optics device listed had variable magnification, for example 4-12X. In that case one can assume that the field of view value is for the midrange of the magnification scale, which in this example would be 8X.

Note: Many optical gear retailers offer 10 to 25 percent discounts below MSRP (Manufacturer's Suggested Retail Price).

*(Please note that we have used the manufacturers' stated model magnification rather than the actual magnification. For instance, the Kahles, model Helia Compact 2.5–10X50 actually has a magnification range of 2.7-10. In order to keep the data in the tables easy to compare, we have listed this model as 2.5-10, as indicated in the model name. Many scope manufacturers make scopes that are slightly over or under the stated model magnification. The differences are indiscernible for anybody save those with highly specialized measuring instruments. Notice also that the exit-pupil value in millimeters varies from one scope to the other, even though the listed model magnification and objective lens values are identical. This is because the value of the exit pupil is based on the actual magnification rather than the stated model magnification. (See page 13 (Mazour article) for an explanation on how exit pupil is calculated.)

Conversion Tables

Weight Conversions

Ounces times 0.035274 equals Grams
Grams times 28.35 equals Ounces

Ounces ... Grams	Grams .. Ounces
1,000 ... 28,349	1000 ... 35.27
900 ... 25,514	900 ... 31.75
800 ... 22,679	800 ... 28.22
700 ... 19,845	700 ... 24.69
600 ... 17,010	600 ... 21.16
500 ... 14,175	500 ... 17.64
400 ... 11,340	400 ... 14.11
300 ... 8,504.8	300 ... 10.58
200 ... 5,669.9	200 ... 7.055
100 ... 2,834.9	100 ... 3.53
90 ... 2,551.4	90 ... 3.17
80 ... 2,267.9	80 ... 2.82
70 ... 1,984.5	70 ... 2.47
60 ... 1,701.0	60 ... 2.12
50 ... 1,417.5	50 ... 1.76
40 ... 1,134.0	40 ... 1.41
30 ... 850.5	30 ... 1.06
20 ... 567.0	20 ... 0.71
10 ... 283.5	10 ... 0.35
9 ... 255.1	9 ... 0.32
8 ... 226.8	8 ... 0.28
7 ... 198.4	7 ... 0.25
6 ... 170.1	6 ... 0.21
5 ... 141.7	5 ... 0.18
4 ... 113.4	4 ... 0.14
3 ... 85.0	3 ... 0.11
2 ... 56.7	2 ... 0.07
1 ... 28.3	1 ... 0.04
0.9 ... 25.5	0.9 ... 0.032
0.8 ... 22.7	0.8 ... 0.028
0.7 ... 19.8	0.7 ... 0.025
0.6 ... 17.0	0.6 ... 0.021
0.5 ... 14.2	0.5 ... 0.018
0.4 ... 11.3	0.4 ... 0.014
0.3 ... 8.5	0.3 ... 0.010
0.2 ... 5.7	0.2 ... 0.007
0.1 ... 2.8	0.1 ... 0.003

Yard/Meter Length Conversions

Yards times .9144 equals Meters
Meters times 1.094 equals Yards

Yards .... Meters	Meters ... Yards
1,000 ..... 914.4	1,000 .... 1,094.0
900 ..... 823.0	900 .... 984.6
800 ..... 731.5	800 .... 875.2
700 ..... 640.1	700 .... 765.8
600 ..... 548.6	600 .... 656.4
500 ..... 457.2	500 .... 547.0
400 ..... 365.8	400 .... 437.6
300 ..... 274.3	300 .... 328.2
200 ..... 182.9	200 .... 218.8
100 ..... 91.4	100 .... 109.4
90 ..... 82.3	90 ..... 98.5
80 ..... 73.2	80 .... 87.5
70 ..... 64.0	70 .... 76.6
60 ..... 54.9	60 .... 65.6
50 ..... 45.7	50 .... 54.7
40 ..... 36.6	40 .... 43.8
30 ..... 27.4	30 .... 32.8
20 ..... 18.3	20 .... 21.9
10 ..... 9.1	10 .... 10.9
9 ..... 8.2	9 .... 9.8
8 ..... 7.3	8 .... 8.8
7 ..... 6.4	7 .... 7.7
6 ..... 5.5	6 .... 6.6
5 ..... 4.6	5 .... 5.5
4 ..... 3.7	4 .... 4.4
3 ..... 2.7	3 .... 3.3
2 ..... 1.8	2 .... 2.2
1 ..... 0.9	1 .... 1.1

Inch-millimeter Conversions

Inches times 25.40 equals millimeters
Millimeters times .03937 equals inches

in ... mm	mm .. in
1,000 25,400	10,000 ... 393.70
900 22,860	9,000 ... 354.33
800 20,320	8,000 ... 314.96
700 17,780	7,000 ... 275.59
600 15,240	6,000 ... 236.22
500 12,700	5,000 ... 196.85
400 10,160	4,000 ... 157.48
300 7,620	3,000 ... 118.11
200 5,080	2,000 ... 78.74
100 2,540	1,000 ... 39.37
90 2,286	900 ... 35.43
80 2,032	800 ... 31.50
70 1,778	700 ... 27.56
60 1,524	600 ... 23.62
50 1,270	500 ... 19.69
40 1,016	400 ... 15.75
30 762	300 ... 11.81
20 508	200 ... 7.87
10 254	100 ... 3.94
9 229	90 ... 3.54
8 203	80 ... 3.15
7 178	70 ... 2.76
6 152	60 ... 2.36
5 127	50 ... 1.97
4 102	40 ... 1.57
3 76	30 ... 1.18
2 51	20 ... 0.79
1 25	10 ... 0.39
0.9 23	9 ... 0.35
0.8 20	8 ... 0.31
0.7 18	7 ... 0.28
0.6 15	6 ... 0.24
0.5 13	5 ... 0.20
0.4 10	4 ... 0.16
0.3 8	3 ... 0.12
0.2 5	2 ... 0.08
0.1 3	1 ... 0.04

Varmint and Target Scopes
Fixed

Millett
4–16X56 Varmint Target Special 30mm A/O

Manufacturer	Model	Tube Dia.	Magnifi-cation	Objective Lens Dia. (mm)	Parallax Adj.	Exit Pupil Dia. (mm)	Eye Relief (in)	FOV (ft/100yds)	O/All Length (in)	Weight (oz)	Price (MSRP)
Bushnell	Elite 3200 10X40	1"	10X	40	Yes	4	3.5	11	11.7	15.5	$320
Leupold	Mark 4 M1 10X40	30mm	10X	40	Yes	4	3.4	11.1	13.1	21	$1,925
Schmidt & Bender	10X42	30mm	10X	42	Yes	4.2	2.9	12	13	16.6	$955
Springfield Armory	10X50 Mil Dot Govt. Model Ill. Reticle	30mm	10X	50	Yes	5	3.5	NA	14.8	14.7	$654
Leupold	M8 12X40	1	12X	40	Yes	3.4	4.2	11.6	13	13.5	$609
Leupold	Mark 4 M1 16X40	30mm	16X	40	Yes	2.6	4	6.6	12.9	22	$1,925
Sightron	Target/Competition 24X42	1"	24X	42	Yes	1.8	3.9	4.4	13.3	15.9	$342
Weaver	T36 36X40	1"	36X	40	Yes	1.1	3	3	15.1	17	$394
Sightron	Target/Competition 36X42	1"	36X	42	Yes	1.2	3.9	3.7	15	16.6	$467

Zeiss
6–24X56 V Series

Zeiss
6–24X56mm V Series

Shepherd
6–18X40mm

Redfield
6–20X50mm Silver

Varmint and Target Scopes

Variable

Manufacturer	Model	Tube Dia.	Magnifi-cation	Objective Lens Dia. (mm)	Parallax Adj.	Exit Pupil Dia. (mm)	Eye Relief (in)	FOV (ft/100yds)	O/All Length (in)	Weight (oz)	Price (MSRP)
Millett	Buck Gold 4–16X44	1"	4–16X	44	Yes	11–2.8	3.5	25–7	14.9	20.5	$270
Millett	Buck Gold 4–16X56 Varmint Special	30mm	4–16X	56	Yes	14–3.5	3.5	35–12	16.4	29.4	$318
Nightforce	5.5–22X56 NXS	30mm	5.5–22X	56	Yes	10.2–2.5	3.9	17.5–4.7	15.2	32	$1,334
Millett	Buck Silver 6–18X40	1"	6–18X	40	Yes	6.7–2.2	3.5	17–7	14.7	18.2	$172
Weaver	Grand Slam 6–20X40	1"	6–20X	40	Yes	6.6–2	3–2.8	16.5–5.3	14.3	17..8	$467
Redfield	Illuminator 6–20X50	1"	6–20X	50	Yes	8.3–2.5	3.1–3.3	20.5–6.3	16	24	$800
Springfield Armory	6–20X50 Mil Dot Govt. Model III. Reticle	30mm	6–20X	50	Yes	8.3–2.5	3.5	NA	18.2	33	$899
Tasco	VAR624X42m	1"	6–24X	42	Yes	7–1.8	3	13–3.7	16	19.6	$114
Tasco	VAR624X44DS	1"	6–24X	44	Yes	7.3–1.8	3	15–4.5	16.5	19.6	$200
Zeiss	VM/Z 6–24X56	30mm	6–24X	56	Yes	9.3–2.3	3.3	18.6–5.2	14.8	29.1	$1,500
BSA	Contender 6–24X40	1"	6–24X	40	Yes	6.7–1.7	3	16–4	15.6	20	$150
Bushnell	Elite 4200 6–24X40	1"	6–24X	40	Yes	6.7–1.7	3.3	18–4.5	16.9	20.2	$730
Sightron	Target/Competition 6–24X42	1"	6–24X	42	Yes	7–1.8	3.6	15.7–4.4	14.6	18.7	$435
Sightron	Tactical/Mil Dot 6–24X42	1"	6–24X	42	Yes	7–1.8	3.6	15.7–4.4	14.6	18.7	$463
Tasco	Varmint 6–24X42	1"	6–24X	42	Yes	7–1.8	3	13–3.7	16	19.6	$114
Weaver	Classic V V24 6–24X42	1"	6–24X	42	Yes	6.6–2	3–2.8	16.5–5.3	14.1	17.6	$469
BSA	Platinum 6–24X44	1"	6–24X	44	Yes	7.3–1.8	3	15–4.5	15.3	18.5	$222
Burris	Signature 6–24X44	1"	6–24X	44	Yes	6.7–1.9	3.2–3.7	18–5.5	16.2	23	$795
Tasco	Varmint 6–24X44	1"	6–24X	44	Yes	7.3–1.8	3	15–4.5	16.5	19.6	$200
BSA	Catseye 6–24X50	1"	6–24X	50	Yes	8.3–2.5	4.5	12	15.8	23	$223
BSA	Contender 6–24X50	1"	6–24X	50	Yes	6.3–1.6	3	11–3	16.1	24	$172
Burris	Black Diamond 6–24X50	30mm	6–24X	50	Yes	7.6–2.1	3.2–3.7	19–5.3	16.9	26	$1,202

Varmint and Target Scopes
Variable

Manufacturer	Model	Tube Dia.	Magnifi-cation	Objective Lens Dia. (mm)	Parallax Adj.	Exit Pupil Dia. (mm)	Eye Relief (in)	FOV (ft/100yds)	O/All Length (in)	Weight (oz)	Price (MSRP)
Pentax	Lightseeker 6–24X50	30mm	6–24X	50	Yes	7.6–2.1	3.2–3.7	18–5	16.9	27	$928
Swarovski	PH 6–24X50	30mm	6–24X	50	Yes	8.3–2.1	3.15	23.2	15.4	23.6	$1,610
Tasco	Varmint 6–24X40	1"	6–25X	40	Yes	6.7–1.7	3	17–4	19.1	16	$114
Leupold	VX-III 6.5–20X	1"	6.5–20X	40	Yes	6.2–2.1	3.6–5.3	14.2–5.5	14.2	16	$750
Nikon	Monarch 6.5–20X44 Ill. Reticle	1"	6.5–20X	44	Yes	6.7–2.2	3.5–3.2	16.1–5.4	14.7	22.5	$981
Nikon	Monarch 6.5–20X44	1"	6.5–20X	44	Yes	6.7–2.2	3.5–3.2	16.1–5.4	14.7	20.8	$705
Simmons	44 Mag 6.5–20X44	1"	6.5–20X	44	Yes	6.8–2.2	2.6–3.4	14–5	12.8	19.5	$285
Burris	Fullfield II 6.5–20X50	1"	6.5–20X	50	Yes	7.6–2.6	3.1–3.6	17–6	14.5	19	$660
Leupold	VX-III 6.5–20X50 LR Target	30mm	6.5–20X	50	Yes	7.4–2.6	3.7–4.9	14.7–5.4	14.3	21	$975
Pentax	Whitetails Unlimited 6.5–20X50	1"	6.5–20X	50	Yes	7.6–2.6	3.1–3.6	17–6	14.6	19	$738
Zeiss	Conquest 6.5–20X50	1"	6.5–20X	50	Yes	7.7–2.5	3.3	17.6–5.8	15.6	21	$950

Springfield
6–20X50mm BDC

Springfield
10X50mm Mil Dot BDC

Swarovski
Habicht PV4 6–18X50Pmm

Sightron
SII 6–24X42mm MD

Varmint and Target Scopes
Variable

Manufacturer	Model	Tube Dia.	Magnifi-cation	Objective Lens Dia. (mm)	Parallax Adj.	Exit Pupil Dia. (mm)	Eye Relief (in)	FOV (ft/100yds)	O/All Length (in)	Weight (oz)	Price (MSRP)
Zeiss	Conquest 6.5–20X50 MC	1"	6.5–20X	50	Yes	7.7–2.5	3.5	17.6–5.8	15.6	21	$950
Sightron	SII Series 6.5–25X50	1"	6.5–25X	50	Yes	7.7–2	3.8–3.3	15–4.2	14.7	20.7	$510
BSA	Platinum 6.5–26X52 Side focus	1"	6.5–26X	52	Yes	8.0–2.0	4	3.5–15	15.5	30	$330
BSA	Contender 8–32X40	1"	8–32X	40	Yes	5.0–1.3	3	11–3	16.1	20	$172
Bushnell	Elite 4200 8–32X40	1"	8–32X	40	Yes	5–1.25	3.3	14–4.7	18	22	$803
Burris	Signature 8–32X55	1"	8–32X	44	Yes	5.1–1.4	3–3.5	14–4.5	17.2	24	$833
Simmons	8–Point 8–32X44	1"	8–32X	44	Yes	5.5–1.4	3–4.5	11.8–3	16.5	23.2	$188
Tasco	TG832X44DS	1"	8–32X	44	Yes	5.5–1.4	3.3	11–3.5	17	20	$220
Burris	Black Diamond 8–32X50	30mm	8–32X	50	Yes	6.2–1.7	3–3.5	14–4	18	27	$1,091
Nightforce	8–32X56 NXS	30mm	8–32X	56	Yes	7–1.8	3.8	12.1–3.1	15.9	34	$1,447
Nightforce	8–32X56 Benchrest	30mm	8–32X	56	Yes	5.6–1.7	3	9.4–3.1	16.6	36	$1,048
Leupold	VX-III 8.5–25X50 LR Target	30mm	8.5–25X	50	Yes	6–2.1	3.6–4.4	11.4–4.3	14.3	21	$1,040
BSA	Platinum 8.5–32X44	1"	8.5–32X	44	Yes	5.5–1.4	3	3.5–11	15.3	19.5	$242
Pentax	Lightseeker 8.5–32X50	30mm	8.5–32X	50	Yes	6.2–1.7	3–3.5	14–4	18	27	$968
BSA	Platinum 8.5–34X52	1"	8.5–34X	52	Yes	6.5–1.5	4	1.5–10	15.5	30	$400
Sightron	Target/Competition 10–40X42	1"	10–40X	42	Yes	4.2–1	3.3–4.5	8.5–2.3	16	19	$564
Tasco	TG104050-DS	1"	10–40X	50	Yes	5–1.3	3.3	11–2.5	15.5	25.5	$212
Tasco	Varmint 10–40X50 FOV @ 16X	1"	10–40X	50	Yes	5–1.3	3.25	25	15.5	25.5	$212
Nightforce	12–42X56 NXS	30mm	12–42X	56	Yes	4.7–1.3	3.9	8.2–2.4	16.1	34	$1,570
Nightforce	12–42X56 Benchrest	30mm	12–42X	56	Yes	4–1.4	3	6.7–2.3	17	36	$1,006

Manufacturer	Model	Tube Dia.	Magnifi-cation	Objective Lens Dia. (mm)	Parallax Adj.	Exit Pupil Dia. (mm)	Eye Relief (in)	FOV (ft/100yds)	O/All Length (in)	Weight (oz)	Price (MSRP)
Sightron	SI Series 1X20	1"	1X	20		20	5.7	111.3	9.5	9.5	$140
Nikon	Buckmasters 1X20 BP	1"	1X	20		30	4.3–13	52.5	8.8	9.2	$241
Thompson/Center	Hawken Hunter 1X32	1"	1X	32		32	3.8	60	9.4	10.2	$145
Millett	Buck Silver Compact 2X20	1"	2X	20		10	5	35	7.5	8.6	$100
Weaver	K2.5 2.5X20	1"	2.5X	20		8	4	36.8	9.6	7.1	$172
Kahles	American Hunter 4X	1"	4X	30		9	3.2	34.5	11.2	12.7	$555
Millett	Buck Silver Compact 4X32	1"	4X	32		8	4.5	22	8.8	10.6	$105
Thompson/Center	Hawken Hunter 4X32	1"	4X	32		8	3	16	8.8	9.1	$182
Leupold	M8 4X	1"	4X	33		8.3	4	24	10.5	9.3	$249
Schmidt & Bender	4X36	1"	4X	36		9	3.3	30	11.4	13.7	$760
Weaver	K4 4X38	1"	4X	38		9.5	3.3	23.1	11.5	9.9	$180

Sightron
SII 6X42mm

Springfield
6X40mm

Kahles
AH Series

Kahles
3–12X56mm, 2.5–10X50mm, 1.5–6X4mm, 1.1–40X24mm

General Hunting Scopes

Fixed Power

Manufacturer	Model	Tube Dia.	Magnifi-cation	Objective Lens Dia. (mm)	Parallax Adj.	Exit Pupil Dia. (mm)	Eye Relief (in)	FOV (ft/100yds)	O/All Length (in)	Weight (oz)	Price (MSRP)
Nikon	Monarch 4X40	1"	4X	40		10	3.5	26.9	11.6	11.6	$351
Nikon	Buckmasters 4X40	1"	4X	40		10	3.3	30.6	12.7	11.8	$249
Redfield	Widefield 4X30	1"	4X	30		7.4	2.9	36	11.4	12.4	$360
Weaver	Grand Slam 4.75X40	1"	4.75X	40		7.7	3.3	20	11	10.8	$335
Burris	Fullfield II 6X HBF	1"	6X	32		5.2	3.8	17	12.2	13.6	$488
Leupold	M8 6X	1"	6X	36		6	4.3	17.7	11.4	10	$364
Weaver	K6 6X38	1"	6X	38		6.3	3.3	18.4	11.6	9.8	$192
Burris	Signature 6X	1"	6X	40		6.7	4	20	12.6	16	$462
Burris	Fullfield II 6X	1"	6X	40		6.5	3.8	17	12.1	12.8	$370
Springfield Armory	6X40 Govt. Model	1"	6X	40		6.7	3.5	NA	13	14.7	$435
Weaver	Target Silhouette T6 6X40	1"	6X	40		6	3	17	12.8	15	$425
Swarovski	PH 6X42	1"	6X	42		7	3.2	23.2	12.8	12	$988
Kahles	American Hunter 6X	1"	6X	42		7.1	3.2	23.4	12.4	14.5	$694
Leupold	M8 6X	1"	6X	42		7	4.5	17	11.9	11.3	$424
Nikon	Monarch 6X42	1"	6X	42		7	3.5	17.8	12.1	12.3	$371
Schmidt & Bender	6X42	1"	6X	42		7	3.3	21	13.1	16.9	$835
Sightron	Target/Competition 6X42	1"	6X	42		7	4	20	12.9	16	$394
Leupold	M8 6X Target	1"	6X	42	Yes	7	4.5	17	12.2	15	$470
Burris	Black Diamond 6X	30mm	6X	50		8.3	4.5	19	13	17.5	$745
Swarovski	PH 8X50	30mm	8X	50		6.3	3.2	23.2	13	14.3	$1,010
Kahles	American Hunter 8X	1"	8X	50		6.4	3.2	17.4	13.1	16.6	$749
Kahles	American Hunter 8X Ill. Reticle	1"	8X	50		6.4	3.2	17.4	13.1	16.6	$1,100
Schmidt & Bender	8X56	1"	8X	56		7	3.2	15	14.6	20.8	$960
Swarovski	PH 8X56	30mm	8X	56		7	3.2	23.2	13.3	15.9	$1,055

Redfield
6–18X40mm

Schmidt & Bender
4–16X50mm

Springfield
4–16X50mm 3rd Generation

BSA
4–16X40mm

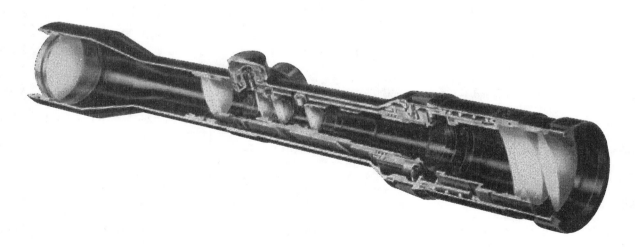

Swarovski
Havicht AV6–18X50mm

General Hunting Scopes

Variable Long Range

Manufacturer	Model	Tube Dia.	Magnifi-cation	Objective Lens Dia. (mm)	Parallax Adj.	Exit Pupil Dia. (mm)	Eye Relief (in)	FOV (ft/100yds)	O/All Length (in)	Weight (oz)	Price (MSRP)
Leupold	Rifleman 3-9X40	1"	3–9X	40		13.3–4.4	4.2–3.7	32.9–13.1	12.2	12.6	$250
Nightforce	3.5–15X50 NXS	30mm	3.5–15X	50	Yes	14.3–3.6	3.9	27.6–7.3	14.7	30	$1,218
Nightforce	3.5–15X56 NXS	30mm	3.5–15X	56	Yes	13.5–4.0	3.8	27.6–7.3	14.8	31	$1,247
Bushnell	Elite 3200 4–12X40	1"	4–12X	40	Yes	10–3.3	3.3	26.9–9	13.2	15	$470
Bushnell	Trophy 4–12X40	1"	4–12X	40	Yes	10–3.3	3.4	32–11	12.6	16.1	$301
Bushnell	Banner 4–12X40	1"	4–12X	40	Yes	10–3.3	3.3	29–11	12	15	$158
Bushnell	Sportsman 4–12X40	1"	4–12X	40	Yes	10–3.3	3.3	25–8.5	13.8	14.6	$142
BSA	Contender 4–16X40	1"	4–16X	40	Yes	10–2.5	3	21–5	13.3	18	$152
Bushnell	Elite 4200 4–16X40	1"	4–16X	40	Yes	10–2.5	3.5	26–7	14.4	18.6	$646
Sightron	Target/Competition 4–16X42	1"	4–16X	42		10.5–2.6	3.6	26–7	13.6	16	$372
Sightron	Tactical/Mil Dot 4–16X42	1"	4–16X	42		10.5–2.6	3.6	26–7	13.6	16	$331
Weaver	V Series V16 4–16X42	1"	4–16X	42		10.5–2.6	3.1	24.4–7	14	16.1	$402
Burris	Signature 4–16X44	1"	4–16X	44	Yes	10–2.8	3.5–4	26–8	15.2	23	$741
Burris	Signature 4–16X44 Electro–Dot	1"	4–16X	44	Yes	10–2.8	3.5–4	26–8	15.2	23	$861
Redfield	Tracker 4–16X44	1"	4–16X	44		5.5–2.7	3–2.6	26.2–7.4	14.4	16	$299
BSA	Catseye 4–16X50	1"	4–16X	50	Yes	12.5–3.1	4.5	25–6	15.2	22	$192
Burris	Mr. T Black Diamond Titanium 4–16X50	30mm	4–16X	50	Yes	12–3.1	3.3–3.8	27–7.5	13.6	27	$1,875
Burris	Black Diamond T–Plate 4–16X50	30mm	4–16X	50	Yes	12–3.1	3.3–3.8	27–7.5	13.6	27	$1,351
Burris	Black Diamond 4–16X50	30mm	4–16X	50	Yes	12–3.1	3.3–3.8	27–7.5	13.6	27	$1,000
Bushnell	Elite 4200 4–16X50	1"	4–16X	50	Yes	12.5–3.	13.6	26–7	15.6	22	$835
Nikon	Tactical 4–16X40	30mm	4–16X	50	Yes	12.5–3.	13.4	26.2–6.6	15	24.3	$1,000
Pentax	Lightseeker 4–16X50	30mm	4–16X	50	Yes	12–3.1	3.3–3.8	27–7.5	15.2	23	$888
Schmidt & Bender	4–16X50 Varmint	30mm	4–16X	50		12.6–3.1	3.7	33.3–11.4	13.7	23.4	$1,595
Swarovski	PH 4–16X50	30mm	4–16X	50		12.5–3.1	3.5	27.3–7.8	14.2	22.2	$1,477
Tasco	World Class DWC416X50	1"	4–16X	50		6.7–1.7	3	28–7	16	20.5	$124
Springfield Armory	4–16X50 Tactical Govt. Mdl. Ill. Reticle	1"	4–16X	42	Yes	10–2.6	3.5	NA	16.1	26.5	$619

Manufacturer	Model	Tube Dia.	Magnifi-cation	Objective Lens Dia. (mm)	Parallax Adj.	Exit Pupil Dia. (mm)	Eye Relief (in)	FOV (ft/100yds)	O/All Length (in)	Weight (oz)	Price (MSRP)
Springfield	4–16X50 Mil Dot Govt. Model III. Reticle	30mm	4–16X	50	Yes	12.5–3.6	3.5	NA	16	30.6	$869
Springfield Armory	4–16X50 3rd Gen. Govt. Mdl. III. Reticle	30mm	4–16X	50	Yes	12.5–3.6	3.5	NA	16	30.6	$869
Springfield Armory	4–16X50 1st Gen Govt. Model	30mm	4–16X	50	Yes	12.5–3.6	3.5	NA	16	28.2	$568
Leupold	VX-III 4.5–14X40	1"	4.5–14X	40	Yes	8.2–2.8	5–3.7	20.8–7.4	12.6	13.2	$699
Nikon	Buckmasters 4.5–14X40	1"	4.5–14X	40	Yes	8.9–2.9	3.6–3.4	22.5–7.5	14.8	18.7	$431
Weaver	Grand Slam 4.5–14X40	1"	4.5–14X	40		8.8–2.6	3.5–3	22.5–10.5	14.3	17.5	$456
Weaver	Tactical 4.5–14X40	1"	4.5–14X	40		9.7–3.1	3	22.3–8.5	15.4	25.8	$716
Burris	Fullfield II 4.5–14X42	1"	4.5–14X	42	Yes	9.1–3.1	2.5–3.6	22–7.5	13	18	$572
Zeiss	Conquest 4.5-14X44	1"	4.5–14X	44	Yes	10.8–3.6	3.3	25.5–8.8	14	20.5	$800
Zeiss	Conquest 4.5–14X44	1"	4.5–14X	44		9.7–3.1	3.5	8.3–25	13.9	17.5	$750
Leupold	VX-III 4.5–14X50 LR Tactical	30mm	4.5–14X	50	Yes	10.2–3.5	4.4–3.7	19–6	12.6	17.5	$790
Pentax	Whitetails Unlimited 4.5–14X50	1"	4.5–14X	50		9.1–3.1	3.1–3.8	25–9	14.1	15	$698
Sightron	SII series 4.5–14X50	1"	4.5–14X	50		11.1–3.6	3.9–3.3	23–8	13.9	15.2	$372
BSA	Big Cat 4.5–14X52	1"	4.5–14X	52	Yes	11.6–3.7	5	30–8.5	12.9	24.7	$250
Bushnell	Elite 3200 5–15X40	1"	5–15X	40	Yes	9–2.7	4.3	21–7	14.5	19	$502
Nikon	Titanium 5.5–16.5X44	1"	5.5–16.5X	44	Yes	8–2.7	3.2–3	19.1–6.4	13.4	20.4	$939
Nikon	Monarch 5.5–16.5X44	1"	5.5–16.5X	44	Yes	8–2.7	3.2–3	19.1–6.4	13.5	18.6	$623
Leupold	VX II 6–18X40	1"	6–18X	40	Yes	6–2.3	4.7–3.7	14.5–6.6	13.4	15.8	$540
Simmons	Pro 50 6–18X40	1"	6–18X	40	Yes	8.2–2.8	3.6	17–5.8	13.2	18.3	$230
Bushnell	Trophy 6–18X40	1"	6–18X	40	Yes	6.6–2.2	3	17.3–6.2	14.8	17.5	$379
Redfield	Golden 5–Star 6–18X40	1"	6–18X	40	Yes	6.6–2.2	3	18–6	13.5	16.3	$484
Shepherd	Shepherd 6X18X40 Varmint/Target FOV @ 16X	1"	6–18X	40	Yes	6.7–2.2	3.2–3.4	5.5	16.3	20.8	$649
Simmons	Prohunter SE 6–18X40	1"	6–18X	40	Yes	6–2	3	14.9–6.5	14.4	22.6	$138
Simmons	Prohunter 6–18X40	1"	6–18X	40	Yes	7	3–2.8	18.5–6	13.8	2	$173
Simmons	Whitetail Expedition 6–18X42	1"	6–18X	42		7–2.3	3	18–6.5	15.1	26.5	$330
Bushnell	Banner 6–18X50	1"	6–18X	50	Yes	8.3–2.8	3.5	17.5–6.2	16	18	$210
Simmons	Prohunter SE 6–18X50	1"	6–18X	50	Yes	8.3–2.7	3	15.6–5	15.3	21.2	$150
Swarovski	AV 6–18X50	1"	6–18X	50		8.2–2.8	3.5	17.4–6.6	14.8	20.3	$888

General Hunting Scopes
Variable Medium to Long Range

Manufacturer	Model	Tube Dia.	Magnifi-cation	Objective Lens Dia. (mm)	Parallax Adj.	Exit Pupil Dia. (mm)	Eye Relief (in)	FOV (ft/100yds)	O/All Length (in)	Weight (oz)	Price (MSRP)
Weaver	V Series V10 2–10X38	1"	2–10X	38		19–3.8	3.3–3	38–9.6	12.5	11	$240
Weaver	V Series V1050 2–10X50	1"	2–10X	50		12–5	3.3–3	37.4–9.1	13.8	15.5	$339
Swarovski	PH 3–12X50	30mm	2–12X	50		13.1–4.2	3.2	33–10.5	12	16.9	$1,421
Tasco	Titan 3–12X52	30mm	2–12X	52		17.3–4.3	4.5	27–10	14	20.7	$336
Burris	Elite 4200 2.5–10X40	1"	2.5–10X	40		15.6–4	3.3	41.5–10.8	13.5	16	$643
Swarovski	PH 2.5–10X42	30mm	2.5–10X	42		13.1–4.2	3.2	39.6–12.6	13.2	15.2	$1,377
BSA	Deer Hunter 2.5–10X44	1"	2.5–10X	44		17.6–44	3	42–12	12.5	13	$100
Burris	Signature 2.5–10X44	1"	2.5–10X	44	Yes	15–4.6	3.0–4.5	35–10	14.1	21	$647
Nikon	Tactical 2.5–10X44 Ill. Reticle	30mm	2.5–10X	44		17.6–4.4	3.39	37.7–9.4	14	25.3	$1,050
Nikon	Tactical 2.5–10X44	30mm	2.5–10X	44		17.6–4.4	3.39	37.7–9.4	14	23.9	$900
Leupold	LPS 2.5–10X45	30mm	2.5–10X	45		17.3–4.6	4.5–3.8	37.2–9.9	11.8	17.2	$1,120
Burris	Elite 4200 2.5–10X50	1"	2.5–10X	50		15–5	3.3	40.3–10.8	14.3	18	$764
Burris	Elite 4200 2.5–10X50 Ill. Dot Reticle	30mm	2.5–10X	50		5–15	3.3	40–13.3	14.5	22	$799
Burris	Black Diamond Titanium 2.5–10X50	30mm	2.5–10X	50	Yes	16–4.6	3–4.7	35–10	13.6	27	$1,786
Burris	Black Diamond T–Plate 2.5–10X50	30mm	2.5–10X	50	Yes	16–4.6	3–4.7	35–10	13.6	23	$1,165
Kahles	Helia Compact 2.5–10X50	30mm	2.5–10X	50		5.1–9.4	3.5	12.9–43.5	12.8	17.3	$999

Zeiss
3–12X56 Conquest

Redfield
Illuminator 3–10X50mm

Schmidt & Bender
Zenith 2.5–10X56mm

Burris
4.5–14X42mm

Leupold
VX-III 3.5–10X40mm

Redfield
4–12X40mm AO

Weaver
4.5–14X40mm AO

Schmidt & Bender
3–12X50mm

Weaver
3–10X40mm

General Hunting Scopes
Variable Medium to Long Range

Manufacturer	Model	Tube Dia.	Magnifi-cation	Objective Lens Dia. (mm)	Parallax Adj.	Exit Pupil Dia. (mm)	Eye Relief (in)	FOV (ft/100yds)	O/All Length (in)	Weight (oz)	Price (MSRP)
Kahles	Helia Compact 2.5–10X50 Ill. Reticle	30mm	2.5–10X	50		5.1–9.4	3.5	12.9–43.5	12.8	17.3	$1,353
Pentax	Lightseeker 2.5–10X50	1"	2.5–10X	50		16.3–4.6	4.2–4.7	35–10	14.1	23	$818
Simmons	Pro 50 2.5–10X50	1"	2.5–10X	50		9–4	2.8	39–12.2	12.8	15.9	$143
Zeiss	Diavari VM/V 2.5–10X50 T*	30mm	2.5–10X	50		15–5	3.5	43.5–12	12.5	14.8	$1,550
Schmidt & Bender	2.5–10X56	30mm	2.5–10X	56		13.9–5.9	3.7	39.6–12	14.8	23	$1,390
Schmidt & Bender	2.5–10X56 Ill. Reticle	30mm	2.5–10X	56		13.9–5.9	3.7	39.6–12	14.8	24	$1,725
Swarovski	PH 2.5–10X56	30mm	2.5–10X	56		13.1–5.6	3.2	39.6–12.3	13.6	18.3	$1,410
Simmons	Aetec 2.8–10X44	1"	2.8–10X	44		14.6–4.4	5	44–14	11.9	15.5	$316
Shepherd	3–10X40	1"	3–10X	40	Yes	13.3–4	3–3.5	41.5–15	14	17	$575
Weaver	Grand Slam 3–10X40	1"	3–10X	40		12.6–4	3.5–3	35–11.3	11.9	13	$347
Swarovski	AV 3–10X42	1"	3–10X	42		12.6–4.2	3.5	33–11.7	12.4	12.7	$821
BSA	Catseye 3–10X44 Ill. Reticle	1"	3–10X	44		14.7–4.4	4.5	27–9	13.3	16	$172
BSA	Catseye 3–10X44	1"	3–10X	44		14.7–4.4	4.5	27–9	13.3	16	$152
Simmons	44 Mag 3–10X44	1"	3–10X	44		14.7–4.4	3	16.5–5	12.8	15.5	$225
Redfield	Illuminator 3–10X50	1"	3–10X	50		12–5	3.1–3	24.5–11.3	14.8	18.1	$742
BSA	Contender 3–12X40	1"	3–12X	40	Yes	13.3–3.3	3	28–7	13.6	17.5	$213
Schmidt & Bender	3–12X42	30mm	3–12X	42		14.1–3.5	3.7	31.5–11.4	13.5	21.4	$1,290
Sightron	SII Series 3–12X42	1"	3–12X	42		14–3.5	3.6–4.2	32–9	11.9	13	$312
Sightron	Tactical/Mil Dot 3–12X42	1"	3–12X	42		14–3.5	3.6–4.2	32–9	11.9	13	$324
Redfield	Tracker 3–12X44	1"	3–12X	44		5.5–3.0	3–2.8	33–8.7	12.4	3.5	$268
Schmidt & Bender	3–12X50	30mm	3–12X	50		14.2–4.2	3.7	33.3–11.4	13.7	23.4	$1,360
Schmidt & Bender	3–12X50 Ill. Reticle	30mm	3–12X	50		14.2–4.2	3.7	33.3–11.4	13.7	23.4	$1,640
Sightron	SII Series 3–12X50	1"	3–12X	50		16.7–4.2	4.5–3.7	34–8.5	13.9	16.3	$343
Tasco	Titan T312X52N	1"	3–12X	52		17.3–4.3	4.5	27–10	14	20.7	$336
Zeiss	Conquest 3-12X56	1"	3–12X	56		12.7–4.7	3.2	27.6–9.9	15.3	25.8	$1,050
Zeiss	Diavari VM/V 3–12X56 T*	30mm	3–12X	56		14.7–4.7	3.5	37.5–10.4	13.5	17.8	$1,600
Zeiss	Diavari ZM/Z 3–12X56 MC	30mm	3–12X	56		12.7–4.7	3.2	27.6–9.9	15.3	25.8	$1,100

Weaver
2.5–8X28mm

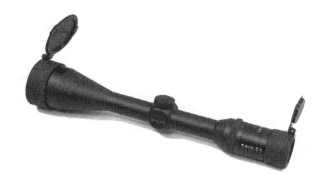

Kahles AH
3.5-10X50mm

Manufacturer	Model	Tube Dia.	Magnifi-cation	Objective Lens Dia. (mm)	Parallax Adj.	Exit Pupil Dia. (mm)	Eye Relief (in)	FOV (ft/100yds)	O/All Length (in)	Weight (oz)	Price (MSRP)
Millett	Buck Gold 3–12X44	1"	3–12X	44		14.7–3.7	3.5	31–10	14.4	20.8	$258
BSA	Contender 3–12X50	1"	3–12X	50		16.7–4.2	3	28–7	13.6	21	$132
Burris	Black Diamond 3–12X50	30mm	3–12X	50	Yes	16–4.2	3.5–4	34–10	13.6	23	$960
Nikon	Titanium 3.3–10X44	1"	3.3–10X	44	Yes	13.3–4.4	3.6	30.4–10.1	13	20.3	$899
Nikon	Monarch 3.3–10X44	1"	3.3–10X	44	Yes	13.3–4.4	3.6	30.4–10.1	13	18.5	$579
Kahles	Helia Compact 3–12X56	30mm	3.3–12X	56		4.6–9.4	3.5	11.4–37.3	14	19.4	$1,100
Kahles	Helia Compact 3–12X56 Ill. Reticle	30mm	3.3–12X	56		4.6–9.4	3.5	11.4–37.3	14	19.4	$1,471
Leupold	VX-III 3.5–10X40	30mm	3.5–10X	40		12.1–4.1	4.6–3.6	25.9–10.7	12.6	13	$550
BSA	Big Cat 3.5–10X43	30mm	3.5–10X	42		12–4.2	5	30–11	12.8	17.3	$270
BSA	Big Cat 3.5–10X42	1"	3.5–10X	42		12–4.2	5	30–11	9.7	16.8	$220
Sightron	SII Series 3.5–10X42	1"	3.5–10X	42		12–4.2	3.6	32–11	12	13.8	$325
Sightron	SIII Series 3.5–10X44	30mm	3.5–10X	44		12.6–4.4	3.5	29–9.2	13.6	24	$697
Zeiss	Conquest 3.5-10X44	1"	3.5–10X	44		11.4–4.7	3.3	35.1–11.6	17.6	17.6	$700
Zeiss	Conquest 3.5-10X44	1"	3.5–10X	44		12.6–4.4	3.5	11.6–35.1	12.7	15.8	$600
BSA	Catseye 3.5–10X50 Ill. Reticle	1"	3.5–10X	50		14–3.5	4.5	30–10.5	13.3	17.2	$192
BSA	Catseye 3.5–10X50	1"	3.5–10X	50		14–3.5	4.5	30–10.5	13.3	17.2	$172

General Hunting Scopes
Variable Medium to Long Range

Manufacturer	Model	Tube Dia.	Magnifi-cation	Objective Lens Dia. (mm)	Parallax Adj.	Exit Pupil Dia. (mm)	Eye Relief (in)	FOV (ft/100yds)	O/All Length (in)	Weight (oz)	Price (MSRP)
Burris	Fullfield II 3.5–10X50	1"	3.5–10X	50		13–5.1	3.1–3.8	28–11	13.1	15	$550
Kahles	American Hunter 3.5–10X50	1"	3.5–10X	50		15.2–5	3.4	33.6–11.7	12.6	14.5	$665
Leupold	VX-III 3.5–10X50	1"	3.5–10X	50		15.2–5.2	4.8–3.6	29.5–10.7	12.2	15.1	$625
Leupold	VX-III 3.5–10X50 Ill. Reticle	1"	3.5–10X	50		15.2–5.2	4.8–3.6	29.5–10.7	12.3	19.5	$800
Millett	Buck Gold 3.5–10X50	1"	3.5–10X	50		14.3–5	3.5	35–12	12.8	18.6	$258
Nikon	Monarch 3.5–10X50 Ill. Reticle	1"	3.5–10X	50		14.3–5	3.9	25.5–8.9	13.9	17.6	$865
Nikon	Monarch 3.5–10X50	1"	3.5–10X	50		14.3–5	3.9	25.5–8.9	13.7	15.8	$665
Sightron	SII Series 3.5–10X50	1"	3.5–10X	50		14.3–5	4.0–4.3	30–10	12.6	15.1	$342
Simmons	ProHunter SE 3.5–10X50	1"	3.5–10X	50		14–5	3.1	30.5–10.6	13.3	21.4	$120
Tasco	Titan DWCP251050	1"	3.5–10X	50		14.3–3.5	3.8	30–10.5	13	17.1	$192
Tasco	Titan 3.5–10X50	1"	3.5–10X	50		14.3–5	3.8	30–10.5	13	17.1	$192
Weaver	Grand Slam 3.5–10X50	1"	3.5–10X	50		11.5–4.5	3.1–3	23.6–10.9	12.8	16.3	$421
Leupold	LPS 3.5–14.5X50 Side Focus	30mm	3.5–14X	50	Yes	13.9–3.6	4.5–3.8	27.2–7.1	13.5	19.5	$1,250

Shepherd
Counter Sniper 3–10X40mm

Schmidt & Bender
2.5–10X56 33.3mm Hunter series

BSA
Big Cat 4.5–14X52mm AO

Leupold
VX-III 4.5–14X50mm LR-IR

Manufacturer	Model	Tube Dia.	Magnifi-cation	Objective Lens Dia. (mm)	Parallax Adj.	Exit Pupil Dia. (mm)	Eye Relief (in)	FOV (ft/100yds)	O/All Length (in)	Weight (oz)	Price (MSRP)
Pentax	Whitetails Unlimited 3.7–11X42	1"	3.7–11X	42		13–5.1	3.1–3.8	28–11	13	15	$558
Simmons	Aetec 3.8–12X44	1"	3.8–12X	44		15–3.7	4	33–11	13.5	20	$330
Leupold	VX II 4–12X40	1"	4–12X	40		9.3–3.6	4.7–3.7	23–11	12.3	14	$500
Leupold	VX–I 4–12X40	1"	4–12X	40		8.8–3.5	4.9–3.7	19.9–9.4	12.3	13	$310
Millett	Buck Silver 4–12X40	1"	4–12X	40	Yes	10–3.3	3.5	25–9	13.8	18.1	$172
Nikon	Monarch 4–12X40	1"	4–12X	40	Yes	10–3.3	3.6–3.4	25.6–8.5	13.7	17.4	$573
Redfield	Golden 5–Star 4–12X40	1"	4–12X	40	Yes	10.3–3.3	3–2.9	27–9.1	12.6	16	$443
Simmons	ProHunter 4–12X40	1"	4–12X	40		10–3.3	3–2.8	26–9	12.8	12.8	$156
Simmons	ProHunter SE 4–12X40	1"	4–12X	40		10–3.3	3	29–10	11.8	12.1	$153
Simmons	Whitetail Expedition 4–12X42	1"	4–12X	42		10.5–5.3	3	29–9.5	13.3	21.3	$309
Simmons	44 Mag 4–12X44	1"	4–12X	44		11–3.7	3	29.5–9.5	13.2	18.2	$275
Simmons	Pro 50 4–12X50	1"	4–12X	50		12.5–4.2	3.5	27–9	13.2	18.3	$211
Simmons	ProHunter SE 4–12X50	1"	4–12X	50		12.5–4.2	3.5	27–9	13.8	12.1	$120
Swarovski	AV 4–12X50	1"	4–12X	50		12.5–4.2	3.5	29.1–9.9	13.5	13.9	$843

Kahles
3–9X42mm

Nikon
T2 3.3–10X44mm AO

General Hunting Scopes
Variable Medium Range

Sightron
SI 3–9X40mm WA

Weaver
3.5–10X50mm Duplex Silver

BSA
3.5–10X50mm

Zeiss
2.5–10X50 V Series Varipoint

Manufacturer	Model	Tube Dia.	Magnifi-cation	Objective Lens Dia. (mm)	Parallax Adj.	Exit Pupil Dia. (mm)	Eye Relief (in)	FOV (ft/100yds)	O/All Length (in)	Weight (oz)	Price (MSRP)
Browning	2–7X32	1"	2–7X	32		16–4.6	3.7	42–11	13.1	12.4	$336
Bushnell	Elite 3200 2–7X	1"	2–7X	32		12.2–4.6	3	44.6–12.7	11.6	12	$304
Nikon	Monarch 2–7X32	1"	2–7X	32		15–4.6	3.9–3.6	44.5–12.7	11.1	11.6	$447
Simmons	ProHunter 2–7X32	1"	2–7X	32		16–4.6	3	53–16.3	11.5	12.5	$122
Leupold	Rifleman 2–7X33	1"	2–7X	33		16.5–4.7	10.8	4.2–3.7	10.8	11.1	$225
Leupold	VX–I 2–7X	1"	2–7X	33		13.2–5.1	4.2–3.7	43–17	11	10.5	$250
Leupold	VX II 2–7X	1"	2–7X	33		13.2–5	4.9–3.8	42–18	10.9	10.5	$350
Kahles	American Hunter 2–7X	1"	2–7X	36		15.6–5.1	3.4	48–27.3	11	11.9	$532
BSA	Big Cat 2–7X (compact)	1"	2–7X	42		21–6	5	57–15	9.7	16.8	$190
Redfield	Widefield 2–7X30	1"	2–7X	30		9.8–3.1	3.8–2.9	58–13	11.5	13.7	$412

Manufacturer	Model	Tube Dia.	Magnification	Objective Lens Dia. (mm)	Parallax Adj.	Exit Pupil Dia. (mm)	Eye Relief (in)	FOV (ft/100yds)	O/All Length (in)	Weight (oz)	Price (MSRP)
Pentax	Lightseeker 2–8X39	1"	2–8X	39		11–4	3.5–4	53–17	11.7	14	$594
Leupold	VX-III 2.5–8X	1"	2.5–8X	36		13.8–4.6	4.7–3.7	37–14	11.3	11.5	$500
Sightron	SII Series 2.5–8X42	1"	2.5–8X	42		16.8–5.3	3.6–4.2	36–12	11.9	12.2	$262
Redfield	Widefield 3–9X36	1"	3–9X	36		12–4	3.3–3	42.5–14.3	12.4	15	$443
Swarovski	AV 3–9X36	1"	3–9X	36		12–4	3.5	39–13.5	11.9	11.6	$743
Weaver	V Series V9 3–9X38	1"	3–9X	38		12.7–4.2	3.3–3	34–11.4	12.3	11.3	$240
Browning	3-9X40	1"	3–9X	40		13.3–4.4	3.4	32–11	13.1	12.4	$352
BSA	Deer Hunter 3–9X40	1"	3–9X	40		13.3–4.4	3	39–13	11.8	13	$100
BSA	Deer Hunter 3–9X40 Ill. Reticle	1"	3–9X	40		13.3–4.4	4.5	39–13	11.8	13	$130
Burris	Fullfield II 3–9X40	1"	3–9X	40		12.9–4.7	3.1–3.8	33–13	12.2	13	$392
Burris	Fullfield II 3–9X40 Electro Dot	1"	3–9X	40		12.9–4.7	3.1–3.8	33–13	12.2	13	$506
Burris	Signature 3–9X40	1"	3–9X	40	Yes	12–4.5	3.5–4	35–14	13	17	$631
Burris	Signature 3–9X40 Electro Dot	1"	3–9X	40	Yes	12–4.5	3.5–4	35–14	13	17	$741
Bushnell	Elite 3200 3–9X40	1"	3–9X	40		13.3–4.4	3.3	33.8–11	12.6	13	$320
Bushnell	Trophy 3–9X40	1"	3–9X	40		13.3–4.4	3.4	42–14	11.7	13.2	$160
Bushnell	Banner 3–9X40	1"	3–9X	40		13.3–4.4	3.3	40–14	12	13	$121
Leupold	VX–1 3–9X40	1"	3–9X	40		12.1–4.7	4.2–3.7	43–17	11.1	10.5	$275
Redfield	Illuminator 3–9X42	1"	3–9X	42		13–4.6	3.3–3.1	31–12	12.6	14.9	$669
Sightron	SII Series 3–9X42	1"	3–9X	42		13–4.6	4.2–3.6	34–12	12.1	13.2	$275
Sightron	Tactical/Mil Dot 3–9X42	1"	3–9X	42		13–4.6	4.2–3.6	34–14	12	13.2	$324
Simmons	Whitetail Expedition 3–9X42	1"	3–9X	42		14–4.6	3	40–13.5	13.4	17.5	$278
Tasco	Titan 3–9X42	1"	3–9X	42		14–4.7	3.5	37–13	12.5	16.8	$282
Zeiss	Diavari V/MV 3–9X42 T*	1"	3–9X	42		10–4.7	3.7	39.6–13.2	13.3	15.2	$1,250
Pentax	Lightseeker 3–9X43	1"	3–9X	43		12–5	3.5–4	36–14	12.7	15	$594
Tasco	Titan T39X42N	1"	3–9X	43		14–4.7	3.5	37–13	12.5	16.8	$282
Millett	3–9X44 Buck Lightning	1"	3–9X	44	Yes	14.7–4.9	3.5	39.13	13.6	17.3	$270

General Hunting Scopes

Variable Medium Range

Manufacturer	Model	Tube Dia.	Magnifi-cation	Objective Lens Dia. (mm)	Parallax Adj.	Exit Pupil Dia. (mm)	Eye Relief (in)	FOV (ft/100yds)	O/All Length (in)	Weight (oz)	Price (MSRP)
Tasco	Titan 3–9X44	1"	3–9X	44		14.6–4.9	3.5	39–14	12.8	16.5	$174
Browning	3-9X50	1"	3–9X	50		16.7–5.6	3.4	30–10.5	18.9	15.7	$420
BSA	Deer Hunter 3–9X50	1"	3–9X	50		16.7–5.6	3	41–15	12.4	13	$110
Burris	Fullfield II 3–9X50	1"	3–9X	50		16–5.3	3.1–3.8	32–13	13.1	17	$472
Burris	Signature 3–9X50	1"	3–9X	50	Yes	16–5.6	3.5–4	35–12	13	19	$645
Bushnell	Elite 3200 3–9X50	30mm	3–9X	50		16–5.6	3.3	31.5–10.5	15.6	22	$383
Bushnell	Elite 3200 3–9X50	1"	3–9X	50		16–5.6	3.3	31.5–10.5	15.7	19	$383
Bushnell	Banner 3–9X50	1"	3–9X	50		16–5.6	3.8	26–12	16	19	$187
Leupold	VX II 3–9X50	1"	3–9X	50		15.2–5.8	4.7–3.7	32–14	12.9	13.7	$415
Millett	Buck Gold 3–9X44	1"	3–9X	50		14.7–4.9	3.5	39–13	13.6	17.3	$238
Nikon	Buckmasters 3–9X50	1"	3–9X	50		15.1–5.9	3.5–3.4	33.9–12.9	12.9	18.2	$463
Pentax	Lightseeker 3–9X50	1"	3–9X	50		15.1–5.6	3.5–4	35–12	13	19	$718
Pentax	Whitetails Unlimited 3–9X50	1"	3–9X	50		16–5.3	3.1–3.8	32–13	13.2	17	$498
Redfield	Golden 5–Star 3–9X50	1"	3–9X	50		11.9–5.1	3.6–3.4	36.7–12	13.1	18.7	$381
Redfield	Tracker 3–9X50	1"	3–9X	50		15.8–6.3	3.3–3	35–11.8	13	18.5	$237
Sightron	SII Series 3–9X50	1"	3–9X	50		16.7–5.6	4.2–3.6	34–12	12.9	15.4	$340
Weaver	V Series V950 3–9X50	1"	3–9X	50		10.5–5	3.3–3	28.5–9.7	13.3	15.5	$240
Zeiss	Conquest 3-9X50	1"	3–9X	50		11.4–5.5	3.3	37.5–12.9	12.4	17.5	$550
Leupold	Rifleman 4-12X40	1"	4–12X	40		10–3.3	4.9–3.7	19.9–9.4	12.2	13.1	$310

Weaver
1.5–5X32mm

Swarovski
Havicht PVI 1.25–4X24mm

Kahles
2-7X36mm

Burris
1.75–5X20mm

Manufacturer	Model	Tube Dia.	Magnification	Objective Lens Dia. (mm)	Parallax Adj.	Exit Pupil Dia. (mm)	Eye Relief (in)	FOV (ft/100yds)	O/All Length (in)	Weight (oz)	Price (MSRP)
Zeiss	Varipoint VM/V 1–1.4X24 T*	30mm	1–1.4X	24		14.8–6	3.7	108–30.8	11.8	15.3	$1,800
Weaver	Classic V3 1–3X20	1"	1–3X	20		15–6.6	3.1	87–31	9.1	8.5	$228
Leupold	VX II 1–4X	1"	1–4X	20		12.5–4.8	4.3–3.8	75–29	9.2	9	$325
Kahles	Helia Compact 1.1–4X	30mm	1.1–4X	24		6.1–10.4	3.5	31.8–108	10.8	14.6	$722
Schmidt & Bender	1.25–4X20	30mm	1.25–4X	20		14.3–5	3.7	96–30	11.5	15.9	$995
Schmidt & Bender	1.25–4X20 Flash Dot	30mm	1.25–4X	20		14.3–5	3.7	96–30	11.5	15.9	$1,480
Swarovski	PH 1.25–4X24	30mm	1.25–4X	24		12.5–6	3.2	98.4–31.2	11.4	12.7	$988
Tasco	Titan 1.25–4.5X26	30mm	1.25–4.5X	26		20–5.8	3.25	77.5–22	10.5	15.2	$274
Nikon	Monarch 1.5–4.5X20 FOV @ 50 yards	1"	1.5–4X	20		13.3–4.4	3.7–3.5	33.5–11.2	9.7	9.8	$385
Nikon	Monarch 1.5–4.5X20 Ultra Wide FOV @ 50 yards	1"	1.5–4X	20		13.3–4.4	3.7–3.5	50.3–16.7	9.7	9.8	$385
Millett	Buck Silver Compact 1.5–4X32	1"	1.5–4X	32		21.3–8	4.5	50–22	8.6	11.2	$136
BSA	Catseye 1.5–4.5X	1"	1.5–4.5X	32		21–7.1	5	55–19	11.5	12	$95
BSA	Catseye 1.5–4.5 Ill. Reticle	1"	1.5–4.5X	32		21–7.1	5	55–19	11.5	12	$122
Bushnell	Banner 1.5–4.5X	1"	1.5–4.5X	32		16.9–8	4.3	78.5–24.9	10.5	12.2	$117
BSA	Big Cat 1.5–4.5X	30mm	1.5–4.5X	42		28–9.3	5	72–22	12.2	15.9	$220
Leupold	VX-III 1.5–5X20	1"	1.5–5X	20		13.3–4.4	5.3–3.7	66–23	9.3	9.5	$500
Leupold	VX-III 1.5–5X20 Ill. Reticle	1"	1.5–5X	20		13.3–4.4	5.3–3.7	66–23	9.3	11	$720

General Hunting Scopes
Variable Short to Medium Range

Manufacturer	Model	Tube Dia.	Magnifi-cation	Objective Lens Dia. (mm)	Parallax Adj.	Exit Pupil Dia. (mm)	Eye Relief (in)	FOV (ft/100yds)	O/All Length (in)	Weight (oz)	Price (MSRP)
Thompson/Center	Hawken Hunter 1.5–5X32	1"	1.5–5X	32		21–6.4	3	53–16.3	11.5	12.5	$169
Weaver	Grand Slam 1.5–5X32	1"	1.5–5X	32		17.4–6.2	3.3	71–21	10.5	11.5	$394
Burris	Signature 1.5–6X	1"	1.5–6X	26		15–4.5	3.5–4	71–20	11	14	$538
Simmons	Whitetail Expedition 1.5–6X32	1"	1.5–6X	32		12.5–5.3	3	72–19	11	15	$268
Bushnell	Elite 4200 1.5–6X	1"	1.5–6X	36		14.6–6	3.3	61.8–16.1	12.8	15.4	$609
Kahles	Helia Compact 1.5–6X	30mm	1.5–6X	42		7.1–13	3.5	21.3–72	16.4	12.1	$632
Kahles	Helia Compact 1.5–6X Ill. Reticle	30mm	1.5–6X	42		7.1–13	3.5	21.3–72	16.4	12.1	$1,249
Schmidt & Bender	1.5–6X42	30mm	1.5–6X	42		14.1–7	3.7	60–19.5	12.4	19.3	$1,125
Schmidt & Bender	1.5–6X42 Ill. Reticle	30mm	1.5–6X	42		14.1–7	3.7	60–19.5	12.4	19.3	$1,525
Sightron	SII Series 1.5–60X42	1"	1.5–6X	42		28–7	4–3.8	50–15	11.7	14	$288
Swarovski	PH 1.5–6X42	30mm	1.5–6X	42		13.1–7	3.2	66.3–21	13	16.2	$1,221
Tasco	Titan 1.5–6X42	30mm	1.5–6X	42		1.5–7	3.5	59–20	12	16.4	$294
Zeiss	Diavari VM/V 1.5–6X42 T*	30mm	1.5–6X	42		15–7	3.5	72–20.7	12.3	15	$1,350
Sightron	SIII Series 1.5–6X50	30mm	1.5–6X	50		33.3–8.3	4.3–3.7	64–17	12	21	$580
Burris	Fullfield II 1.75–5X	1"	1.75–5X	20		11.1–4.2	3.1–3.8	55–20	10.7	10	$400
Burris	Signature 1.75–5X	1"	1.75–5X	32		18–6.4	3.8–4.5	45–19	11.6	12	$601
Bushnell	Trophy 1.75–5X	1"	1.75–5X	32		18.3–6.4	4.1	68–23	10.8	12.3	$178
Leupold	VX-III 1.75–6X	1"	1.75–6X	32		16.8–5.7	4.8–3.7	47–18	11.1	11.3	$500
Pentax	Lightseeker 1.75–6X35	1"	1.75–6X	35		15.3–5	3.5–4	71–20	10.8	13	$546
Pentax	Whitetails Unlimited 2–5X20	1"	2–5X	20		11.1–4.2	3.1–3.8	65–23	10.7	10	$398

Sightron
SII 4X32mm

Weaver
4.75X40mm

Weaver
2–10X38mm

Redfield
Gold Five Star 3–9X40mm Silver

BSA
DH3–9X40mm Silver

Sightron
SII 1.5–6X42mm

Manufacturer	Model	Tube Dia.	Magnifi-cation	Objective Lens Dia. (mm)	Parallax Adj.	Exit Pupil Dia. (mm)	Eye Relief (in)	FOV (ft/100yds)	O/All Length (in)	Weight (oz)	Price (MSRP)
Weaver	Classic V3 1–3X20	1"	1–3X	20		15–6.6	3.1	87–31	9.1	8.5	$228
Leupold	VX II 1–4X	1"	1–4X	20		12.5–4.8	4.3–3.8	75–29	9.2	9	$325
Millett	Buck Silver Compact 1.5–4X32	1"	1.5–4X	32		21.3–8	4.5	50–22	8.6	11.2	$136
Thompson/Center	Hawken Hunter 1.5–5X32	1"	1.5–5X	32		21–6.4	3	53–16.3	11.5	12.5	$169
Weaver	Grand Slam 1.5–5X32	1"	1.5–5X	32		17.4–6.2	3.3	71–21	10.5	11.5	$394
Sightron	SII Compact 2.5–7X32	1"	2.5–7X	32		12.8–4.6	3.8–3.2	41–11.8	10.9	11.6	$243
Sightron	SII Compact 2.5–10X32	1"	2.5–10X	32		12.8–3.2	3.8–3.5	41–10.5	10.9	11.6	$261
Burris	Compact 2–7X	1"	2–7X	26		10.4–3.8	5	32–14	9.5	11	$424
Leupold	Vari–X 2–7X Compact	1"	2–7X	28		11.2–4.2	3.8–3	41–17	9.9	8.2	$299
Burris	Compact 3–9X	1"	3–9X	32		8.9–3.6	5	25–11	10.4	12	$434
Leupold	Vari–X 3–9X Compact	1"	3–9X	33		10.3–3.8	4–3	35–13.5	11	8.8	$315
Burris	Compact 4–12X	1"	4–12X	32		7.1–2.8	5	19–8	11.3	16	$527

General Hunting Scopes

Fixed Compact

Millett
3–9X40mm Buck Silver

Millett
3–9X40mm Buck Silver

Manufacturer	Model	Tube Dia.	Magnifi-cation	Objective Lens Dia. (mm)	Parallax Adj.	Exit Pupil Dia. (mm)	Eye Relief (in)	FOV (ft/100yds)	O/All Length (in)	Weight (oz)	Price (MSRP)
Thompson/Center	Hawken Hunter 1X32	1"	1X	32		32	3.8	60	9.4	10.2	$145
Millett	Buck Silver Compact 2X20	1"	2X	20		10	5	35	7.5	8.6	$100
Leupold	Compact 2.5X	1"	2.5X	20		8.7	4.9	30.5	8	6.5	$330
Weaver	K2.5 2.5X20	1"	2.5X	20		8	4	36.8	9.6	7.1	$172
Burris	Compact 4X	1"	4X	20		5.6	5	24	8.4	8	$319
Millett	Buck Silver Compact 4X32	1"	4X	32		8	4.5	22	8.8	10.6	$105
Sightron	SII Compact 4X32	1"	4X	32		8	4.5	25	9.7	9.8	$206
Thompson/Center	Hawken Hunter 4X32	1"	4X	32		8	3	16	8.8	9.1	$182
Sightron	SII Compact 6X42	1"	6X	42		7	3.6	20	12.8	12.7	$225

Manufacturer	Model	Tube Dia.	Magnifi-cation	Objective Lens Dia. (mm)	Parallax Adj.	Exit Pupil Dia. (mm)	Eye Relief (in)	FOV (ft/100yds)	O/All Length (in)	Weight (oz)	Price (MSRP)
Burris	Scout 1X XER	1"	1X	20		20	4–24	32	8.9	7	$319
Nikon	Buckmasters 1X20 BP	1"	1X	20		30	4.3–13	52.5	8.8	9.2	$241
Leupold	Compact 2.5X	1"	2.3X	20		8.7	4.9	30.5	8	6.5	$250
Burris	Fullfield II 2.5X Shotgun	1"	2.5X	20		8	3.8	55	10.8	10	$308
Sightron	SII 2.5X20SG	1"	2.5X	20		8	4.3	41	10.2	9	$195
Pentax	Lightseeker 2.5X25 SG	1"	2.5X	25		7	3.5–4	55	10	9	$350
Burris	Scout 2.75X	1"	2.75X	20		7.3	7–14	15	20	7	$342
BSA	Deer Hunter 4X SG	1"	4X	32		8	3	32	11.3	11	$90
Simmons	Pro–Diamond Shotgun Reticle 4X32	1"	4X	32		8	5.5	17	8.5	8.8	$113
Weaver	Classic 4X32	1"	4X	32		8	3.5	22.3	9.1	8.5	$265

Simmons
Camo-Shotgun 1.5–5X32mm

Shotgun and Intermediate Eye Relief Scopes

Variable

Manufacturer	Model	Tube Dia.	Magnifi-cation	Objective Lens Dia. (mm)	Parallax Adj.	Exit Pupil Dia. (mm)	Eye Relief (in)	FOV (ft/100yds)	O/All Length (in)	Weight (oz)	Price (MSRP)
Leupold	VX II 1–4X	1"	1–4X	20		12.5–4.8	4.3–3.8	75–29	9.2	9	$324
Nikon	Monarch 1.5–4.5X20 FOV @ 50 yards	1"	1.5–4X	20		13.3–4.4	3.7–3.5	33.5–11.2	9.7	9.8	$385
Nikon	Monarch 1.5–4.5X20 Ultra Wide FOV @ 50 yards	1"	1.5–4X	20		13.3–4.4	3.7–3.5	50.3–16.7	9.7	9.8	$385
BSA	Deer Hunter 1.5–4.5X SG	1"	1.5–4.5X	32		21.3–7.1	5	55–19	11.3	12	$100
Simmons	Shotgun, Ill. Reticle 1.5–5X32	1"	1.5–5X	32		9–5.3	2.8	55–20	10.5	15.2	$150
Weaver	Classic 1.5–5X32	1"	1.5–5X	32		16–6.4	4.3–3.4	62–18.5	10.4	10	$276
Bushnell	Trophy 1.75–4X	1"	1.75–4X	32		18–8	4.1	73–30	10.8	10.9	$172
Leupold	Vari–X 2–7X Compact	1"	2–7X	28		11.2–4.2	3.8–3.0	41–17	9.9	8.2	$300
Leupold	VX II 2–7X Shotgun	1"	2–7X	33		13.2–5	4.9–3.8	42–18	10.9	10.5	$350
Sightron	SII 2.5–7X32SG	1"	2.5–7X	32		12.8–4.6	3.8–3.2	41–11.8	10.9	11.6	$243
Zeiss	Conquest 3–9X40S MC	1"	3–9X	40		12.6–4.4	4	11–34	13.2	15	$500

Burris
2X20mm Handgun

Bushnell
Trophy 2X32

Sightron
SII 1X28P

BSA
Deer Hunter 1.5–4.5X SG

Manufacturer	Model	Tube Dia.	Magnifi-cation	Objective Lens Dia. (mm)	Parallax Adj.	Exit Pupil Dia. (mm)	Eye Relief (in)	FOV (ft/100yds)	O/All Length (in)	Weight (oz)	Price (MSRP)
Burris	1X XER	1"	1X	20		20	4–24	27	8.9	7	$319
Sightron	SII 1X28P	1"	1X	28		28	9–24	28	9.5	9.3	$213
Burris	2X	1"	2X	20		11.8	10–24	21	8.9	7	$275
Leupold	M8 2X EER	1"	2X	20		11.8	18	21	8	6	$334
Nikon	Monarch 2X20 EER	1"	2X	20		11.4	10–26	22	8.1	7	$269
Sightron	SII 2X28P	1"	2X	28		14	9–24	15	9.5	9.3	$213
Weaver	H2 2X28	1"	2X	28		14	12–8	15	8.4	6.7	$209
Bushnell	Trophy 2X	1"	2X	32		16	18	20	8.7	7.7	$219
Burris	4X	1"	4X	26		7	12–20	11	9.7	9	$333
Leupold	M8 4X EER	1"	4X	28		7.6	18	9	8.4	7	$454
Weaver	H4 4X28	1"	4X	28		7	12–8	8.3	8.5	6.4	$227
Burris	10X	1"	10X	32		3.4	9–12	4	10.6	14	$507

Handgun and Long Eye Relief Scopes

Variable

Manufacturer	Model	Tube Dia.	Magnifi-cation	Objective Lens Dia. (mm)	Parallax Adj.	Exit Pupil Dia. (mm)	Eye Relief (in)	FOV (ft/100yds)	O/All Length (in)	Weight (oz)	Price (MSRP)
Thompson/Center	Recoil Proof 1.25–4X28	1"	1.25–4X	28		18.7–7	15–23	24–8	9.4	8.9	$367
Burris	1.5–4X	1"	1.5–4X	20		12.5–5.3	11–24	21–11	11.1	11	$442
Bushnell	Elite 3200 2–6X	1"	2–6X	32		16–5.3	20	10–4	9	10	$445
Bushnell	Trophy 2–6X	1"	2–6X	32		16–5.3	18	11–4	9.1	10.9	$287
Burris	2–7X	1"	2–7X	32		16–4.9	16–4.9	21–7	9.7	13	$461
Thompson/Center	Recoil Proof 2.5–7X28	1"	2.5–7X	28		11.2–4	8–21	15–5	9.3	9.2	$343
Thompson/Center	Recoil Proof 2.5–7X28 Ill. Reticle	1"	2.5–7X	28		11.2–4	8–21	15–5	9.3	10.5	$408
Leupold	Vari–X 2.5–8X EER	1"	2.5–8X	32		12.3–4	15	13	9.7	10.9	$636
Weaver	Classic 2.5–8X28	1"	2.5–8X	28		11.2–3.5	8.2–18	12.2–3.9	9.4	9.1	$276
Nikon	Monarch 2.5–8X28 EER	1"	2.5–9X	28		11.2–3.5	9–30	13.1–4.1	9.6	10.9	$425
Burris	3–9X	1"	3–9X	32		9.4–3.8	10–19	13–6	10.8	16	$540
Thompson/Center	Recoil Proof 3–9X32	1"	3–9X	32		10.7–3.5	13.5–20	10–4	10.4	9.4	$399
Burris	3–12X	1"	3–12X	32		9.2–2.8	10–19	14–4	10.8	16	$560

Burris
Ragebull 2–7X32mm

Manufacturer	Model	Tube Dia.	Magnification	Objective Lens Dia. (mm)	Parallax Adj.	Exit Pupil Dia. (mm)	Eye Relief (in)	FOV (ft/100yds)	O/All Length (in)	Weight (oz)	Price (MSRP)
Leupold	Compact 4X Rimfire Special	1"	4X	28		7.8	4.5	25.5	9.2	7.5	$290
Weaver	RV4 4X28	1"	4X	28		7	3.3	21.8	10.3	8.5	$148
Burris	Rimfire/Airgun 6X	1"	6X	32	Yes	6.5	3.8	17	12.2	13.6	$359

Schmidt & Bender
3–12X50mm

Rimfire Rifle Scopes

Variable

Manufacturer	Model	Tube Dia.	Magnification	Objective Lens Dia. (mm)	Parallax Adj.	Exit Pupil Dia. (mm)	Eye Relief (in)	FOV (ft/100yds)	O/All Length (in)	Weight (oz)	Price (MSRP)
Bushnell	Banner 1–4X	1"	1–4X	32		16.9–8	4.3	78.5–24.9	10.5	12.2	$124
Kahles	American Hunter 2–7X RF	1"	2–7X	36		15.6–5.1	3.4	48–27.3	11	11.9	$532[1]
Leupold	Compact 2–7X Rimfire Special	1"	2–7X	28		11.2–4.2	3.8–3	41–17	9.9	8.2	$300
Weaver	RV7 2.5–7X28	1"	2.5–7X	28		11.2–4	3.5	41.2–15.7	11.5	9.8	$171
Burris	Rimfire/Airgun 3–9X	1"	3–9X	32	Yes	8.9–3.6	3.8–5	23–10	10.4	12	$443
Burris	Rimfire/Airgun 4–12X	1"	4–12X	32	Yes	7.1–2.8	3.8–5	18–8	11.3	16	$527
Burris	Rimfire/Airgun 8–32X	1"	8–32X	44	Yes	5.1–1.4	3–3.5	14–4.5	17.2	24	$854

[1.] with rings.

Bushnell
Banner 1–4X32mm

Reticle Styles

While many reticle styles are available, the reticles shown below represent the most common types. (Courtesy Leupold & Stevens, Inc.)

Leupold offers sixteen reticle options in a variety of Leupold scopes. Each is designed to help you achieve your goals, no matter what type of shooting you enjoy. Several reticles are available as illuminated reticle options in our Vari-X III line of scopes. If you don't see the reticle you prefer listed for a particular scope, the Leupold Custom Shop can install any of our reticles in nearly all of our scopes.

Leupold Dot

A Leupold exclusive, this reticle still has a prominent dot, like the so-called "floating dot." But the thinning portion of the cross hair makes locating the dot much easier.

CPC

As an alternative to the sharp step-down of the Duplex, the CPC reticle has a steady taper down to a fine intersection. This gives a faster reference than a conventional cross hair since it leads your eye to the center.

Fine Duplex

Thinner posts and cross hairs allow for less target coverage, making precision shots on small targets easy.

Cross Hair

The conventional cross hair is still a popular choice among shooters because of its simplicity and versatility.

Duplex

Leupold invented the Duplex design more than thirty-five years ago. Heavy posts stand out against cover and in twilight conditions, pointing boldly to the intersection. Centering is a snap. The thin cross hairs obscure little. Heavy Duplex with its heavy posts makes the Heavy Duplex reticle especially useful in low-light conditions.

Target Dot

The Target Dot seems to "float," and it is a conventional shooter's dot. The cross hairs are extremely thin.

The German No. 1, No. 4, Illuminated No. 4, and Illuminated No. 4 Dot are typical European-style reticles. They are bold and easy to see, especially against tangled backgrounds and shadows.

Mil. Dot

Several Leupold riflescopes are available with the Mil. Dot reticle, which was designed to help the people in the U.S. Marine Corps estimate distances. It is now standard for all military branches.

Illuminated Circle Dot

Designed for fast target acquisition in any environment, the Illuminated Circle Dot reticle can also be used to estimate range. It is available in the Vari-X III 1.5-5X20 Illuminated Reticle model as well as Mark 4 CQ/T scopes

Post & Duplex

The Post & Duplex is a favorite of many hunters because it offers the benefits of both the Duplex and the German No. 4.

Estimating Range with the Mil. Dot Reticle

With practice, this is a simple system to use. Dots are spaced in one mil (milliradian) increments on the cross hair. Using the mil formula, a table can be created that is based on the size of the object being targeted. Just look through the scope, bracket the object between the dots, and refer to the table for an estimated distance to target. Leupold scopes fitted with the mil-dot reticle include more specific instruction on its use.

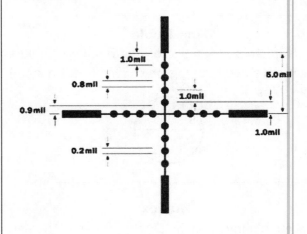

Chapter 10

Mounts & Rings

Aimtech Mount Systems

Aimtech mount systems make it possible to mount scope or electronic sights on a wide variety of firearms. Most models require no gunsmithing. The Aimtech Second Sight series fits most modern sporting rifles, while the ARM-14 and ARM-30 series accommodate Ruger Mini-14 and Min-30 autoloaders. See-through mounts are available for muzzleloading rifles. Saddle-style shotgun mounts fit over the receivers of pumps or autoloaders. Mounts are also offered for the majority of popular centerfire and rimfire pistols, as well as for most revolvers.

B-Square (An Armor Holdings Company)

B-Square offers mounts and rings for more than three hundred rifles, shotguns, auto pistols, and revolvers. These include those manufactured by Anschutz, Benelli, Beretta, BRNO, Browning, BSA, Charter Arms, Colt, Daewoo, Dragunov, Enfield, Fabrique Nationale, Gamo, Glock, Hakim, H &

Saddle mounts are available for adding red dot sights or Holosights to shotguns.

K, Ithaca, Marlin, Mauser, Mossberg, Remington, Rossi, Ruger, Smith & Wesson, Springfield, Taurus, and Winchester. Most mounts require no drilling or tapping.

B-Square also has more than twenty models to fit a wide variety of modern and vintage military rifles. Again, these mounts require no gunsmithing, so the value of a collectible firearm is preserved.

Burris Company

Burris manufactures both one- and two-piece steel dovetail bases that fit a wide variety of bolt, pump, autoloading, lever-action, and single-shot centerfire and rimfire rifles. Bases are also available for selected Smith & Wesson and Ruger

With Redfield/Burrs/Leupold-style mounts and QD mounts, the front ring post fits into a mating receptacle in the base.

Burris Signature rings come complete with Pos-Align nylon inserts.

revolvers, Ruger Mk II automatic pistols and Thompson/Center pistols.

Matching Burris rings are available in low, medium, high, and extra-high models for both 1-inch and 30mm scopes. In addition to standard steel rings, Burris Signature rings house pivoting synthetic inserts that prevent the scope tube from marring and that offer greater gripping strength. Signature rings also accept Pos-Align offset inserts that allow centering the scope without adjusting ring position. Zee rings are available to fit Weaver-style mounts.

Conetrol Mounts

Conetrol offers projection-free bases and smooth-topped steel rings for a large number of firearms, including obsolete rifles.

Each base contains internal socket-cone screws, allowing for windage adjustments during mounting. Three basic styles are offered: Hunter, Gunnur, and Custum—along with rings for five scope-tube diameters. Mounts come in multiple heights and are available in-the-white, blued, or stainless steel. Special finishes also offered, along with a new quick-detach mounting system.

Ironsighter Company

Ironsighter offers see-through mounts for a variety of rifles, shotguns, and muzzleloading rifles. Both fixed and detachable rings are also available to fit Weaver-style bases. Scopes necessarily ride higher when see-through mounts are used, so an add-on cheekpiece may be advisable.

Leupold & Stevens
Leupold Mounting Systems

Leupold mounts and rings are similar to those offered by Burris and Redfield. One difference is the Torx drive system featured on Leupold rings. Torx screws are more resistant to deformation than standard hex-head screws. Leupold Standard 1-Piece and 2-piece bases fit most rifles, and quick-detachable mounts are also available. In addition, bases are available for a variety of handguns. The forward part of each base accepts a dovetail ring, locking it solidly in place. The rear ring is anchored by opposing windage adjustment screws. Five ring heights are offered.

Mounting rings are also available for integral Ruger and Sako bases, as well as for rimfire rifles with dovetail receivers. Rings designed for cross-slot bases fit Remington shotguns with cantelever mounts and Browning Buckmark pistols

Millett Sights

Millett Ultra Light one- and two-piece bases are available for most popular rifles. Matching rings are offered in low, medium, high, and extra-high configurations in 1-inch or 30mm sizes. Angle-Loc Weaver-style rings and mounts are made of either heat-treated steel or a high-strength aluminum alloy. In addition to fitting Weaver-style bases, Angle-Loc rings are made to accommodate the integral mounts found on Ruger M77, Sako, Tikka, CZ, and Brno rifles.

Redfield Mounts

Like Leupold and Burris, Redfield offers all-steel Rotary Dovetail bases in two styles. The Redfield Jr. base is a one-piece bridge-style base, while Redfield Sr. bases are two-piece bridge-style bases. Opposing twin screws at the rear of each base allow windage adjustments. Redfield offers both styles for all popular rifles as well as many handguns.

When installing scope mounts, it's important to have a screwdriver with a properly fitting blade.

Redfield offers its rotary dovetail rings in 1-inch and 30mm sizes, and in low, medium, high, and extra-high heights. Rings to fit Weaver-style bases, as well as Ruger rifles and handguns are also available. A variety of ¾-inch, 1-inch, 26mm, and 30mm rings are offered for grooved rimfire receivers.

S & K Scope Mounts

S & K offers two basic types of mounts: Insta-Mounts that attach to military-type rifles without drilling or tapping, and projectionless mounts with

Quick-detachable rings and mounts are offered by Leupold, Warne, and other manufacturers.

These are Warne's quick-detachable mounts and rings.

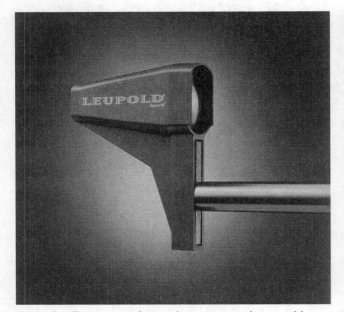

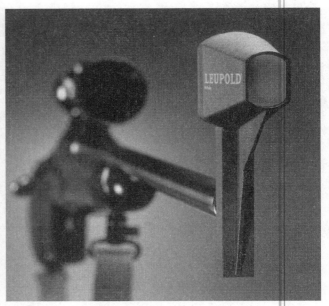

Optical collimators, or boresighters, are used to roughly zero in scopes during the mounting process.

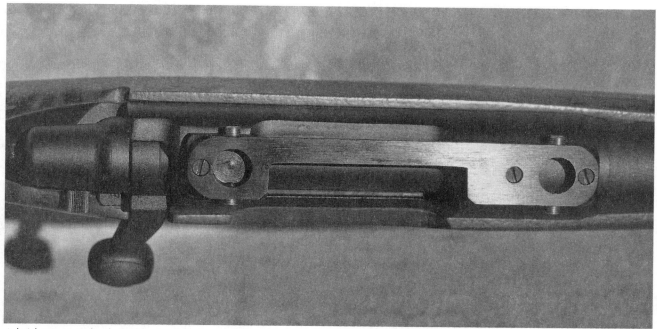

A bridge mount bridges the ejection port. These one-piece bases look stronger than two-piece bases, but they accommodate only one mounting screw at the rear (two-piece bases feature two mounting screws).

Buhler mounts for Weatherby actions.

windage adjustments. These mounts fit most sporting rifles that have been drilled and tapped.

Talley Manufacturing

Talley Quick-Detachable Scope Rings allow scopes to be removed and replaced, then returned to zero without adjustment. Quick interchangeability makes it possible to carry more than one pre-sighted scope for your firearm, and it allows scopes to be easily dismounted during travel.

The Talley Fixed Ring System is for shooters who prefer the sleeker profile of a nondetachable, vertically split ring. This system offers extra strength to withstand magnum recoil.

Talley bases are machined from solid bar stock. Talley's Light-Weight Aluminum Scope Mount is a rigid, one-piece design that leaves no joint between scope and the rifle.

Warne Scope Mounts

The Warne Manufacturing Company offers an extensive range of quick-detachable and permanently attached scope mounts for most currently produced firearms, as well as many discontinued models. The Warne Quick Detachable System allows easy removal of the scope from the firearm without the use of tools. The scope can be reattached quickly without loss of zero. Warne rings are split vertically. Maxima series rings are available in low, medium, high, extra-high, and ultrahigh ring heights, as well as 1-inch or 30mm

diameters. Maxima rings are also offered in a fixed, nonquick-detachable version.

Weaver

Weaver mounts and rings are lightweight, but extremely strong. Scopes can be removed, and they return to zero upon reinstallation. Grand Slam all-steel two-piece bases feature square-cut notches that mate with the cross bolt in every Weaver detachable ring. These are available for all popular rifles. Extension rings allow the scope to be mounted ¾ of an inch either forward or rearward of the normal mounting position.

Available for 1-inch and 30mm-diameter scopes in low, medium, high, and extra-high elevations. They are offered in matte black, gloss black, and silver finishes.

Wideview Scope Mounts

Wideview See-Through Rings and Bases are available in Premium, Ring-Style, High-Ring, and Extra High-Ring models for most centerfire and muzzleloading rifles. These include Browning A-Bolt, CVA, Glenfield, H&R Bolt FN rifles, Hsquvarna, Interarms Mk 10, Knight, Marlin, Mauser, Mossberg, Parker-Hale, Remington, Revelation, Ruger, Savage, Smith & Wesson, Thompson/Center muzzleloaders, Traditions, Weatherby, and Winchester rifles. They are also offered for Mossberg Model 500 shotguns manufactured through 1996, and all Remington Model 870, 1100, and 11-87 shotguns.

Chapter 11
Binoculars

If you are serious about hunting, you need a good binocular. First-time hunters may try to get by without one. The truth is, they can—as long as they are willing to walk many fruitless miles and shoot the first inexperienced animal they stumble upon. As a cash-poor teenage deer hunter, I simply couldn't afford a decent binocular. I could barely afford a rifle and shells. I never got within rifle range of a trophy buck, but I sometimes managed to bring a doe or forkhorn buck home for the freezer. I was hunting, but not very successfully. Like most budding sportsmen, I was taking baby steps. I didn't really begin to stride out until I finally bought a binocular and learned how to use it.

A binocular is not an optional hunting accessory. It is a vital part of your gear, second only to your rifle in importance. You *hunt* game with a binocular. Once you locate the game, you then evaluate it and plan a successful stalk . . . all with the help of your binocular. You finish the hunt with your rifle.

In addition to being an indispensable hunting tool, a binocular greatly adds to the enjoyment of simply being afield. When you are examining distant slopes in search of game, your binocular often reveals riveting tableaus. You may see a doe and her fauns at play, watch sparring bucks, or follow the lazy spirals of a hawk or eagle scanning for unsuspecting prey. I have watched ducks cup their wings to land and marked the location of the pond for future reference. Once I was treated to the rare and unforgettable sight of a tawny cougar moving

The most effective way to use a binocular is to take a comfortable seat, rest your elbows on your knees, and take the time to scrutinize possible cover carefully.

Alaskan guide Ed Stevenson looks for bear on a distant hillside.

purposefully along a mountain trail. Such sights are an integral part of the hunting experience, but you will miss seeing them if you don't have a binocular.

OK, we have established the need to have a binocular. But what kind should you buy? Binoculars come in a confusing variety of sizes and shapes, and prices vary widely. Which binocular should you choose?

For most people, cost is an important factor. Price is one sign of quality—the more it costs, the better the binocular is supposed to be. I say *supposed* to be because sometimes price can fool you. Not too many years ago, binoculars from big-name European companies like Zeiss, Swarovski, and Leica were accepted as the world's best—and were priced accordingly. Binoculars bearing these famous names are still among the best you can buy, but they now have serious competition from companies like Leupold, Bausch & Lomb, Pentax, Nikon, and others.

Over the last few years there has been a revolution in optics manufacturing. While European wages are high and import duties add to the expense of top-quality German optics, computers and improved manufacturing technology have combined to drive costs down while at the same time increase quality. To remain competitive, moreover, Zeiss and other European companies are manufacturing certain products in other countries, including the United States. Optical manufacturers have become a lot more efficient in recent years, and competition has drastically lowered prices.

This revolution means you don't always have to pony up $1,000 or more to get a high-quality binocular. It is still advisable to buy the best you can afford, but that doesn't necessarily mean breaking the bank. Knowing what to look for can help you shop carefully and get the best value for your buck.

Getting a bargain, however, doesn't mean buying a binocular cheaply. Don't fall for the "camo-patterned $39.95 specials" that discount sporting goods stores display when deer season rolls around. While camouflage may be a good thing, it isn't really necessary on a hunting binocular. This could change, but right now I only know of a couple of top-quality binoculars that wear a camouflage finish. Most models are solid black, green, or gray. And while I always appreciate a good bargain, I have yet to see a $40 (or $50 or $70) binocular worth carrying home. That is why no binocular (or riflescope or spotting scope) cataloged in this book lists for less than $100.

Bargain binoculars may seem fine when you try them out in a store, but looking through a store window is a lousy way to test optical quality. Almost any binocular delivers a bright image under sunny, daylight conditions.

Cheaply made binoculars are more likely to be out of alignment, which guarantees eyestrain and headaches. If a bottom-dollar binocular seems in alignment when you check it out in the store, it isn't likely to stay that way. You can almost count on cheap binoculars falling apart at the worst possible time. In addition to being unreliable, they lack quality optics, fully coated lenses, and other features that help you see game clearly.

It is possible to buy a usable binocular for around $100, but you will get much better quality by paying two or three times that amount. Top-grade binoculars sell for $400 or more (sometimes a *lot* more). Be aware that all binoculars in a particular price range aren't likely to deliver equal performance. Line up several different models and compare them before you buy.

An excellent way to do this is select two similar binoculars and hold one atop the other. Alternately look through the top one and then the bottom one. Try reading the labels on boxes at the far end of the store. Do not look through the store window at an object in the sunlight outside. Instead, focus each binocular on something up in the rafters or somewhere else in the dimmest part of the store. Even poor binoculars can seem to perform well in full daylight. The true test is to see how bright, clear, and sharp something appears in deep shadow. Take the time to look carefully through at least three or four binoculars. Compare image brightness and clarity. One model should stand out from the others. That is the one to buy.

Exit pupils visible in each eyepiece should appear perfectly round, with no flattened sides.

Another test you can make while you are still at the store is to check the shape of the exit pupil. We will have more to say about exit pupils, but for now just be sure each pupil appears perfectly round. To verify exit pupil roundness, hold the binocular eight or ten inches in front of your face and point the front (objective) lenses at a source of light. A small dot of light will appear in the eyepiece. This dot should be round. If it has flattened sides, that is one indication the binocular has been cheaply constructed. Using it for more than a ten-second glance may strain your eyes and give you a pounding headache. Binoculars exhibiting slightly squared exit pupils may otherwise be capable of performing half decently, but I wouldn't count on it. Rather than risking your money on something that could be junk, I would advise digging a little deeper into what is available.

Ergonomics is also important. How does each binocular feel in your hand? How well does it balance? How heavy is it? Does it feel awkward and burdensome when hanging from your neck? In short, which model seems to suit you best?

While these tests are useful and easy to perform, you first must decide which *kind* of binocular you want to buy. Binoculars come in four basic sizes: compact, midsize, full-size, and very large. Unless you have specialized hunting needs, it is best to narrow your choice to the mid- or full-size models. Compact folding glasses sporting 20 to 25mm objective lenses (the lenses at the front of the

When it comes to optical performance, the size of the objective lens matters. From top, binoculars with 32mm, 50mm, and 80mm objectives. The downsize to size is added bulk and heft.

The Swarovski 15X56mm binocular is a top choice for distant viewing, but requires some type of stable rest.

binocular) simply lack the brightness, sharpness, and clarity that larger objectives provide. This is true regardless of price. An expensive 8X20 or 10X25 compact binocular won't deliver images as bright and sharp as you will get with a less costly binocular sporting larger 32mm or 40mm lenses.

Exit pupil size is one reason for this. To determine exit pupil size, divide the diameter (in millimeters) of the objective lens by the magnification (power). A 10X40 binocular has a 4mm exit pupil. This is an acceptable size for normal daytime use. Exit-pupil size indicates how much light reaches your eyes. In daylight, a 5mm exit pupil delivers all the light your eye can accommodate. If you are much over forty, a 4mm exit pupil is all you will need for daytime use. As you age, your pupils lose the ability to dilate as far as they did when you were a teenager . . . a fact I have sadly discovered.

At dawn or dusk the pupil of your eye expands in order to compensate for dimmer light. Even if your eyes are young and strong, the widest exit pupil known is 7mm. Anything larger 7mm is wasted potential. European sportsmen like to hunt into late evening, long after American hunters are sitting around the fire enjoying an after-dinner cup of coffee. To accommodate that kind of hunting, many Europeans buy big, top-quality 8X56 German binoculars. Yep, they have exit pupils measuring a full 7mm in diameter. In addition to being pricey, these binoculars weigh a ton. Hanging a three-pound binocular from your neck becomes old very quickly.

While 8X56 binoculars are bulky and heavy, pocket-size binoculars sporting tiny exit pupils simply aren't very useful afield. A compact 10X25 binocular delivers an exit pupil measuring just 2.5mm in diameter. With such a small diameter, you will be unable see animals at long range very clearly in daytime, let alone when the light begins to fade.

Exit-pupil size is one good indicator of viewing clarity—the larger the exit pupil (up to the 7mm maximum as mentioned earlier), the brighter and sharper the image. This brings us back to the relationship between magnification and the

This 15X80mm Steiner binocular offers great power and resolution, but again it requires a rest like this Stoney Point Steady-Stix bipod.

diameter of the objective lens. If the optics are of equal quality, an 8X42 binocular sporting a 5.25mm exit pupil provides a brighter, sharper image than a 10X42 binocular with a 4.2mm pupil. A 7X42 binocular—with its large 6mm exit pupil—offers an even crisper, brighter image.

Exit-pupil size is not the only measure of image brightness in bad light. "Twilight factor" may be a better indication of a binocular's viewing ability in the dim, low-contrast conditions hunters often experience. Twilight factor is calculated by multiplying magnification by the size (in millimeters) of the objective lens, then taking the square root of the product. The higher the twilight factor, the brighter the image.

When you compare Swarovski's highly regarded 8X56 B SLC binocular with the similar size 15X56 WB model, a surprising fact emerges. While the 8X model sports the optimum 7mm exit pupil

From left, a full-size Bausch & Lomb Elite, a midsize Leica Trinovid, and a large Swarovski binocular are the most useful sizes for hunting. All three models sport 10X magnification.

(compared with 3.7mm in the 15X binocular), the more powerful 15X glass handily edges its 8X brother with a twilight factor rating of 29—by far the highest of any Swarovski binocular. The 8X56 Swarovski gets a still respectable, but less impressive, 21.2 rating. Other things being equal, the higher the magnification, the brighter the image.

In spite of the brightness rule mentioned above, the most useful magnification for a hunting binocular is from 7X to 10X. Most users have difficulty holding 12X (or more) binoculars steady without the aid of a tripod or some other rest. While 10X binoculars are extremely popular with hunters, 7X or 8X models offer some very real advantages. As my colleague John Barsness has pointed out, increasing a binocular's magnification reduces the effectiveness of a tiny area—called the macula—at the rear of our eye. The macula transmits detail to our brain, while other parts of the eye are responsible for seeing motion. In a nutshell, with binoculars of identical quality, an 8X model typically delivers greater detail than a 10X model

will. A 7X binocular (if you can find one) will do even better.

Two different prism types are available: Roof-prism binoculars have straight tubes (or barrels) and internal prisms that split the light beams at one end and reassemble them at the other. Porro-prism binoculars are identified by their dogleg tubes. They use a different arrangement of mirrors and prisms to deliver light to your eye. Both types work very well. Roof-prism models are popular because they are typically handier and more compact. Porro-prism binoculars may be slightly bulkier, but they cost less to manufacture; thus, it is often possible to get equal optical quality for less money when you buy a porro-prism design.

Until recently, prisms were offered in two basic types. Once the universal standard, BK7 prisms have been largely replaced in better-quality binoculars by BaK4 prisms. BK7 prisms have a lower refractive index and aren't as efficient in reflecting light back to the prism. Too, binoculars with BK7 prisms may exhibit exit pupils with squared or shadowed edges. Because BK7 prisms are less expensive, they are still used in many models. BaK4 prisms feature higher-quality glass and additional coatings to control reflection. They have a higher index of refraction and produce round, full exit pupils. These higher-priced prisms transmit more light, delivering better resolution and improved color correction.

Brunton has now introduced a third prism type featuring SF prism glass, formerly used only in astronomical telescopes and expensive cameras. This is said to be of even higher quality than BaK4 prisms, and after testing Brunton's new Epoch binoculars I am inclined to believe it. I expect to see SF prism glass showing up in other high-end binoculars before long.

Be sure the binocular you buy has multicoated lenses. Waterproofing is also important. Binoculars that aren't fully waterproof can fog in the cold or rain. If you wear prescription glasses, eye relief is another big consideration. Eye relief is the distance your eye must be from the eyepiece lens to see the fullest possible field of view. Glasses keep your eye farther from the eyepiece. Unless the binocular offers sufficient eye relief, this limits your field of view. Folding rubber or twist-up eyecups help position your eye the right distance from the lens. A twist-adjustable diopter setting on one eyepiece (usually the right) allows the binocular to be focused so it delivers a sharp image to both eyes. To make this adjustment, focus the binocular while you squint your right eye. Then close the other eye and twist the right eyepiece until it comes into focus.

Which binocular should you buy? To recap, I suggest bypassing small pocket models with 20mm and 25mm objectives. Regardless of price and quality, you cannot get top performance from optics this small. I also advise against big, heavy binoculars with 50mm or 56mm objective lenses if you intend to hang them from your neck all day afield. Binoculars of this size are best carried in a daypack, which means digging them out every time you stop to look for game. That narrows the choice to mid- and full-size models. Full-size 8X

Rees uses his binocular to watch for bear from an Alaskan streamside ambush.

and 10X models sport 40mm or 42mm objective lenses. They are lighter than 56mm models, but still heavier and more tiring to carry than midsize binoculars. Most midsize models have 30mm to 32mm objectives, making them relatively light, handy, and compact. The images they deliver, however, aren't quite as bright as you will get with a full-size binocular, particularly in low light. Those are the trade-offs. Here is a closer look at the available options:

Superlight, Ultra-Compact Binoculars

The older I get, the greater my appreciation for lightweight hunting gear. I hunt a lot of western mule deer, and these hunts never involve spending an afternoon sitting in a tree stand. What's more, I have never shot deer at extreme range from a comfortable Texas tower. Whenever I hunt deer, I usually do a lot of walking. I often find myself struggling up steep slopes at oxygen-starved elevations or fighting through thick stands of oak brush. During elk season I ride horseback up the mountains, then hunt on foot. I do my best to avoid lugging extra weight around.

If heft and size are real issues, there are featherlight, folding binoculars you can buy that fit handily in a shirt pocket and tip the scales at less than eight ounces. If you insist on this kind of lightweight portability, I have already pointed out the downside: relatively poor optical performance delivered by the tiny 21–25mm objectives these models wear. Regardless of lens quality—and there are some very fine and costly folding models on the market—combining 25mm objectives with 8X or 10X magnification means not-very-bright viewing in dim light. While they are temptingly compact, I do not recommend pocket-size binoculars to any serious sportsman.

A compact, top-quality 10X binocular that tucks into your shirt pocket, weighs a handful of ounces, and delivers superb viewing performance would be a wonderful thing to own. Low price would be an added bonus. Unfortunately, a binocular's size, weight, magnification, cost, and optical performance are all interrelated. A pocket-size folding model that sports 22mm objectives simply cannot compete with a heavier binocular wearing 50mm or 56mm objective lenses. While lens quality, prisms, type of coating, and binocular construction play a part, bigger optics almost always produce brighter, sharper images. The downside

is greater size and heft. Optimum viewing performance necessarily means lugging a couple of pounds of bulky, hefty glassware.

While I give most pocket-size binoculars a wide berth, I once enjoyed using a 6X26 Bushnell Custom Compact—the first compact hunting binocular I ever owned. This porro-prism model weighed just twelve ounces and fit neatly inside the breast pocket of my hunting shirt. In spite of its lightweight handiness, this little binocular really delivered. Combined with excellent lenses and a 4.3mm exit pupil, the Custom Compact yielded bright, crisp images. It worked great in deer woods, where I used the little Bushnell to spot part of a deer's leg or antler in thick brush. It also worked very well for locating deer hidden in shadow 300 or 400 yards away.

Custom Compacts are still available, now marketed under the Bausch & Lomb name. Sadly, the 6X26 model I liked so well has been discontinued because few people appreciate a good 6X glass anymore. The 7X26 version currently offered is pretty good (I own and regularly use one), but its smaller 3.7mm exit pupil isn't quite as bright.

A guide checks out mountain goats with his binocular during a British Columbia hunt. A good binocular is a vital part of any hunter's equipment.

The Custom Compact worked well in the Utah deer woods, but it disappointed me during an Alaska bear hunt. Its 6X26 optics simply couldn't deliver crisp images in Alaska's perennially dark, overcast fall weather. At one point, Ed Stevenson, my guide, pointed to a bear that he had spotted with his 10X Zeiss binocular. The big boar was ambling along the shoreline on the far side of Gravina Bay, but I could barely make it out with my pocket-size Bushnell. It simply lacked the optical oomph to penetrate the dim Alaska light and show me a clear, sharp image.

When I returned from that hunt, I promptly bought a heavy 8X56 binocular. I carried it on a number of hunts, enjoying the exceptionally bright, crisp images it provided. The big binocular delivered superlative viewing, but I was more than happy to remove it from my neck at the end of the day.

Full-Size Hunting Binoculars

While I still prefer binoculars with big 56mm objectives in heavy, overcast, or nearly dark conditions, I find them too heavy for all-day, all-round hunting duty. Most of the time I rely on 8X or 10X binoculars with 40mm or 42mm objective lenses. These are the full-size models that most experienced hunters rely on for quality viewing.

I have owned a number of excellent full-size binoculars, including Zeiss's classic roof-prism, black-rubber-armored 10X40 model long favored by many hunters. It has performed superbly not only in Europe and Alaska but also when I was scouting for western deer, elk, and pronghorn. While this remains a very fine binocular, Zeiss has recently replaced it with the new Victory 10X40 BT* binocular. The binoculars in the Victory Series feature lenses treated with improved antireflection multicoating and new phase-correction coatings on prisms. New push-pull eyecups are also featured, along with a guarantee that these binoculars are 100 percent waterproof and fogproof. The 10X40 Victory weighs 26 ounces and lists at just under $1,100.

A binocular comes in handy for locating distant targets when hunting prairie dogs.

I have been similarly impressed with the 10X42 Elite binocular offered by Bausch & Lomb. This roof-prism model is fully waterproof and has first-class optics. I recently used the Elite in Alaska during a fall brown-bear hunt. For ten straight days it was subjected to the unbelievably wet, freezing weather only Alaska provides. While my scope briefly fogged up, the binocular's innards remained clear and dry. This binocular weighs 28 ounces. The list price is around $1,500, but it typically sells for several hundred dollars less.

Another favorite of mine is the Swarovski 10X42 WB SLC binocular, which I have carried on many deer and pronghorn hunts the past few years. It has always delivered a sharp, bright viewing image, and, if you want more magnification, a 2X doubler is available to convert one tube to a 20X spotting scope.

While the binoculars I have just described are all costly, high-end models, I have also been impressed with the performance delivered by Nikon's 10X42 Monarch, Bushnell's 10X42 Legend,

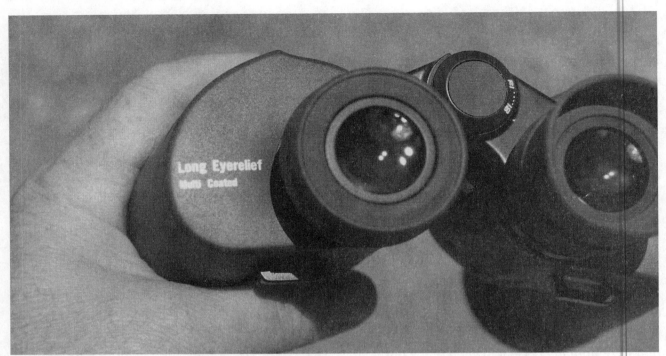

Long eye relief and fold-down (or push-down) eyecups are important for eyeglass wearers. Multicoated lenses help ensure good optical performance.

and Leupold's 10X42 Wind River. These are all fully waterproof roof-prism binoculars that list for around $500 but usually sell for substantially less.

While I appreciate 10X magnification, I am beginning to carry 8X binoculars with increasing regularity. As noted elsewhere in this chapter, an 8X binocular usually delivers a noticeably sharper viewing image. Objects appear smaller, but you see them in greater detail. Good, affordably priced 8X binoculars I have been using include Bausch & Lomb's 8X40 Discoverer, Burris's 8X40 Fullfield, and the excellent Minox BD 8.5X42 BR. Both the Discoverer and Fullfield are porro-prism models, while the Minox has a roof-prism design. All are waterproof. Listing at a recommended $529, the Minox is the most expensive of this trio. However, any of these models should be available for well under $500.

I have been highly impressed with Brunton's new Epoch binocular . . . if you are willing to spend a lot more money. This full-size, roof-prism binocular has 43mm objective lenses and comes in either 7.5X or 10.5X magnification. My 7.5X

Epoch produces exceptionally bright, sharp images, offers 20mm of eye relief, and tips the scales at just 26 ounces. This lightweight binocular is a heavy hitter in both performance and price. The recommended retail price is $1,449.

Midsize Hunting Binoculars

Full-size 8X40 or 10X42 binoculars are your best bet for most kinds of hunting. They are the most versatile "go-to" binoculars you can buy. There is a downside to this, however. While the performance of many of these binoculars is excellent, not everyone wants to be burdened by the heft of a full-size model.

If you are curious about how you would do while hunting in steep terrain carrying a heavy, full-size binocular, think about the kind of shape you are in. Could you backpack the high country in search of sheep, goats, or mountain mule deer while carrying all the necessary gear? Could you keep up with guide Ed Stevenson while hurrying along Alaska bear trails? I have walked many miles daily on hunts like these while toting a pack, rifle, ammo, food, other necessary gear, and a good binocular. Pounds quickly add up, so a lightweight binocular makes good sense. During a long day afield, a heavy binocular literally becomes a pain in the neck. When I am climbing steep inclines after mountain game, I usually opt for lighter, less hefty binoculars that are still capable of delivering bright, crisp images.

For hunters who want a relatively light, handy binocular, I would suggest a good 8X30 or 8X32mm midsize model of either roof-prism or porro-prism design. Your binocular is a lifetime investment, so buy quality optics. How much cash will you need to expend? While you should stretch your budget to spend as much as you can afford, several moderately priced models deserve consideration. Brunton's midsize 8X32mm roof-prism binocular is waterproof and has fully multicoated lenses. It weighs just over 20 ounces and lists for around $200. Bushnell's 8X32 Legend, Nikon's 8X36 Sporter I, and Burris's 8X32

Landmark are also very affordable. Slightly higher-priced models include Pentax's DCF 8X32 binocular and Leupold's 8X32 Wind River Plus. The Zeiss Diafun 8X30 binocular weighs less than a pound and sells for around $400. Kahles's excellent, fully waterproof 8X32 model is priced slightly higher, while Swarovski's top-quality 7X30 roof-prism binocular lists for just under $700.

A great choice for weight-conscious hunters would be one of the better quality 8X models that sport 30mm or 32mm objective lenses and weigh somewhere in the neighborhood of 20 to 24 ounces. An 8X32 glass gives you a 4mm exit pupil, which provides adequate brightness in all but the dimmest light.

Kahles's 8X32 compact binocular is 4¾ inches tall and weighs just 21½ ounces. The roof-prism binocular is waterproof, shockproof, and has fully multicoated optics. I like this lightweight binocular because it offers plenty of eye relief for eyeglass wearers like myself. The field of view is 399 feet at 100 yards.

These high-power binoculars are specialized tools for extreme-range viewing. From left: 12X50mm Bausch & Lomb Elite, 15X80mm Steiner, 12X50mm Shepherd, image-stabilizing Zeiss 20X60 S, and 15X56mm Swarovski with optional 2X extender.

This prairie dog hunter uses a binocular to spot hits for his pistol-shooting companion.

A porro-prism binocular I really like is Nikon's 8X32 Superior E (SE). It weighs just 22 ounces and provides very high-quality viewing. Eye relief is a generous 17½mm, and you see a generously wide field of view. Quality multicoated lenses and BaK4 prisms deliver very sharp resolution.

Steiner's 10X30mm Predator is compact and weighs a bare 10½ ounces; however, an eye relief of just 12mm and a limited viewing field makes it a less attractive choice than the larger 8X32 Predator. While this roof-prism model weighs twice as much, it offers 22mm of eye relief and a larger viewing field. The lens coatings on the Steiner Predator model are supposed to make animals "pop" from dark, wooded backgrounds.

Leica's 10X32 BA Ultra Trinovid binocular weighs 22 ounces and is fully waterproof. Field of view is a wide 405 feet at 100 yards. Also from Leica, the Minox 8X32 BR compact binocular is slightly lighter and stands just 4 inches high.

Swarovski's 8X30WB SLC is a compact, roof-prism model that is an ounce lighter. The trademark green rubber-armored binocular is a favorite of many hunters. Zeiss's 8X30 B MC Diafun binocular may not be as rugged as the company's excellent 8X30 B/GA model, but it weighs less than a pound. If you want a good, truly lightweight binocular, the Diafun is hard to beat.

Unless you are independently wealthy, cost is always a consideration. Earlier in this chapter I gave some tips for comparing binoculars before you buy. However, it is usually wise to pay as much as you can when purchasing any kind of hunting optics. This is particularly true with binoculars. The performance difference between budget-priced and expensive top-end binoculars may not be readily apparent, but the difference is there. In full sunlight, even bottom-end models may seem to deliver a crisp, bright-looking image. These same binoculars may offer dim, fuzzy viewing early or late in the day, and be all but useless in overcast conditions. Furthermore, bargain-priced models tend to be poorly constructed and misaligned. Attempting to use them for extended viewing is almost guaranteed to cause eyestrain and skull-splitting headaches.

While bargain-basement models are usually junk, lightweight and moderately priced midsize binoculars are available that deliver good performance. Burris's Landmark 8X32 binocular has fully coated lenses and BaK4 roof prisms. I have used this binocular and it performed well. Leupold's 8X32 Wind River binocular is another good buy. This waterproof binocular offers Leupold quality at very reasonable cost. The Pentax 8X32 DCF WP binocular is another lightweight roof-prism model worth looking at. With its magnesium frame, it tips the scales at 21 ounces. It is also waterproof and has phase-coated optics.

The lightweight 8X32 binoculars mentioned here cannot be counted on to perform as well as heavier 8X and 10X models featuring 40mm, 42mm, or even larger objective lenses. However, they are lighter, handier, and won't become bothersome when worn around your neck all day long. Pocket-size models with 20mm to 24mm objectives are even lighter and handier, but their smaller size means less performance. For many types of hunting, 8X32 binoculars make an excellent choice.

Large, Long-Range Binoculars

Big binoculars designed for extreme-range viewing fall at the other end of the heft and power scale. These long-distance models are impressive in both size and performance. Bring out Steiner's massive 15X80 Senator binocular or its 20X80 twin, and watch eyebrows raise. These green rubber-armored monsters stand a full foot high. From the front, the 80mm objective lenses look like the eyes of a giant, prehistoric barn owl. These and other high-power models, like the image-stabilizing Zeiss 20X60 S, are the Arnold Schwarzeneggers of

Alaskan hunters search the hillside for brown bear. Every serious trophy hunter depends heavily on a binocular.

binoculars. They look powerful enough to suck the eyes right out of your head.

Another superb high-power hunting binocular is Swarovski's powerful 15X56 WB SLC model. It has the same dimensions (8½ inches high and 5 inches wide) as the company's 8X56 SLC model, and at 47 ounces it is only two ounces heavier. It is a more manageable size than the big 15X80 Steiner binocular, and I have hung one from my neck for an hour or so at a time without fatigue. Although the Swarovski's smaller 56mm objective lenses don't collect quite as much light as the big 80mm Steiner optics, they deliver a satisfyingly bright image.

When it comes to hunting optics, size truly matters. Huge binoculars like those mentioned above are capable of surprising performance.

However, the higher the magnification, the shakier the image. Too, the 15X80 and 20X80 Steiners are big and bulky, tipping the scales at a solid 3½ pounds. Even if you *could* hold these high-powered binoculars steady, you would soon be looking for some kind of rest to relieve your tired muscles. In my opinion, binoculars that big and heavy are too unhandy to tote very far on foot. They are best transported in a truck, ATV, or on horseback.

High-magnification optics must be kept perfectly motionless. I am here to tell you that NO one can hand hold a 20X binocular steady enough for truly useful viewing. The lone exception is Zeiss's stratospherically priced 20X60 S image-stabilizing model, which lists at—are you ready for this—$6,000! I have seen it discounted to $4,500, but that is still way out of *my* league.

I have used the 20X60 S Zeiss, and it really works! It doesn't use gyroscopes or battery-powered devices to minimize the effects of hand or body tremor. Focus the big 58-ounce binocular on a distant object, then press a rubber-armored panel on top. The internal optical system becomes mechanically isolated from the binocular's housing, so hand tremors don't affect image stability. The

The image-stabilizing Zeiss 20X60 S binocular is the only 20X binocular that allows successful hand-held viewing.

image remains frozen for ten or fifteen seconds, then loses its stability. That is no problem—simply press the panel again to restart the process.

Both Nikon and Canon also offer image-stabilizing binoculars, but these use different systems to reduce shake. Canon's image-stabilizing binoculars include 12X36, 15X50, and 18X50 All-Weather IS models. The 12X binocular is relatively compact and weighs 32 ounces. The larger 15X and 18X models tip the scales at 42 ounces. Canon's image-stabilizer system features a microprocessor-controlled motor and vari-angle prism. The battery-powered system makes continuous adjustments to maintain a stable viewing image. Suggested retail prices are around $2,000 and $2,300 respectively for the 15X50 and 18X50 models. The 12X36 IS binocular lists at $1,250.

Nikon's StabilEyes binocular comes in 12X32 and 14X40 versions. Both use a gimbaled servo system to keep the image steady. These are

A midsize 10X32mm Leica, left, and a full-size 10X42mm Bausch & Lomb Elite are good all-round hunting choices. The Elite's larger objective lens gives it the edge for twilight viewing.

The Nikon binocular on the left features porro-prism construction, while the straight-tubed Bausch & Lomb is of roof-prism design.

relatively heavy binoculars—39 and 46 ounces, respectively—but they don't offer the high magnification the Zeiss and Canon image-stabilizing models do.

With the possible exception of image-stabilizing models (which are all too heavy for easy carrying), large, high-power binoculars work best when mounted on a sturdy tripod. Nearly all come drilled and tapped for this purpose. The best use I have found for binoculars of 15X and greater magnification is when I am scouting from a vehicle. Weight isn't a problem when you are riding in a truck, and you can steady the binocular (most are rubber armored) on the edge of a partly raised window. This won't be quite as stable as using a tripod, but you will be able to keep the binocular steady enough for extended viewing. While lacking real portability, these big boys can be useful—if highly specialized—hunting tools.

Using Your Binocular

Regardless of the binocular you choose, you must learn to use it properly; otherwise, purchasing

good optics is largely a waste of money. Magazine photographs often show a hunter looking through his binocular while standing erect. Try hard not to imitate this classic pose. Standing and scanning the far countryside is a lousy way to find game. If an animal meandering across a distant hillside catches your eye, go ahead and throw up the binocular for a closer look. The critter probably spotted you first, so standing there in plain sight while peering through binocular lenses isn't likely to spook it. I can almost guarantee you saw that animal simply because it was moving.

Like most animals, our eyes are programmed to detect movement. As I pointed out earlier, only a very tiny segment (the macula) of the eye is devoted to seeing detail. When you move along a mountain trail, it is harder to spot an animal that is also on the move. It is almost impossible to see distant detail. The same thing is true when you make slow sweeps with your binocular while scanning for game.

Instead of taking a closer look at an animal you have already spotted, use your binocular to find game you *haven't* seen. The way to do this is keep

This is a Minox 10X42mm binocular.

the binocular motionless while you methodically examine the stationary field of view.

I recently prospected for mule deer in rimrock country. In late afternoon on the third day of the hunt, I slowly eased to the rim of a canyon overlooking dozens of square miles of sagebrush desert. Keeping low and using the sparse cover to mask my movements, I made my way to the base of a cedar tree. Settling to a comfortable sitting position, I leaned my back against its trunk. Bracing my elbows against upraised knees, I focused the binocular on a line of pinon abutting the desert below. This position offered excellent support, and I could look through the binocular several minutes at a time without experiencing fatigue. Focusing on one piece of real estate at a time, I searched long and hard for some sign of deer. I didn't expect to see an entire animal. I was looking for a flickering ear or a brief flash of antler. I kept the binocular steady, moving it only after I was sure I had missed nothing in my field of view.

I didn't hurry but took my time. After thirty minutes of careful glassing, my patience paid off. The light was beginning to fail when a heavy-bodied 4-point buck finally stepped from the shadowed tree line. As he posed unaware just 150 yards away, I gently pressed the trigger.

One of the few times I will use my binocular while standing up is when still-hunting close cover. I will use my binocular after every few steps to check nearby limbs and brush for any sign of a hidden deer. Magnifying lenses are wonderful tools for finding hidden bucks.

Bushnell
8X27mm

Bushnell
8X42mm

Manufacturer	Model	Prism	Water	Magnifi-cation	Objective Lens Dia. (mm)	Exit Pupil Dia. (mm)	Eye Relief (in)	FOV (ft/100yds)	O/All Length (in)	Weight (oz)	Price (MSRP)
Zeiss	15X45B T*P* Conquest	Roof	Yes	15X	45	3	14.5	192	6.8	20	$750
Swarovski	SLC 15X56WB	Roof	Yes	15X	56	3.7	13	231	8.5	47.3	$1,832
Minox	BD 15X58EDBR	Roof	Yes	15X	58	3.8	16	236	8.8	52.7	$1,099
Simmons	Endeavor 15X70	Porro	No	15X	70	4.7	NA	231	10.9	51.2	$165
Steiner	Senator 15X80	Porro	Yes	15X	80	6.3	13	216	12	56	$979
Steiner	15X80C Commander w/compass	Porro	Yes	15X	80	6.3	13	216	12	58	$1,279
Pentax	XCF 16X50	Porro	No	16X	50	3.1	13	183	6.5	31.7	$174
Pentax	PCF WP 16X60	Porro	Yes	16X	60	3.8	20	147	8.4	44.4	$362
Pentax	PCF WP 20X60	Porro	Yes	20X	60	3	21	114	8.8	45.1	$388
Simmons	Endeavor 20X60	Porro	No	20X	60	3	NA	174	7.8	37.8	$130
Steiner	Senator 20X80	Porro	Yes	20X	80	4	13	165	12	56	$999

Note: Many optical gear retailers offer 10 to 25 percent discounts below MSRP (Manufacturer's Suggested Retail Price).

Binoculars

Full-size

Zeiss
Victory 8X56 BT*P*

Leica
Duvovid 8X42mm

Steiner
Nighthunter 12X56mm

Pentax
DCF SP 12.4X50mm

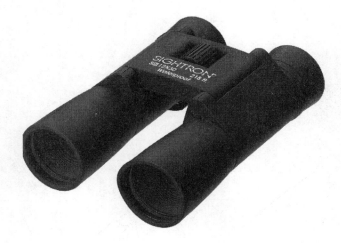

Sightron
SIII 1230PC 12X40mm

Manufacturer	Model	Prism	Water	Magnification	Objective Lens Dia. (mm)	Exit Pupil Dia. (mm)	Eye Relief (in)	FOV (ft/100yds)	O/All Length (in)	Weight (oz)	Price (MSRP)
Simmons	Expedition 7X35	Porro	Yes	7X	35	5	NA	484	5.5	27.6	$120
Bausch & Lomb	Discoverer	Roof	Yes	7X	42	6	20	420	NA	28	$613
Brunton	Eterna	Roof	Yes	7X	42	6	20	416	7.13	30	$444
Leica	Trinovid	Roof	Yes	7X	42	6	17	459	5.6	31.4	$995
Swarovski	Habicht 7X42GA	Porro	Yes	7X	42	6	14	342	6.1	26.8	$788
Swarovski	SLC 7X42B	Roof	Yes	7X	42	6	19	420	6.5	33.5	$1,077
Zeiss	Classic 7X42B/GA T* P*	Roof	Yes	7X	42	6	19	450	7.5	28.2	$1,150
Alpen Outdoor	Pro 550	Porro	Yes	7X	50	7.1	19	367	NA	41	$158
Nikon	Action	Porro	No	7X	50	7.1	20	336	8.1	35.4	$193
Pentax	PCF WP 7X50	Porro	Yes	7X	50	7.1	20	324	7.2	35.3	$248
Steiner	Commander 7X50	Porro	Yes	7X	50	7.1	22	385	5.2	39	$799
Steiner	Nighthunter 7X50	Porro	Yes	7X	50	7.1	21	375	7.3	33	$669
Steiner	Military/Marine 7X50	Porro	Yes	7X	50	7.1	22	354	5.2	37	$469
Steiner	Navigator 7X50	Porro	Yes	7X	50	7.1	22	354	7.3	33	$399
Swarovski	SLC 7X50B	Roof	Yes	7X	50	7.1	23	372	7.9	40.6	$1,310
Tasco	Offshore 7X50	Porro	Yes	7X	50	7.1	NA	366	NA	35.2	$174
Zeiss	Classic 7X50B/GA T*	Porro	Yes	7X	50	7.1	18	390	5.7	42.3	$1,400
Brunton	Epoch	Roof	Yes	7.5X	43	5.7	20	370	6	26	$1,449
Bushnell	Legend	Roof	Yes	8X	32	4	16	396	4.8	23.8	$431

Pentax
DCF SP 10X43mm

Pentax
DCF HR II 10X42mm

BSA
CC10X50ACP 10X50mm

Binoculars
Full-size

Tasco
Sonoma 10X25mm

Steiner
Predator 10X26mm

Burris
Signature 10X50mm

Tasco
Amphibian 10X15mm

Bushnell
8X25mm

Bushnell
Legend 10X42mm

Manufacturer	Model	Prism	Water	Magnifi-cation	Objective Lens Dia. (mm)	Exit Pupil Dia. (mm)	Eye Relief (in)	FOV (ft/100yds)	O/All Length (in)	Weight (oz)	Price (MSRP)
Bausch & Lomb	Legacy	Porro	No	8X	40	5	14	445	NA	24	$190
Burris	Fullfield	Porro	Yes	8X	40	5	26	430	5.9	31	$396
Nikon	Action	Porro	No	8X	40	5	11.9	429	5.6	26.2	$183
Pentax	PCF WP 8X40	Porro	Yes	8X	40	5	20	330	5.3	28.2	$244
Pentax	XFC 8X40	Porro	No	8X	40	5	13	429	5.1	27.2	$140
Sightron	SII 840 RWA	Porro	No	8X	40	5	12	430	5.25	23.2	$80
Simmons	Aetec 8X40 WA	Porro	No	8X	40	5	NA	430	5.5	21	$116
Simmons	Expedition 8X40	Porro	Yes	8X	40	5	NA	421	6.1	29.8	$130
Simmons	Aetec 8X40	Porro	No	8X	40	5	NA	430	5.5	25	$100
Zeiss	Victory 8X40T*P*	Roof	Yes	8X	40	5	16	405	6.4	25	$1,180
Alpen Outdoor	SE 482	Roof	Yes	8X	42	5.2	19	367	NA	30	$275
Alpen Outdoor	Pro 362	Roof	Yes	8X	42	5.2	21	328	NA	23	$205
Alpen Outdoor	Pro 317	Porro	No	8X	42	5.2	19	430	NA	30	$132

Bushnell
Perma Focus 7X35mm

Bushnell
10X50mm

Shepherd
10X42mm

Binoculars
Full-size

Bushnell
12X50mm

Pentax
DCF SP 10X50mm

Weaver
Grand Slam 10.5X25mm

BSA
CC10X42WP 10X42mm

Steiner
Military/Marine 10X50mm

Sightron
SIII 1042RM 10X42mm

Leupold
Wind River Mesa 10X50mm

Kahles
Advantage Timber Camo. 8X42mm

Manufacturer	Model	Prism	Water	Magnifi-cation	Objective Lens Dia. (mm)	Exit Pupil Dia. (mm)	Eye Relief (in)	FOV (ft/100yds)	O/All Length (in)	Weight (oz)	Price (MSRP)
Alpen Outdoor	Pro 540	Porro	Yes	8X	42	5.2	19	430	NA	35	$150
Bausch & Lomb	Elite	Roof	Yes	8X	42	5.2	19.5	365	NA	29	$1,524
Bausch & Lomb	Discoverer	Porro	Yes	8X	42	5.2	19	410	NA	26.6	$454
Burris	Signature	Roof	Yes	8X	42	5.2	26	328	6	24	$684
Burris	Landmark RF	Roof	Yes	8X	42	5.2	19	356	6.7	29	$189
Burris	Landmark PF	Porro	No	8X	42	5.2	18	340	5.9	24	$123
Bushnell	Legend	Roof	Yes	8X	42	5.2	18	330	NA	30	$502
Bushnell	Trophy	Roof	Yes	8X	42	5.2	19	335	NA	27	$251
Kahles	8X42	Roof	Yes	8X	42	5.2	19	330	5.6	26.5	$721
Leica	Geovid 8X42 BRF	Roof	Yes	8X	42	5.3	NA	373	6.9	31.8	$1,800[1]
Leica	Trinovid	Roof	Yes	8X	42	5.25	15.9	427	5.6	31.4	$1,045
Leupold	Wind River	Porro	Yes	8X	42	5	18	341	5.2	26.4	$313
Leupold	Wind River W2	Roof	Yes	8X	42	5	18	341	5.5	22.4	$450
Leupold	Wind River P1	Roof	Yes	8X	42	5	18	332	NA	21.6	$489

[1]. Inc laser rangefinder/ 1,300-yard range.

Bushnell
12X50mm

Swarovski
EL 8X32mm

Simmons
10X80mm & 7X35mm

Binoculars
Full-size

Manufacturer	Model	Prism	Water	Magnification	Objective Lens Dia. (mm)	Exit Pupil Dia. (mm)	Eye Relief (in)	FOV (ft/100yds)	O/All Length (in)	Weight (oz)	Price (MSRP)
Nikon	Venturer LX	Roof	Yes	8X	42	5.3	20	366	6.2	34.6	$1,441
Nikon	Monarch ATB	Roof	Yes	8X	42	5.3	19.6	330	5.7	21.3	$431
Pentax	DCF WP 8X42	Roof	Yes	8X	42	5.2	22	330	5.8	26.8	$652
Pentax	DCF HR 8X42	Roof	No	8X	42	5.2	22	324	6.8	23.3	$428
Remington	Premier 8X42	Roof	Yes	8X	42	5.2	23	430	6.7	28	$191
Shepherd	8X42	Roof	Yes	8X	42	5.2	19.4	NA	5.5	27.7	$630
Sightron	SIII 8X42 RM	Roof	Yes	8X	42	5.2	19.2	340	NA	23	$520
Simmons	Hydrosport 8X42	Roof	Yes	8X	42	5.2	NA	341	6.3	23.8	$208
Steiner	Predator 8X42	Roof	Yes	8X	42	5.3	20	367	6.1	24	$729
Tasco	World Class 8X42	Roof	Yes	8X	42	5.3	NA	360	NA	27	$160
Weaver	Classic 8X42	Roof	No	8X	42	5.3	NA	332	6	23.6	$440
Leica	Ultravid 8X50 BR	Roof	Yes	8X	50	6.3	NA	345	7.2	35.6	$1,600
Leica	Trinovid	Roof	Yes	8X	50	6.25	NA	377	7	40.6	$1,145
Steiner	Nighthunter 8X56	Porro	Yes	8X	56	7	21	333	8	41	$799

Bushnell
8X21mm

Steiner
Big Horn 9X40mm

Bushnell
12X25mm

Burris
Land PF 8X42mm

Steiner CUTAWAY
Predator Ultra-light 8X30mm

Tasco
Essentials 10X25mm

Tasco
Sonoma 8–20X25mm

Weaver
Classic 8X42mm

Bausch & Lomb
Discoverer 8X42mm

Alpen
Pro 8X42mm

Burris
Signature 8X42mm

Steiner
Predator Ultra-light 8X30mm

Binoculars

Full-size

Manufacturer	Model	Prism	Water	Magnifi-cation	Objective Lens Dia. (mm)	Exit Pupil Dia. (mm)	Eye Relief (in)	FOV (ft/100yds)	O/All Length (in)	Weight (oz)	Price (MSRP)
Swarovski	SLC 8X56B	Roof	Yes	8X	56	7	22	345	8.5	45.5	$1,543
Zeiss	Victory 8X56T*P*	Roof	Yes	8X	56	7	17.5	396	7.9	40.9	$1,450
Zeiss	Classic 8X56B/GA	Roof	Yes	8X	56	7	19	330	9.4	36.3	$1,360
Minox	BD 8X58 EDBR	Roof	Yes	8X	58	7.2	14	374	8.8	49	$899
Leica	Duovid	Roof	Yes	8–12X	42	3.5–5.25	NA	362–268	6.1	34	$1,495[1]
Minox	BD 8.5X42 BR	Roof	Yes	8.5X	42	4.9	15	315	5.8	29.9	$529
Swarovski	EL 8.5X42WB	Roof	Yes	8.5X	42	4.9	15	330	6.2	27.5	$1,532
Alpen	Apex 8.5X50	Roof	Yes	8.5X	50	5.9	20	290	7	28	$543
Steiner	Big Horn 9X40	Porro	Yes	9X	40	4.4	20	300	6.5	26	$379
Remington	Premier 9X63	Roof	Yes	9X	63	7	26.2	360	10.6	44	$212
Steiner	Predator 10X30	Roof	Yes	10X	30	3	12	261	4.7	10.5	$399
Swarovski	Habicht 10X40WGA	Porro	Yes	10X	40	4	13	324	6.1	27.9	$877
Zeiss	Classic 10X40 B/GA T* P*	Roof	Yes	10X	40	4	16	330	6.3	26.8	$700

[1] Variable magnification.

Steiner
Nighthunter 8X30mm

Steiner
Predator 8X30mm

Kahles
8X42mm

Nikon
B8X32 Superior E

Manufacturer	Model	Prism	Water	Magnification	Objective Lens Dia. (mm)	Exit Pupil Dia. (mm)	Eye Relief (in)	FOV (ft/100yds)	O/All Length (in)	Weight (oz)	Price (MSRP)
Zeiss	Victory 10X40T*P*	Roof	Yes	10X	40	4	16	330	6.4	25.7	$1,200
Alpen	Pro 10X42	Roof	Yes	10X	42	4.2	17	298	6.8	23	$163
Alpen Outdoor	Pro 364	Roof	Yes	10X	42	4.2	18	298	NA	23	$220
Bausch & Lomb	Elite	Roof	Yes	10X	42	4.2	19.5	300	NA	28	$1,570
Bausch & Lomb	Discoverer	Roof	Yes	10X	42	4.2	17	341	NA	28	$682
Bausch & Lomb	Discoverer	Porro	Yes	10X	42	4.2	17	341	6.5	27.5	$513
Brunton	Eterna	Roof	Yes	10X	42	4.2	18	338	7.1	30	$444
Brunton	Lite-Tech	Roof	Yes	10X	42	4.2	NA	314	6.1	24.5	$229
Burris	Landmark RF	Roof	Yes	10X	42	4.2	18	284	6.7	29	$214
Burris	Landmark PF	Porro	No	10X	42	4.2	15	288	5.9	24	$132
Bushnell	Legend	Roof	Yes	10X	42	4.2	15	315	NA	29.8	$524
Bushnell	Trophy	Roof	Yes	10X	42	4.2	21	305	NA	28	$285
Kahles	10X42	Roof	Yes	10X	42	4.2	16	315	5.5	26.5	$772
Leica	Geovid 10X42 BRF	Roof	Yes	10X	42	4.2	NA	331	6.9	31.8	$1,850[1]

[1.] Inc laser rangefinder/ 1,300-yard range.

Nikon
Nascar (R) 8X25mm

Brunton
Lite-Tech 8X32mm

Nikon
Sportstar Blk. 8X25mm

Sightron
SIII 8X42mm

Binoculars
Full-size

Manufacturer	Model	Prism	Water	Magnifi-cation	Objective Lens Dia. (mm)	Exit Pupil Dia. (mm)	Eye Relief (in)	FOV (ft/100yds)	O/All Length (in)	Weight (oz)	Price (MSRP)
Leica	Trinovid	Roof	Yes	10X	42	4.2	13.9	361	5.6	31.4	$1,095
Leupold	Wind River	Roof	Yes	10X	42	4.2	16	268	5.5	23.1	$450
Minox	BD 10X42 BR	Roof	Yes	10X	42	4.2	15	318	5.6	26.6	$549
Nikon	Venturer LX	Roof	Yes	10X	42	4.2	19	314	6.2	34.6	$1,541
Nikon	Superior E	Porro	No	10X	42	4.2	17.4	314	6.2	25	$1,271
Nikon	Monarch ATB	Roof	Yes	10X	42	4.2	15.5	314	5.6	21.1	$471
Pentax	DCF WP 10X42	Roof	Yes	10X	42	4.2	18	314	5.8	26.8	$726
Pentax	DCF HR 10X42	Roof	No	10X	42	4.2	20	261	6.7	23.2	$490
Redfield	Waterproof 10X42	Roof	Yes	10X	42	4.2	NA	188	6	22.6	$130
Remington	Premier 10X42	Roof	Yes	10X	42	4.2	23	341	6.7	28	$208
Shepherd	10X42	Roof	Yes	10X	42	4.2	18.9	NA	5.5	22.7	$648
Sightron	SIII10X42 RM	Roof	Yes	10X	42	4.2	17.5	262	NA	23	$531
Simmons	Hydrosport 10X42	Roof	Yes	10X	42	4.2	NA	315	6.3	23	$209

Zeiss
Victory II 8X40mm

Kahles
8X32mm

Zeiss
Classic Compact 10X25 & 8X20mm

BSA
C3–818X25 8–18X25mm

Swarovski
EL 8X32mm

BSA
CC8X32WP 8X32mm

Manufacturer	Model	Prism	Water	Magnification	Objective Lens Dia. (mm)	Exit Pupil Dia. (mm)	Eye Relief (in)	FOV (ft/100yds)	O/All Length (in)	Weight (oz)	Price (MSRP)
Simmons	Hydrosport 10X42	Roof	Yes	10X	42	4.2	NA	105	6.3	23.4	$130
Simmons	Prohunter 10X42	Roof	No	10X	42	4.2	NA	315	6.3	19.5	$100
Steiner	Predator 10X42	Roof	Yes	10X	42	4.2	20	295	6.1	25	$729
Swarovski	EL 10X42WB	Roof	Yes	10X	42	4.2	15	330	6.2	27.5	$1,610
Swarovski	SLC 10X42WB	Roof	Yes	10X	42	4.2	14	330	5.8	30.7	$1,144
Tasco	World Class 10X42	Roof	Yes	10X	42	4.2	NA	304	NA	28	$180
Weaver	Classic 10X42	Roof	No	10X	42	4.2	NA	263	6	24.1	$462
Alpen	Apex 10X50	Roof	Yes	10X	50	5	20	262	6.8	6.8	$550
Alpen Outdoor	Pro 312	Porro	No	10X	50	5	16	342	NA	32	$145
Bausch & Lomb	Legacy	Porro	No	10X	50	5	9	380	NA	28	$217
Brunton	Lite-Tech	Porro	Yes	10X	50	5	19	342	7.5	39	$139
Burris	Signature	Roof	Yes	10X	50	5	26	262	7	28	$735
Burris	Fullfield	Porro	Yes	10X	50	5	26	334	7.4	35	$432
Leica	Ultravid 10X50 BR	Roof	Yes	10X	50	5	NA	345	7	35.4	$1,650
Leica	Trinovid	Roof	Yes	10X	50	5	14.6	377	7	40.6	$1,195
Leupold	Wind River P1	Roof	Yes	10X	50	5	NA	263	NA	25.5	$568

Pentax
DCFR HR II 8X42mm

Pentax
DCF SP 8X43mm

Binoculars
Full-size

Manufacturer	Model	Prism	Water	Magnifi-cation	Objective Lens Dia. (mm)	Exit Pupil Dia. (mm)	Eye Relief (in)	FOV (ft/100yds)	O/All Length (in)	Weight (oz)	Price (MSRP)
Leupold	Wind River	Porro	Yes	10X	50	5	18	316	6.5	31.6	$355
Nikon	Tundra ATB	Roof	Yes	10X	50	5	17.4	324	7.7	39.5	$385
Nikon	Action	Roof	No	10X	50	5	11.8	342	7.3	34.7	$215
Pentax	PCF WP 10X50	Porro	Yes	10X	50	5	30	261	6.9	34.2	$266
Pentax	XCF	Porro	No	10X	50	5	13	342	6.5	30.7	$158
Pentax	DCF WP 10X50	Roof	Yes	10X	50	5	22	261	6.7	33.5	$880
Redfield	Aurora 10X50	Roof	Yes	10X	50	5	NA	263	5.5	27.6	$500
Remington	Premier 10X50	Porro	Yes	10X	50	5	22.1	342	7.4	39	$159
Sightron	SII 1050RA	Porro	No	10X	50	5	12	341	6.5	27.4	$100
Simmons	Expedition 10X50	Porro	Yes	10X	50	5	NA	342	7.5	33.2	$150
Simmons	Aetec 10X50 WA	Porro	No	10X	50	5	NA	341	7.1	26.5	$136
Steiner	Nighthunter 10X50	Porro	Yes	10X	50	5	22	315	7.3	35	$699
Steiner	Military/Marine 10X50	Porro	Yes	10X	50	5	17	327	5.1	36	$469
Steiner	Police 10X50	Porro	Yes	10X	50	5	17	300	5.1	36	$399
Swarovski	SLC 10X50WB	Roof	Yes	10X	50	5	17	336	7.7	40.9	$1,388
Minox	BD 10X52 BR	Roof	Yes	10X	52	5.2	19	308	6.7	32.2	$659
Zeiss	Victory 10X56T*P* AOSAK	Roof	Yes	10X	56	5.6	15.6	330	7.9	42.3	$1,550
Minox	BD 10X58 EDBR	Roof	Yes	10X	58	5.8	19	357	8.8	52.6	$999
Brunton	Epoch	Roof	Yes	10.5X	43	4.1	17	290	5.8	25	$1,499
Steiner	Predator 12X40	Porro	Yes	12X	40	3.3	20	270	6.5	26	$399
Brunton	Eterna	Roof	Yes	12X	42	3.5	18	271	7.1	30	$449
Pentax	DCF HR 12X42	Roof	No	12X	42	3.5	18	219	6.7	23.3	$528
Pentax	DCF HR 12X42	Roof	No	12X	42	3.5	18	219	6.7	23.3	$528
Zeiss	12X44 T*P* Conquest	Roof	Yes	12X	45	3.8	14.5	240	6.8	19.5	$700
Alpen	Apex 12X50	Roof	Yes	12X	50	4.2	16	252	6.8	28	$561
Bausch & Lomb	Elite	Porro	Yes	12X	50	4.2	15	250	NA	33.5	$1,639

Manufacturer	Model	Prism	Water	Magnifi-cation	Objective Lens Dia. (mm)	Exit Pupil Dia. (mm)	Eye Relief (in)	FOV (ft/100yds)	O/All Length (in)	Weight (oz)	Price (MSRP)
Bausch & Lomb	Legacy	Porro	No	12X	50	4.2	10	314	NA	28	$206
BSA	Silverstar	Porro	No	12X	50	4.2	NA	NA	NA	NA	$110
Burris	Signature	Roof	Yes	12X	50	4.2	18	209	7	28	$864
Leica	Ultravid 12X50 BR	Roof	Yes	12X	50	4.2	NA	300	7.2	36.9	$1,675
Leica	Trinovid	Roof	Yes	12X	50	4.2	NA	328	7	40.6	$1,345
Nikon	Premier SE	Porro	No	12X	50	4.2	17.4	262	7.2	31.7	$1,395
Nikon	Action	Porro	No	12X	50	4.2	9.4	288	7.1	34.3	$245
Pentax	PCF WP 12X50	Porro	Yes	12X	50	4.2	20	219	7	34.6	$276
Pentax	XCF 12X50	Porro	No	12X	50	4.2	11	294	6.5	31.7	$168
Redfield	Aurora 12X50	Roof	Yes	12X	50	4.2	NA	221	6.5	27.4	$510
Shepherd	A.E.F. 12X50	Roof	Yes	12X	50	4.2	18	NA	6.6	27.7	$699
Sightron	SII 1250R	Porro	No	12X	50	4.2	10.6	271	6.5	27.1	$110
Steiner	Nighthunter 12X56	Porro	Yes	12X	56	4.7	22	258	8	41	$849

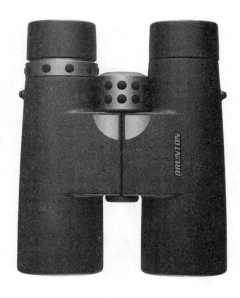

Brunton
Epoch 10.5X43mm

Steiner
Military/Marine 10X50mm

Binoculars
Midsize

Manufacturer	Model	Prism	Water	Magnifi-cation	Objective Lens Dia. (mm)	Exit Pupil Dia. (mm)	Eye Relief (in)	FOV (ft/100yds)	O/All Length (in)	Weight (oz)	Price (MSRP)
Leupold	Wind River Katmai 6X32	Roof	Yes	6X	32	5.3	16.6	425	4.1	18.2	$370
Nikon	Action	Porro	No	7X	35	5	11.9	487	4.8	23.8	$153
Leica	Ultravid 7X42 BR	Roof	Yes	7X	42	6	NA	420	4.8	26.8	$1,425
Nikon	E2	Porro	No	8X	30	3.8	13.8	461	4	20.3	$461
Steiner	Nighthunter 8X30	Porro	Yes	8X	30	3.8	20	390	4.6	18	$449
Steiner	Military/Marine 8X30	Porro	Yes	8X	30	3.8	20	360	4.6	18	$199
Steiner	Safari 8X30	Porro	Yes	8X	30	3.8	20	360	4.6	18	$199
Swarovski	SLC 8X30WB	Roof	Yes	8X	30	3.8	15	408	5.6	20.8	$888
Swarovski	Habicht 8X30WGA	Porro	Yes	8X	30	3.8	12	408	6.4	20.8	$788
Zeiss	8X30 T*P* Conquest	Roof	Yes	8X	30	3.8	14.5	360	5.6	15.9	$550
Zeiss	Classic 8X30B/GA I.F.	Roof	Yes	8X	30	3.8	15	360	4.7	21.2	$1,000
Zeiss	Diafun 8X30B MC	Roof	Yes	8X	30	3.8	14	360	5.6	15.9	$480
Alpen	Apex 8X32	Roof	Yes	8X	32	4	16	393	4.8	20	$484
Brunton	Lite-Tech	Roof	Yes	8X	32	4	NA	392	5.2	20.6	$219
Kahles	Compact	Roof	Yes	8X	32	4	16	399	4.7	21.5	$610
Leica	Trinovid	Roof	Yes	8X	32	4	13.3	553	4.4	22	$995
Leupold	Wind River Katmai 8X32	Roof	Yes	8X	32	4	16	335	4.1	18.9	$390
Minox	BD 8X32 BR	Roof	Yes	8X	32	4	15	399	4.9	21.7	$439
Nikon	Venturer LX	Roof	Yes	8X	32	4	17	408	5	25.2	$1,081
Nikon	Superior E	Porro	No	8X	32	4	17.4	393	4.6	22.2	$977
Pentax	DCF WP 8X32	Roof	Yes	8X	32	4	17	393	4.8	21.2	$566
Redfield	WaterProof 8X32	Roof	Yes	8X	32	4	NA	131	5.5	19.2	$125
Simmons	Hydrosport 8X32	Roof	Yes	8X	32	4	NA	131	5.8	19.8	$120
Steiner	Predator 8X32	Roof	Yes	8X	32	4	20	328	5.5	21	$599
Nikon	Sporter 1	Roof	No	8X	36	4.5	20.5	366	5.7	25.3	$261
Nikon	Team Realtree	Roof	No	8X	36	4.5	20.5	366	5.7	25.3	$291
Alpen	Apex 8X42	Roof	Yes	8X	42	5.3	20	341	5.8	24	$506
Alpen	Pro 8X42	Roof	Yes	8X	42	5.3	21	328	6.2	23	$152

Binoculars
Midsize

Manufacturer	Model	Prism	Water	Magnifi-cation	Objective Lens Dia. (mm)	Exit Pupil Dia. (mm)	Eye Relief (in)	FOV (ft/100yds)	O/All Length (in)	Weight (oz)	Price (MSRP)
Leica	Ultravid 8X42 BL	Roof	Yes	8X	42	5.3	NA	390	4.8	24.9	$1,500
Swarovski	EL 8.5X42 WB	Roof	Yes	8.5X	42	4.2	15	390	6.5	28.9	$1,632
Remington	Premier 9X32	Roof	Yes	9X	32	3.4	20	252	5.3	24	$166
Zeiss	10X30 T*P* Conquest	Roof	Yes	10X	30	3	14.5	288	5.6	16.4	$600
Zeiss	Diafun 10X30B MC	Roof	Yes	10X	30	3	14	288	5.6	15.9	$550
Leica	Trinovid	Roof	Yes	10X	32	3.2	13.5	394	4.4	23.3	$1,045
Leupold	Wind River Katmai 10X32	Roof	Yes	10X	32	3.2	7.6	272	4.1	18.2	$420
Nikon	Venturer LX	Roof	Yes	10X	32	3	16	340	5	25.2	$1,121
Nikon	E2	Porro	No	10X	35	3.5	13.8	366	5	22	$511
Nikon	Sporter 1	Roof	No	10X	36	3.6	16.1	293	5.5	24.6	$281
Nikon	Team Realtree	Roof	No	10X	36	3.6	16.1	293	5.5	24.6	$311
Alpen	Apex 10X42	Roof	Yes	10X	42	4.2	16	315	5.7	24	$528
Leica	Ultravid 10X42 BR	Roof	Yes	10X	42	4.2	NA	330	5.8	26.8	$1,550
Swarovski	EL 10X42 WB	Roof	Yes	10X	42	4.2	15	330	6.2	27.5	$1,699

Nikon
Sporter 1 Camo 8X36mm

Zeiss
Diafun 10X30MC

Binoculars
Stabilized

Manufacturer	Model	Prism	Water	Magnifi-cation	Objective Lens Dia. (mm)	Exit Pupil Dia. (mm)	Eye Relief (in)	FOV (ft/100yds)	O/All Length (in)	Weight (oz)	Price (MSRP)
Nikon	Stabileyes	Roof	Yes	14X	40	2.9	13	209	7.3	39.8	$1,700
Zeiss	Classic 20X60BS	Roof	Yes	20X	60	3	14	150	10.8	58.5	$5,000

Steiner
Military 15X80mm

Steiner
Military R 7X50mm

Zeiss
Conquest 10X30T*P*

Nikon
Sporter I 10X36mm

Chapter 12
Spotting Scopes

If you hunt anything larger than rabbits or squirrels, you need a spotting scope. I did not always believe this. During my high school and college years, money was so tight I could barely afford a rifle and ammo. I had been hunting deer for several years before I bought my first binocular. A spotting scope was something I never even considered.

During those lean, early years, I was more interested in venison than in trophy antlers. When I finally acquired an 8X binocular, it offered all the magnification I needed to tell me whether I was looking at a doe or a legal buck. That was the distinction that interested me. The binocular was also a big help in finding distant deer, particularly when they were hidden in deep shadow. I saw little need for a spotting scope.

A few years later, I spent a long September morning struggling to the top of the Skeena mountain range. Reg Collingwood, my British Columbia guide, was a lot fitter than I, but we were both pretty well exhausted by the time we finally reached the crest. You could see forever from where we stood. I was starved, but before digging in my backpack for lunch, I spent several minutes carefully scanning the far reaches with my 8X binocular. My search was methodical. I held the binocular steady as I examined the stationary viewing field foot by foot. Then I would focus on another piece of real estate and do it again. When I finally put the binocular down to concentrate on lunch, I was satisfied no huntable game was in sight.

British Columbia guide Reg Collingwood uses a spotting scope to search for game above timberline.

While the big 80mm objective lens on this B&L spotter offers top brightness and clarity, it reduces portability.

I was biting into my baloney sandwich when Reg said, "Take a look at this." While I had been busy using my binocular, he was parsing distant terrain with a 20X spotting scope. We had climbed the mountain in search of goats, but when I looked through the spotting-scope eyepiece I saw a pair of impossibly long caribou antlers jutting skyward from a large patch of snow. A big double-shovel bull had bedded down for a noonday nap. Frigid air above the snowfield kept hordes of hungry flies at bay, so the bull slumbered undisturbed.

Thanks to Reg's spotting scope, our goat hunt suddenly became a mountain caribou hunt. The 20X spotting scope showed detail—a set of antlers—that my 8X binocular simply missed. Every hunt depends on equal measures of skill and luck. Without the aid of the spotting scope, I could have easily returned home empty-handed.

I cannot count the number of times I have used a spotting scope in just the past year. First, there were numerous trips to the target range, where having a spotting scope alongside my shooting bench saved many, many steps under Utah's broiling desert sun. If I had had to trek between shooting bench and target after firing each group, I would be twenty pounds lighter by now (which would not be a bad thing). At the shooting range, a spotting scope is a great time- and labor-saving device. When you are looking at paper targets, any decent spotting scope will show bullet holes that would not otherwise be visible at one hundred or two hundred yards, but remember that better quality always means better performance.

While I haven't hunted sheep in the past couple of years, my home is only a few miles from a scenic twelve-thousand-foot mountain that houses a growing, transplanted flock. I will never shoot one of these local animals. I would have to draw a tag, and the odds are against me. But I enjoy watching them bed down each evening on the face of an impossibly sheer cliff. I can see them through a 10X binocular, but a tripod-supported spotting scope allows me to identify individual animals. Because weight is not a problem when I am sitting on my front porch, I usually use a hefty 20–60X model with a light-gathering 80mm objective lens for these viewing sessions.

Spotting scopes have figured prominently in several of my hunts. I recently spent a few hours watching Montana and Wyoming whitetails through an 80mm Swarovski mounted on the window of a guide's truck. The clear, magnified image it delivered helped identify worthwhile trophies and plan stalking routes. I ogled distant bands of pronghorn in search of that elusive 16-plus-inch head, and I scouted for bulls before elk season began. A good binocular is a must for hunters, but it will take you only part of the way. A spotting scope reveals long-range detail every serious hunter needs.

What kind of spotting scope should you choose? Spotting scopes are simpler than binoculars—or even riflescopes—to construct. There is no need to keep two images in proper parallel alignment, and spotting scopes typically don't sport aiming reticles. Parallax is not a problem, either. Because spotting scopes are easier to make, they are usually less expensive to buy. I cannot recommend some of the discount-store "bargains" selling for $100 or less. Some of these scopes may look pretty good in the store, but they aren't durable enough to survive very long in the field. Top-of-the-line models with the very best optics sell for $1,000 or more, but you can buy a decent scope for around $300. Many excellent spotters are offered in the $500 to $800 range.

Optical quality is important. You can do a fair job of judging optics by focusing the scope on some object in a dark corner of the store. (Again, do not point the scope outdoors in brilliant sunlight.) Check for brightness, clarity, and image sharpness. If the spotting scope offers variable magnification, and most do these days, try reading distant labels at different power settings.

How much magnification do you need? While variable-power spotting scopes are increasingly popular, I have used a number of fixed-magnification 20X and 25X spotters that did a great

job. For most hunting applications, 20X or 25X is all you really need. This relatively low magnification offers some very practical advantages over 35X, 45X, or—heaven help us—the 60X top range some spotters boast. Variable-power spotting scopes allow you to use low magnification in dim light or to quickly locate animals. Then you can dial up a larger image for a closer look.

Maximum magnification may *sound* like a good idea, but there are some definite drawbacks to cranking up the power. Mirage is one problem. Mirage shimmer distorts the image, and it destroys your ability to see what you are looking at. Mirage is most prominent at midday, and it isn't necessarily caused by desert heat. Mirage is created when air of different densities come together, and it can occur even on a cold winter day. The greater the magnification, the greater the effect of mirage. Objects seen clearly at 20X may be totally obscured at 35X or 40X.

Image brightness is also directly related to magnification, particularly at dawn or dusk. When you look through any optical device, the amount of light reaching your eye is determined by the size of

Spotting scopes are available in a variety of sizes with 50 to 80mm objectives.

the exit pupil. Exit-pupil size is calculated by dividing the diameter of the objective lens, in millimeters, by magnification. At 15X, a spotting scope with a 60mm objective lens offers a 4mm exit pupil. Doubling the magnification to 30X halves exit pupil size to 2mm. Crank the power ring to 45X and you are looking through an exit pupil measuring just 1.3mm across. The super-compact 10X25 folding binocular I consider all but useless afield sports an exit pupil nearly twice as large.

In bright sunlight, a 5mm exit pupil delivers all the light a human eye can handle. As the sky darkens, the pupil of your eye expands far enough to accommodate a 7mm exit pupil. That is why many European sportsmen—who do much of their hunting in near-dark conditions—favor big 8X56 binoculars.

When you are viewing a distant buck in dawn's pale light or near the end of the day, you will actually see it more clearly at 20X than at 45X magnification. The larger the exit pupil (up to 7mm), the brighter the image.

There are two ways to increase exit pupil size: Reduce magnification or use a larger objective lens. Bulk and weight are limiting factors here. I own an excellent Bausch & Lomb Elite 20–60X spotting scope with a big 80mm objective lens. BaK-4 prisms boost resolution, while ED (Extra Low Dispersion) glass improves contrast and color rendition. The

Spotting scopes save time and countless steps at the shooting range.

rubber-armored scope body is waterproof. This monster scope is 17 inches long and weighs 53 ounces, but it delivers monster performance. It produces an incredibly bright, sharp image, but it is too big and too heavy to tote up mountains when you are also carrying a rifle and other gear. However, a top-quality spotter like this is ideally suited for hunting with a truck or on horseback.

Most spotting scopes have objective lenses ranging from 50mm to 85mm in diameter. Size and weight are the trade-offs to consider. Very large objective lenses make for super-bright, long-range viewing, but the packaging for these models is, by necessity, heavier and bulkier than hunters on foot like to carry. As a rule, the smaller the objective, the smaller and lighter the spotting scope. In my opinion, 50mm is a practical minimum for hunters; 60mm is even better.

While I like lightweight, fixed-power spotting scopes in magnification of 20 or 25, variable-power models admittedly offer greater versatility. You can dial magnification up or down to accommodate different light and mirage conditions, or you can take advantage of a wider field of view to locate distant game. Variable-power scopes are longer and heavier than most fixed-power spotters, but many consider their extra size and heft worth the trade-off.

Rees uses a compact spotter to evaluate a distant trophy.

While a few fixed-power spotters are available, variable-power models are far more popular. For several years I have used a neat, fixed-magnification 20X50 Leupold spotter that is a compact 9½ inches long and weighs just 20 ounces. This is a highly practical spotting scope you can carry anywhere, and it really performs. Unfortunately, Leupold stopped manufacturing it a few years ago, a victim of variable-power fever. The 10–20X40 Compact Spotting Scope that recently replaced it is even lighter and handier. This hand-size spotter is a porro-prism design measuring just 7½ inches in length and tipping the scales at a featherweight 15.8 ounces.

Leupold continues to offer its excellent 12–40X60 Golden Ring spotting scope with a distinctive "folded light path" lens-and-mirror system. A compact 12½ inches long, it is a perennial favorite of hunters. At 12X, this scope offers a wide field of view and a full 5mm exit pupil. At the other end of the scale, 40X is about the practical maximum for use in the hunting field. Leupold also offers a lower-priced 15–45X60 Wind River spotter.

Burris offers a couple of good spotting scopes. The 18–45X60 Signature model is the top of the

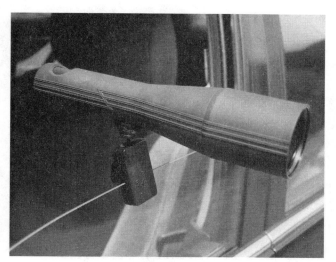

In place of a tripod, a handy window mount keeps this Burris spotting scope steady.

The 50mm objective at left won't deliver as bright an image as the 80mm lens shown to the right; however, the 50mm is a much lighter and handier spotting scope.

line and comes with Burris's "forever warranty." The Landmark 15–45X60 scope offers good quality at a lower price and is guaranteed for a year. While the waterproof, shockproof, rubber-armored Signature model is designed for more rugged use, I like the ¾-inch eye relief the Landmark spotter provides (the Signature scope has ½ inch of eye relief. The Signature model is 12½x2 inches long and weighs 29 ounces.

I am a fan of Shepherd's rangefinder/compensating riflescopes, but I didn't realize Shepherd Enterprises even made spotting scopes until the company sent a 15–40X60 model for me to try. This solid, rubber-armored spotter has good optics, but I needed more eye relief to take full advantage of the viewing quality offered. This wouldn't be a problem for sportsmen who don't need prescription lenses to see across the street.

Another spotter I have been impressed with is the 20–50X63 model that Sightron offers. A generous 20mm eye relief enables prescription eyeglass wearers to see the entire viewing field. I also like the large power-changing ring encircling the scope's body amidships. Sightron's SII spotting scope is 14 inches long and weighs 30 ounces. The lens focuses down to 23 feet. Camera adapters are available. At $349, this scope seems a real bargain.

Not long ago I tested Nikon's 16–47X60 XL Spotter. This 12½-inch-long, 27-ounce spotting scope just may be the optimum size for "carry-it-with-you" hunting. The Nikon Spotter XL is offered in a package deal that includes a good tripod and a handy carrying case. A spotting scope is of little value if it isn't on a tripod or a truck-window mount.

When it comes to tripods, trade-offs are again involved. A light, flimsy tripod may be easy to carry, but it isn't the best choice for keeping your spotting scope steady, particularly in a high wind. A sturdy tripod that positions the spotting scope high enough to be used from a sitting position is nice, but the lower the center of gravity, the easier it is to steady the scope. The low, sturdy tripods that are designed for shooting benches are compact, but they require you to either belly-down behind them when you are hunting or use a spotting scope with an angled eyepiece. Some people like angled eyepieces. I don't because I have a hard time lining the scope up with the animal I am trying to view. I prefer a straight eyepiece that comes on target a lot quicker.

For target range use, Nikon offers the Field Image System MX. A small Nikon CCD camera married to Nikon's 60mm Fieldscope allows shooters to view downrange targets on a 4-inch LCD

Ultra-compact spotting scopes are easy to tote, while larger models with oversize objectives offer better optical performance.

Rees uses compact spotter, mini-tripod to look for game.

color monitor. This is considerably more convenient than repeatedly getting up or stretching your neck to peer through a scope's eyepiece.

One top-grade spotting scope designed for hunters is the CT-85 Extendable model offered by Swarovski. For easy carrying, the scope collapses to a compact 9.7 inches, then extends to 17 inches when it is time for use. Although it is compact when compressed, it weighs a hefty 49 ounces. The Swarovski spotter sports a giant 85mm objective lens. It accepts a fixed-magnification 30mm eyepiece that delivers a wide-angle field. The other option is a 20–60X zoom eyepiece that delivers greater magnification. Both eyepieces feature fold-down cups to accommodate eyeglass wearers.

The Swarovski CT-85 is a spotter for serious hunters. The body lists at $1,100, while the eyepieces sell for $277 (fixed) or $343 (variable magnification). I took this spotting scope to Alaska, and I had to pry it out of bear guide Ed Stevenson's hands when it was time to leave.

Zeiss recently introduced a pair of superlative spotting scopes: the Diascope 65 T* FL and 85 T* FL models. While the 85mm model offers superlative

viewing, the 65mm Diascope is 2½ inches shorter and nearly a pound lighter (2.43 pounds), making it a better choice for many hunters. Three eyepieces are available: fixed-magnification at 23X and 30X and a 15–45X "Vario" eyepiece. The 23X eyepiece works great when prospecting for distant game. The 65 T* FL Diascope lists at $1,200, while the 23X eyepiece adds another $300.

A spotting scope is absolutely vital when you hunt trophy game. Binoculars are useful for locating animals, but they lack the magnification required for critically observing game on the far horizon. A spotting scope's high-powered optics let you examine animals up close and personal while you are seated comfortably an incredible distance away. Evaluating deer, elk, sheep, or bear a mile or more away spares you much wasted time and effort if the animal doesn't measure up to your desires.

When you shop for spotting scopes, you will discover a huge selection of models offered by a number of manufacturers. As I pointed out earlier, I didn't bother carrying a spotting scope when I first started hunting, but when I finally saw what a spotter could do for me I went right out and bought one.

Spotting Scopes

Fixed

Burris
Landmark 20–60X80mm

Burris
Signature 18–45X60mm

Nikon
XL II 16–47X60mm

Manufacturer	Model	Magnifi-cation	Objective Lens Dia. (mm)	Exit Pupil Dia. (mm)	Field of View	FOV (ft/100yds)	Length (in)	Weight (oz)	Price (MSRP)
Leica	Leica Televid 62	16X	62	3.9	140	m/1000m	11.6	32	$745
Leica	Leica APO Televid 62	16X	62	3.9	140	m/1000m	11.6	35	$1,045
Leica	Leica Televid 77	16X	77	4.8	110	m/1000m	15.4	52.8	$895
Leica	Leica APO Televid 77	16X	77	4.8	110	m/1000m	16.1	59.8	$1,395
Weaver	Weaver Classic 20X50	20X	50	2.5	122	ft/1000yds	10.4	19.6	$344
Nikon	Sky & Earth	20X	60	3.0	131	ft/1000yds	11.8	33	$281
Swarovski	ATS/STS 65	20X	65	3.3	108	ft/1000yds	12.8	39.9	$1,398
Swarovski	ATS/STS 65 HD High Definition	20X	65	3.3	108	ft/1000yds	12.8	39.9	$1,831
Swarovski	AT/ST 80	20X	80	4.0	99	ft/1000yds	15.6	52.6	$1,631
Swarovski	AT/ST 80 HD High Definition	20X	80	4.0	99	ft/1000yds	15.6	51.9	$2,098
Swarovski	CT 85 Collapsible	20X	85	4.3	NA	ft/1000yds	9.7–17.2	49.4	$1,299
BSA	SPS 20X40 RD	20X	40	2.0	NA	ft/100yds	12	26	$60
Zeiss	Diascope 65T* FL	23X	65	2.8	168	ft/1000yds	11.1	38.8	$1,398
Zeiss	Diascope 85T* FL	23X	85	3.7	129	ft/1000yds	13.6	51.2	$1,700
Simmons	25X50 ProHunter	25X	50	2.0	113	ft/1000yds	10.3	33.2	$153
Zeiss	Diascope 85T* FL	30X	85	2.8	129	ft/1000yds	13.6	51.2	$1,700
Redfield	Aurora Spotter(catadioptric)	30X	60	2.0	114	ft/1000yds	7.5	10.4	$250
Swarovski	ATS/STS 65	30X	65	2.2	108	ft/1000yds	12.8	39.9	$1,831
Swarovski	ATS/STS 65 HD High Definition	30X	65	2.2	108	ft/1000yds	12.8	39.9	$1,788
Zeiss	Diascope 65T* FL	30X	65	2.2	168	ft/1000yds	13.6	51.2	$2,098
Swarovski	CTC 30X75 Collapsible	30X	75	2.5	123	ft/1000yds	12.2–19.3	42.3	$1,032
Swarovski	AT/ST 80	30X	80	2.7	99	ft/1000yds	15.6	52.6	$1,631

Note: Many optical gear retailers offer 10 to 25 percent discounts below MSRP (Manufacturer's Suggested Retail Price).

Manufacturer	Model	Magnification	Objective Lens Dia. (mm)	Exit Pupil Dia. (mm)	Field of View	FOV (ft/100yds)	Length (in)	Weight (oz)	Price (MSRP)
Swarovski	AT/ST 80 HD High Definition	30X	80	2.7	99	ft/1000yds	15.6	51.9	$2,098
Swarovski	CT 85 Collapsible	30X	85	2.8	23	ft/1000yds	9.7–17.2	49.4	$1,609
Leica	Leica Televid 62	32X	62	1.9	NA	m/1000m	11.6	32	$745
Leica	Leica APO Televid 62	32X	62	1.9	NA	m/1000m	11.6	35	$1,045
Leica	Leica Televid 77	32X	77	2.4	60	m/1000m	15.4	52.8	$895
Leica	Leica APO Televid 77	32X	77	2.4	60	m/1000m	16.1	59.8	$1,395
Leica	Leica Televid 77	40X	77	1.9	60	m/1000m	15.4	52.8	$895
Leica	Leica APO Televid 77	40X	77	1.9	60	m/1000m	16.1	59.8	$1,395

Zeiss
Diascope Family

Zeiss
Diascope with 35mm Camera Adapter

BSA
DH20–60X60mm

Spotting Scopes
Variable

Manufacturer	Model	Magnification	Objective Lens Dia. (mm)	Exit Pupil Dia. (mm)	Field of View	FOV (ft/100yds)	Length (in)	Weight (oz)	Price (MSRP)
BSA	DH 15-45X50	15–45X	50	33.3–11.1	11–4	ft/1000yds	14	23	$80
Leupold	Leupold Compact	10–20X	40	4–2	3.8–2.6	ft/100yds	7.5	15.8	$440
BSA	Big Cat 1030X50 Waterproof	10–30X	50	5–1.7	18–9	ft/100yds	10.5	22	$140
BSA	Catseye 1236X50 Waterproof	12–36X	50	4.2–1.4	16–9	ft/100yds	11	24	$130
Bushnell/Bausch & Lomb	Bushnell Sportview	12–36X	50	4.2–1.4	160–90	ft/1000yds	8.7	21.5	$160
Leupold	Leupold Tactical	12–40X	50	4.8–1.5	16.8–5.2	ft/100yds	12.4	37	$1,250
Leupold	Leupold Golden Ring	12–40X	50	4.8–1.5	16.8–5.2	ft/100yds	12.4	37	$1,250
Alpen	715 w/tripod	15–30X	50	3.3–1.7	136–99	ft/1000yds	NA	18	$159
Alpen	753 w/tripod	15–36X	60	4–1.7	108–60	ft/1000yds	NA	35	$379
Shepherd	Shepherd	15–40X	60	4–1.5	NA	ft/1000yds	12.8	26	$695
Weaver	Weaver Classic 15–40X60	15–40X	60	4–1.5	122–69.8	ft/1000yds	12.5	26.1	$516
Bushnell/Bausch & Lomb	Bushnell Nature View	15–45X	37	4–1.3	150–38	ft/1000yds	14	29	$251

Weaver
Classic 15–40X60mm

BSA
DH20–60X60mm

Simmons
Endeavor 15–45X60mm

Manufacturer	Model	Magnifi-cation	Objective Lens Dia. (mm)	Exit Pupil Dia. (mm)	Field of View	FOV (ft/100yds)	Length (in)	Weight (oz)	Price (MSRP)
Bushnell/Bausch & Lomb	Bushnell Spacemaster	15–45X	40	3.3–1.1	105–48	ft/1000yds	12.4	36	$260
Bushnell/Bausch & Lomb	Bushnell Sportview	15–45X	50	4–1.3	103–35	ft/1000yds	17.4	23.4	$105
Simmons	15–45X50 Waterproof	15–45X	50	3.3–1.1	95–51	ft/1000yds	12	33.5	$256
Alpen	757 Long Eye Relief	15–45X	60	4–1.3	108–63	ft/1000yds	NA	36	$425
Burris	Landmark w/tripod	15–45X	60	4–1..3	14.6–7.2	ft/1000yds	12.7	24	$227
Bushnell/Bausch & Lomb	Bausch & Lomb Elite	15–45X	60	4–1.3	125–65	ft/1000yds	12.2	26.5	$767
Bushnell/Bausch & Lomb	Bushnell Spacemaster Kit	15–45X	60	4–1.3	125–65	ft/1000yds	12.7	43	$561
Bushnell/Bausch & Lomb	Bushnell Xtra–Wide	15–45X	60	4–1.5	160–87	ft/1000yds	13	35	$641
Nikon	Sky & Earth	15–45X	60	4–1.3	133	ft/1000yds	12,7	35.5	$431
Remington	15–45X60 Spotter	15–45X	60	4–1.4	108–63	ft/1000yds	14	42	$456
Zeiss	Diascope 65T* FL	15–45X	65	4.3–1.4	168–78	ft/1000yds	13.6	51.2	$1,500
Leupold	Wind River	15–45X	60	4–1.3	13.1–6.9	ft/100yds	12.1	35.1	$379

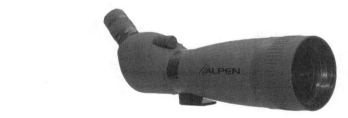

Alpen
20–60X80mm

Simmons
Redline 15–45X50mm

Nikon
Fieldscope III 60mm Angled 20–60X60mm

Spotting Scopes

Variable

Manufacturer	Model	Magnifi-cation	Objective Lens Dia. (mm)	Exit Pupil Dia. (mm)	Field of View	FOV (ft/100yds)	Length (in)	Weight (oz)	Price (MSRP)
Bushnell/Bausch & Lomb	Bausch & Lomb Discovery	15–60X	60	4–1	150–38	ft/1000yds	17.5	48.5	$392
Bushnell/Bausch & Lomb	Bushnell Sentry Field	16–32X	50	1.5–3.1	140–65	ft/1000yds	8.7	21.5	$206
Nikon	Spotter XL	16–47X	60	3.8–1.3	105	ft/1000yds	12.5	26.5	$773
Leica	Leica Televid 62	16–48X	62	4.8–1.3	NA	m/1000m	11.6	32	$745
Leica	Leica APO Televid 62	16–48X	62	4.8–1.3	NA	m/1000m	11.6	35	$1,045
Bushnell/Bausch & Lomb	Bushnell Sentry	18–36X	50	2.8–1.4	115–75	ft/1000yds	14.7	31	$181
Tasco	World Class	18–36X	50	2.8–1.4	12	ft/1000yds	14.5	31	$132
Alpen	719 w/tripod	18–36X	60	3.3–1.7	120–90	ft/1000yds	NA	24	$189
Burris	Signature	18–45X	60	3.3–1.3	11–6.3	ft/1000yds	12.6	29	$819
Nikon	Fieldscope III	20–45X	60	3–1.3	156	ft/1000yds	10.9	38	$1,175
Nikon	Fieldscope III ED Tactical TF3	20–45X	60	3–1.3	156	ft/1000yds	11.5	38	$1,451
Burris	Landmark Compact	20–50X	50	2.5	15.2	ft/1000yds	7	14.5	$120
Bushnell/Bausch & Lomb	Bushnell Trophy	20–50X	50	2.5–1	92–52	ft/1000yds	12.2	17	$338
Sightron	SII Series, SII20–50X63	20–50X	63	3.2–1.3	92–52.5	ft/1000yds	14	30.8	$383
Sightron	SII Series, SII20–50X80	20–50X	80	4–1.6	92–52.5	ft/1000yds	15	34.3	$486
Zeiss	Diascope 85T* FL	20–60X	85	4.3–1.4	129–60	ft/1000yds	13.6	51.2	$1,800
Bushnell/Bausch & Lomb	Bushnell Spacemaster	20–60X	40	3–1	88–40	ft/1000yds	14.5	36.5	$320
Bushnell/Bausch & Lomb	Bushnell Sportview	20–60X	60	3–1	70–24	ft/1000yds	20.5	25	$121
Simmons	20–60X60 Waterproof	20–60X	60	3–1	95–51	ft/1000yds	12	34.5	$283
Bushnell/Bausch & Lomb	Bushnell Trophy	20–60X	63	3–1	90–45	ft/1000yds	12.7	20	$422
Swarovski	ATS/STS 65	20–60X	65	4–1.3	108–60	ft/1000yds	12.8	39.9	$1,332
Swarovski	ATS/STS 65 HD	20–60X	65	4–1.3	108–60	ft/1000yds	12.8	39.9	$1,731
Bushnell/Bausch & Lomb	Bausch & Lomb Elite	20–60X	70	3.5–1.2	90–50	ft/1000yds	16	40	$922
Remington	20–60X70 Spotter	20–60X	70	3.5–1.2	85.2–52.4	ft/1000yds	15	39	$456

Manufacturer	Model	Magnifi-cation	Objective Lens Dia. (mm)	Exit Pupil Dia. (mm)	Field of View	FOV (ft/100yds)	Length (in)	Weight (oz)	Price (MSRP)
Alpen	777	20–60X	77	3.8–1.3	101–57	ft/1000yds	NA	47	$500
Leica	Leica Televid 77	20–60X	77	3.9–1.9	60–22	m/1000m	15.4	52.8	$895
Leica	Leica APO Televid 77	20–60X	77	3.9–1.9	60–22	m/1000m	16.1	59.8	$1,395
Burris	Landmark	20–60X	80	4–1.3	10.5–5.2	ft/1000yds	17.5	42	$290
Bushnell/Bausch & Lomb	Bausch & Lomb Elite	20–60X	80	4.1–1.4	98–50	ft/1000yds	17	53	$1,277
Bushnell/Bausch & Lomb	Bausch & Lomb Elite	20–60X	80	4.1–1.4	98–50	ft/1000yds	17	53	$1,277
Nikon	Sky & Earth	20–60X	80	4–1.3	99	ft/1000yds	16	52.5	$801
Swarovski	AT/ST 80	20–60X	80	4–1.3	99–51	ft/1000yds	15.6	52.6	$1,754
Swarovski	AT/ST 80 HD	20–60X	80	4–1.3	99–51	ft/1000yds	15.6	51.9	$2,220
Swarovski	CT 85 Collapsible	20–60X	85	4–1.3	101–52	ft/1000yds	9.7–17.2	49.4	$1,299
BSA	Big Cat 20-60X60 Waterprf	20–60X	60	3–1	14–7	ft/100yds	12.3	25	$170
BSA	DH 20-60X60	20–60X	60	3–1	7–3	ft/100yds	17	28	$90
Pentax	PF-80ED	21–63X	80	3.8–1.3	93–49.5	ft/1000yds	16.3	56.4	$1,800
Nikon	Fieldscope 78 ED	25–57X	78	3.1–1.7	126	ft/1000yds	12.6	47	$1,620
Pentax	PF-100ED	26–78X	100	3.8–1.3	78–42	ft/1000yds	20	91.7	$2,700

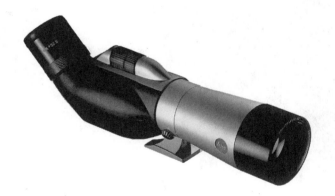

Leica
S10–30X50mm

Leupold
Mark IV tactical 12–40X60mm

Spotting Scopes
Variable

Shepherd
15–40X60mm

Leupold
Goldring Compact 10–20X40mm

Chapter 13
Laser Rangefinders

Even experienced shooters have trouble guessing the range to distant targets. This is true regardless of terrain. People seem unable to estimate distances accurately at anything beyond fifty or sixty yards, whether in rolling plains or steep mountain country. The difficulty is multiplied when you are looking at an elk on the far side of a ravine. I do not know of any hunter—regardless of experience—who can "guesstimate" distances with any degree of accuracy across a lake, canyon, or anything else that spoils visual perspective.

I am constantly reminded of my own rangefinding inadequacies. I have eyeballed mule deer at less than two hundred yards I swore were at least three hundred yards away. I have also overshot four-hundred-yard prairie dogs that proved to be considerably closer.

Accurately knowing the distance to the target is vital to hunting marksmanship. Shoot at an animal more than two hundred yards away, and bullet drop quickly becomes a factor. There is no such thing as a flat-shooting rifle. No matter how high the velocity, as soon as a bullet leaves the bore, gravity begins to pull it down. The farther the bullet travels, the more critical range becomes. At three hundred yards, which is the maximum distance all but the most expert rifleman should attempt to drop a deer, a 30 percent error in estimating range can easily make the difference between killing cleanly or missing—or worse, wounding—an animal.

Leica's Geovid was the first laser rangefinder designed for the sportsman. Combined with Leica's superb 7X42mm binocular, it still ranks at the top.

Until very recently, determining the distance to long-range targets was more of an art than a science. Variable-magnification riflescopes with rangefinding reticles made their appearance many years ago, and they continue to offer one way to estimate shooting distances afield. These reticles sport stadia cross hairs that can be adjusted (by turning the power ring) until they bracket the animal's back-to-brisket height. Then the range is read and the proper elevation dialed in.

While better than an eyeball estimate, this system has its flaws. It assumes every target animal's chest area has a uniform depth of eighteen inches. And as the song says, "It ain't necessarily so." Elk, deer, and pronghorn differ greatly in size and heft—and even individuals of the same species cannot be counted on to share the same dimensions.

Then there's that nagging requirement for the critter to patiently pose as you turn power rings and fiddle with elevation dials. Very few of the animals I have hunted have been that accommodating.

Optical comparison (split image) rangefinders have also been available for some time. These mechanical rangefinders require you to painstakingly transpose a pair of like images. While they measure bowhunting distances with fair

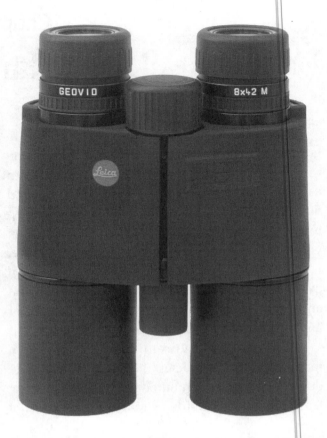

Leica's Geovid BRF combines the latest rangefinding technology into a state-of-the-art roof-prism binocular that is as compact as a regular binocular.

accuracy, I have found they are not all that useful for long-range riflery. At much beyond one hundred yards, you will find that multiple readings of the same target, taken seconds apart with the same rangefinder, can yield widely varying results.

American sportsmen are exposed to a lot of different gadgetry that is often of marginal value. But every once in a while something truly useful comes along. The laser rangefinder is a stellar example.

Laser rangefinders feature a laser diode that emits collimated light pulses in the near-infrared range. This light, which is invisible to the naked eye, travels downrange until it strikes an object. Light reflected from this object retraces its path back to the rangefinder, where it is intercepted by a second diode. The rangefinder measures the elapsed time between transmission and reception, and a microprocessor computes the distance to the

Rees uses Bushnell Yardage Pro 1000 laser rangefinder—one of several different models the company offers.

This pronghorn buck was shot after the author first measured the range with a laser rangefinder.

target. This figure then instantly appears in the rangefinder reticle.

Each laser rangefinder is rated for a specific maximum effective range, but not all ratings are equal. Most laser rangefinders are tested at twilight because that is when they deliver peak performance. The beam they project is in the near-infrared range. Infrared light is present in the atmosphere, degrading rangefinder efficiency. When the sun dips toward the horizon, there is less infrared light to interfere with accurate readings.

Particulate matter suspended in the atmosphere also diminishes performance. The drier the air, the better laser rangefinders work. Angles also matter. Targets square-on to the rangefinder reflect better than steeply angled targets do. The kind of surface

you are projecting against also affects performance. Animal hide absorbs some energy, while flat, hard targets give a better return. Size is also important. Lasers reflect off large objects better than they do off small ones. Directing a laser beam at a highly reflective surface like water is like skipping rocks over a pond.

While military laser rangefinders have been around for years, Leica introduced the first laser rangefinder designed expressly for sportsmen. The Geovid BDA was a technological marvel. It married a top-grade 7X42 binocular, a precisely calibrated electronic compass, and a superbly accurate infrared laser rangefinder into the same rubber-armored package. Problem was, this superlative high-tech optical package was expensive. While few (if any)

Two of Bushnell's highly portable laser rangefinders.

Geovid BDAs actually fetched the initial $6,000 list price, even the $4,500 "street discount" tab was well beyond the reach of most outdoorsmen.

To make the Geovid more affordable, Leica created another version: the Geovid BD, sans electronic compass. This pared a few ounces from the BDA's heft, bringing the weight to an even three pounds. More importantly, it cut a big chunk from the price tag. The original Geovid BDA was recently discontinued. The latest Geovid BRF laser rangefinders—also incorporating top-quality Leica binoculars—sell for about $1,800.

There was a time when manufacturers often exaggerated the efficiency of their fledgling rangefinders. That seems to be changing. Progressively better (and cheaper) technology has made spurious claims less common. Early on, Leica determined the 1,100-yard effectiveness rating of its Geovid BD laser rangefinder by testing it, under less than optimum conditions, at sea level in bright sunlight (visibility: 10 kilometers). It performs even better in dim or evening light.

In my opinion, the Geovid BD remains the gold standard of laser rangefinders. In addition to being a highly accurate rangefinder, it is paired with Leica's superb 7X42 binocular. Yes, it is heavy, but it makes a lot of sense to combine a rangefinder and a binocular. You can zap that laser pulse down the field while you study your potential trophy through the binocular. No wasted time putting the binocular down and reaching for the rangefinder.

Two other manufacturers have also recently introduced laser rangefinding binoculars. Bushnell's Yardage Pro Quest combines an 8X36 binocular with a laser rangefinder capable of measuring distances to highly reflective objects well over 1,000 yards away. The Quest is slightly less bulky than the Geovid, and is a full 14 ounces lighter. It also carries a much lighter price tag—suggested retail is just $599. The Yardage Pro Quest offers one other advantage over the Geovid 7X42 BD. The original Geovid was only "weather resistant." Like Leica's latest Geovid BRF laser rangefiner," the Quest is fully waterproof. To test this claim, I dunked the Quest for several minutes in an ice-rimed river while the air temperature stood at 17 degrees F. When I took the Quest back to my car and turned the heater on full blast, the rangefinder remained fog-free and totally dry inside.

Another fully waterproof model is Leupold's Wind River RB800, which marries a rangefinder with an 8X32 roof-prism binocular with fully coated lenses. The rubber-armored unit gives the precise range of animals more than 550 yards away, and inanimate objects at more than 850 yards. A scan mode allows you to measure the range to a moving target continuously. The RB800C is identical, but it features a built-in compass to give you the direction to a target. The RB800 weighs 23 ounces and lists at $875.

As this is being written, Pentax has just announced its own laser-rangefinding binocular that also computes the uphill or downhill shooting angle to the target. I have yet to see the Pentax unit, but it is apparent that more and more laser rangefinding binoculars will appear over the next few years.

At the moment, monocular-style laser rangefinders outnumber rangefinding binoculars.

A laser rangefinder helps varmint shooters determine the range to distant prairie dogs.

Bushnell entered this market in 1995 with the Lytespeed 400 (later renamed the Yardage Pro 400). At 18 ounces, the Lytespeed was nearly two thirds lighter than the Geovid BD, and you could buy it for about one-tenth the price. Cash-strapped sportsmen who could only drool over Leica's Geovid quickly snapped up the considerably lighter, cheaper Bushnell rangefinder. Not only was the effective range limited to 400 yards, but the Lytespeed also didn't deliver the same, superb optical performance the Geovid provided. The good news was that you could buy the Bushnell for a little over $300.

At the moment, Bushnell offers more laser rangefinders than anyone else. The lineup includes seven monocular models in addition to the Quest binocular. List prices range from $308 up to $648 for the waterproof, pocket-size Legend.

Monocular-style laser rangefinders are also available from Nikon. These include the Buckmaster Laser 800, which offers 8X magnification, weighs just 7 ounces, and retails at a recommended $440. Maximum range is 437 yards. The Buckmaster Laser 600 is a 6X unit selling for $447, and it has a maximum range of 600 yards. The Buckmaster Laser 800 has an 800-yard maximum range and lists at $551. Team Realtree camo versions of all three are also available at a slightly extra cost.

In addition to its excellent Geovid, Leica also offers an LRF 800 Rangemaster that lists for around $450 and has a range of 800 yards. The LRF 1200 model has a range of up to 1,200 yards, and it sells for $530. Swarovski once offered a laser rangefinding riflescope, but its great bulk—a hefty 2½ pounds—and its price tag of several thousand dollars eventually caused its demise.

Not all laser rangefinders are created equal. Beam divergence is an important factor. Laser beam diameter is expressed in milliradians (mil rads), with each milliradian representing 1/1000 of the distance to the target. At 1,000 yards, a one-mil-rad beam measures one yard in diameter. A laser beam with a three-mil-rad convergence covers a cross section nine feet in diameter. The Geovid has a divergence of 1.5 X 0.3 mil rads. This means that at 1,000 yards, the beam is 4½ feet wide and a foot high. With this little convergence, you can determine the range to something as small as a prairie dog without picking up reflections from the ground several yards in front of it.

Beam divergence is why it does not always pay to operate a laser rangefinder while lying prone. Like a full-choke shotgun pattern, the laser beam expands as it travels downrange. Triggered from ground level, the diverging beam may reflect off earth or foliage hundreds of yards ahead of your target.

Low-priced rangefinders are likely to produce greater divergence. The wider the beam, the less accurate the reading. Another difference is the

Leica's LRF 900 laser rangefinder.

way reflected light is measured. Many laser rangefinders are "first read" designs. The first signal reflected back from the target is the one that gets measured. More costly units like the Geovid read multiple pulses, and the readings are then averaged by a microprocessor. This improves accuracy.

Not too long ago I tested several laser rangefinding monoculars to see how they performed on different targets at varying range. First, I visited a nearby lake. Water presents a rangefinding challenge, and I wanted to see how well these rangefinders would do on floating targets. A fisherman sitting in a float tube 200 yards away presented no difficulties. The readings I took varied by only six yards (probably caused by target drift). Then I turned the rangefinders on a boat anchored several hundred yards away. The Geovid BD registered 589 yards, but the less costly models apparently couldn't receive signals from the boat. The broader beams they broadcasted were reflecting off some nearby cattails, giving false readings in the 55–65-yard range. I tried again while standing in the back of my truck, placing the rangefinders some eight feet above the ground. This time the laser passed over the cattails, giving good readings from all the units tested.

Bushnell's Yardage Pro Scout.

Randy Brooks took this ram after first using a laser rangefinder.

More recently, I tested Bushnell's Quest rangefinding binocular on several targets that ranged from 60 to more than 800 yards away. Horses standing in a field gave good, consistent 530-yard readings. The overcast day helped. An hour later, when the sun was shining brightly, animals were less reflective and I had to target a nearby barn or fenceline to get a decent reading.

Today's light, portable, highly accurate laser rangefinders raise one concern. I worry that they may tempt some hunters to shoot at extreme ranges instead of taking the time to stalk closer.

Technology is no substitute for common sense. If your rangefinder tells you a buck is 600 yards away, do not attempt a shot. Too far is too far, even if you know exactly how far that is.

Leica has just introduced its own compact laser rangefinder. The Leica LRF 800 features a 7X21 monocular with Leica's highly respected lenses that include "ballistic tough" coatings. Unlike many other laser rangefinders, the LRF 800 is fully waterproof. Leica also claims this is the world's most compact laser rangefinder: It measures just 4 inches by 3¾ inches by 1⅜ inches and weighs only 10 ounces.

Laser Rangefinders
Monocular

Leica
7XLAF 1200

Bushnell
Yardage Pro 6X

Manufacturer	Model	Prism	Max Range	Magnifi-cation	Objective Dia. (mm)	FOV (ft/100yds)	Exit Pupil Dia. (mm)	Eye Relief (in)	Scan (y/n)	Rain/ Snow (y/n)	Length (in) convert to decimal	Weight (oz)	Price (MSRP)
Nikon	Buckmaster Laser 400	Porro	400	8X	20	330	2.5	10	Yes	NA	L 2.8 W 3.7	7	$411
Nikon	Team Realtree Laser 400	Porro	400	8X	20	330	2.5	10	Yes	NA	L 3.7 W 2.8	7	$441[1]
Bushnell	Yardage Pro 500	Porro	500	6X	NA	NA	NA	NA	Yes	Yes	2¼ x 5 x 4¾	13.5	$399
Nikon	Buckmaster Laser 600	Porro	600	6X	20	330	3.3	17	Yes	NA	L 3.7 W 2.8	7.4	$447
Nikon	Team Realtree Laser 600	Porro	600	6X	20	330	3.3	17	Yes	NA	L 3.7 W 2.8	7.4	$477[1]
Bushnell	Yardage Pro Scout	Porro	700	6X	NA	NA	NA	NA	Yes	Yes	1½ x 4 x 2¾	6.8	$516
Bushnell	Yardage Pro Scout	Porro	700	6X	NA	NA	NA	NA	Yes	Yes	1½ x 4 x 2¾	6.8	$550[1]
Bushnell	Yardage Pro Sport	Porro	800	4X	NA	NA	NA	NA	Yes	Yes	1 1/16 x 3 5/16 x 3 1/8	7.4	$308[2]
Nikon	Monarch Laser 800	Roof	800	6X	21	315	3.5	18	Yes	Yes	L 5	7.4	$491
Bushnell	Yardage Pro Legend	Porro	800	6X	NA	NA	NA	NA	Yes	Yes	1¾ x 3 15/16 x 3 1/8	7.2	$648[3]
Osprey Int.	AimShot Comet EMC2	Porro	800	7X	25	3.6	NA	NA	NA	NA	4.7 x 4.8 x 2.4	18	$399
Nikon	Buckmaster Laser 800	Porro	800	8X	20	330	2.5	10	Yes	Yes	L 3.7 W 2.8	7	$519

[1] w/Realtree camouflage.   [2] Single-button operation.   [3] waterproof.

Note: Many optical gear retailers offer 10 to 25 percent discounts below MSRP (Manufacturer's Suggested Retail Price).

Manufacturer	Model	Prism	Max Range	Magnifi-cation	Objective Dia. (mm)	FOV (ft/100yds)	Exit Pupil Dia. (mm)	Eye Relief (in)	Scan (y/n)	Rain/Snow (y/n)	Length (in) convert to decimal	Weight (oz)	Price (MSRP)
Nikon	Team Realtree Laser 800	Porro	800	8X	20	330	2.5	10	Yes	Yes	L 3.7 W 2.8	7	$551[1]
Bushnell	Yardage Pro Compact 800	Porro	800	8X	NA	NA	NA	NA	Yes	Yes	2 x 4¾ x 3¾	11.4	$525
Leica	LRF 900	Porro	900	7X	21	367	3	NA	Yes	Yes	4¾ x 4⅛ x 1⁹⁄₁₆	11.3	$449
Leica	LRF 1200	Porro	1200	7X	21	367	3	NA	Yes	Yes	4¾ x 4⅛ x 1⁹⁄₁₆	11.3	$529
Bushnell	Yardage Pro 1000	Porro	1500	6X	NA	NA	NA	NA	Yes	Yes	2¼ x 5 x 4¾	13.5	$627
Swarovski	Laser Guide 8X30	Roof	1500	8X	30	NA	3.8	NA	Yes	Yes	L 5.8	12	$888
Osprey Int.	AimShot EMC4	Porro	1600	7X	25	3.6	NA	NA	NA	NA	4.7 x 4.8 x 2.4	18	$449

[1] w/Realtree camouflage.

Nikon
Buckmasters Laser 800

Laser Rangefinders
Binocular

Manufacturer	Model	Prism	Max Range	Magnifi-cation	Objective Dia. (mm)	FOV (ft/100yds)	Exit Pupil Dia. (mm)	Eye Relief (in)	Scan (y/n)	Rain/ Snow (y/n)	Length (in) convert to decimal	Weight (oz)	Price (MSRP)
Leupold	Wind River RB800	Roof	800	8X	32	314	4	16	Yes	NA	L 5.4	23	$875[1]
Leupold	Wind River RB800C	Roof	800	8X	32	314	4	16	Yes	NA	L 5.4	23	$1,000[2]
Bushnell	Yardage Pro Quest	Porro	1300	8X	36	NA	4.5	NA	Yes	Yes	2 x 4¾ x 3¾	34	$600
Leica	Geovid 8X42 BRF	Roof	1300	8X	42	373	5.3	NA	Yes	Yes	L 6.9 W 6.3	31.7	$1,800
Leica	Geovid 10X42 BRF	Roof	1300	10X	42	331	4.2	NA	Yes	Yes	L 6.9 W 6.3	31.7	$1,850
Burris	B-1500	Roof	1500	7X	40	315	5.7	18	Yes	Yes	L 6.2 W 5.7	34	$1,017

[1.] Rubber armored, waterproof.   [2.] With built-in compass.

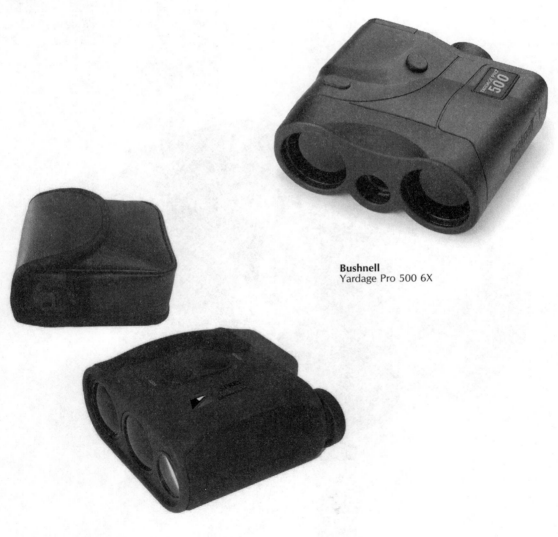

Bushnell
Yardage Pro 500 6X

Osprey
EMC4 25mm w/40mm laser lens

Chapter 14

Red-Dot, Holosight, and Laser Sights

Red-dot sights and Bushnell's Holosight provide very similar sight pictures and offer similar advantages. These 1-power sights offer no magnification and allow shooters to use them with both eyes open. The shooter has a virtually unlimited field of view. There are no front and rear sights to line up. Users see only a bright red-orange dot. Aiming consists simply of placing the dot over the target. The combination of an extremely wide viewing field and aiming simplicity makes these sights extremely fast and easy to use.

Red-dot sights and Holosights are very popular with handgunners. While they add bulk and heft,

they allow you to get on target much faster than open sights permit. Their chief disadvantage is that handguns fitted with these sights cannot be carried in conventional holsters. Specialized holsters are available for competitive handgunners, while other designs accommodate regular field use.

I have used red-dot sights on different .22 pistols and centerfire handguns. They have allowed me to hit animals as small as prairie dogs at one hundred yards or more. Long eye-relief pistol scopes offer greater precision at longer ranges, but are not nearly as fast and easy to use. Long eye-relief scopes offer a very constricted viewing field, while red-dot sights

The Bushnell Holosight displays an orange dot surrounded by a circle. The sight features the same "heads-up" aiming system that jet fighter pilots use.

Mounted on 1911 pistol, the Bushnell Holosight allows ultra-quick target acquisition.

feature a virtually unlimited field of view. While red-dot sights and Holosights are widely used on handguns, they offer similar advantages when mounted on rifles and scatterguns.

A few years ago I watched a trapshooter shatter twenty-five clay pigeons without a miss. He had a Bushnell Holosight mounted over his shotgun's receiver. Showing off, he then switched the gun to his other shoulder and broke another dozen targets.

"It's easy," he said, handing me the gun. "Just put the orange circle where you want the pellets to go, and pull the trigger. The sight won't *let* you miss." I had used Holosights and other red-dot sights on several pistols over the years, and they worked great for short- to midrange handgunning. But I had not recognized their wingshooting potential until I saw that trapshooting exhibition. I spent several minutes powdering clay birds with the Holosighted shotgun, and was amazed at the difference the sight made.

In spite of that impressive demonstration, I did not try mounting a red-dot sight on one of my own scatterguns until the following year. I had just had one of those embarrassing slumps, amusing fellow shooters by flat-out missing not one, but *two* dead-cinch shots as roosters flushed from practically underfoot. Minutes later, I emptied my gun at a

passing bird thirty-five yards away without cutting a feather. The afternoon was similarly disappointing.

I didn't want a repeat performance when I hunted again the following day. Recalling my brief experience on the trapshooting range, I mounted a Holosight on my Model 870 Remington pump. Then I sighted the Holosight in so as to center the shotgun's pattern at forty yards.

The Holosight works on the same principle used in the heads-up holographic displays that help F-14 fighter pilots instantly get on target. A laser-illuminated reticle appears as a holograph that seems to float at the target plane. Eye alignment isn't critical. Simply superimpose the reticle—a bright orange dot surrounded by an orange circle—on the target, and the shot string goes where you want. You can vary reticle intensity by repeatedly pressing "up arrow" or "down arrow" buttons just below the reticle display. There is no magnification, so you can use the Holosight with both eyes open. That gives you a virtually unlimited field of view and makes sighting extremely fast.

In spite of the Holosight, I still missed the first pheasant I shot at the next morning. The sight rode so high I could not see the reticle when I cheeked the stock, which I do as a matter of course. Once I learned to raise my head, I began hitting birds.

The Swedish-made Aimpoint was the first commercial red-dot sight. It can be used on rifles, shotguns, and handguns alike.

Burris Speed Dot red-dot sight mounted on a shotgun makes it easy to find your target.

After that first miss, I redeemed myself by hitting consistently the rest of the day. When a rooster flushed, I would simply center its head in the floating circle and pull the trigger. While I needed to give crossing birds some lead, there was no worry about shooting low or high if I didn't properly cheek the stock. It didn't seem to matter *where* my head was placed. As long as I could see that fluorescent orange holograph, I killed birds. Thanks to the Holosight, I missed no more pheasants during the hunt—a rare experience and one that I thoroughly enjoyed.

Before I took the Holosighted autoloader afield again, I installed a Beartooth comb-raising kit. This kit consists of a rubberized, pull-on sleeve that fits over the buttstock. Each kit comes complete with five high-density foam cheekpads of different thicknesses that fit snugly under the rubber sleeve. I stacked two of the thicker pads together to raise the comb to the proper height.

Later, I tried using red-dot sights on other shotguns I owned. First I mounted a Swedish-made Aimpoint sight on a Model 500 Mossberg pump.

Aimpoint pioneered red-dot sights, and I had used one on a deer rifle many years ago. While a variety of Aimpoint sights is available, they all provide a bright red dot as an aiming point. You vary the dot's intensity by turning a dial atop the sight's tubular body.

I fitted another red-dot sight—the Burris SpeedDot 135—on a Model 1100 Remington

When red-dot/Holosight sights are mounted on a shotgun, the comb must be raised. Beartooth offers specialized kits that adjust to any height.

Bushnell's Holosight makes it easy to hit clay targets.

The Holosight on the Ruger 10/22 is a deadly combination for hunting rabbits.

The Holosight makes it easy to teach youths how to shoot.

This photo illustrates an Aimpoint sight on a Ruger Mark II pistol.

autoloader. This sight was roughly the same size as the Aimpoint and operated pretty much the same way. Either 3 MOA (minute of angle) or 11 MOA aiming dots are available. (Scattergunners should choose the larger size.) The Burris SpeedDot comes complete with Weaver-style rings.

Installing a red-dot sight on your shotgun requires a mount designed for the job. While several mounts are available, I like the Aimtech system, which features a steel saddle mount that fits over the receiver. These mounts are offered to fit most popular pumps and autoloaders.

Like the Holosight, neither the Aimpoint nor the Speed Dot sight offers magnified viewing. You can use them with both eyes open, providing an essentially limitless field of view. While I like the wide, televisionlike screen the Holosight offers, all three sights are extremely fast. No time is wasted in finding the target.

Rees has a Holosight mounted on his .44 Magnum Dan Wesson hunting revolver.

When a red-dot sight or Holosight is mounted on a shotgun, the pull-on Beartooth stock kit raises the comb to the proper height.

I have since used these shotguns and their red-dot sights to hunt a variety of upland game. They proved highly effective for hunting grouse and quail, and even made mourning dove gunning seem easy. I have also used both the Aimpoint and Holosight to take a couple of long-bearded toms.

I had bragged on these sights so long and loud that a pair of friends called my bluff. Scott Treu, Ray Olsen, and I had planned to hunt late-season ducks and geese, and Scott and Ray wanted to see how my red-dot sights would perform. I was curious about this myself. Shooting high-flying waterfowl presents a different challenge from what upland hunting offers, and I had yet to try these sights in the duck blind.

Scott and I drove to Utah's Farmington Bay. Once at the blind, we threw out some decoys and settled down to wait. Ray was using the Aimpoint-equipped Mossberg pump while Scott had the Remington autoloader with its Burris SpeedDot. I kept the Holosighted Model 870 for myself.

The January afternoon was unseasonably warm, and there was little or no wind to put birds in the air. We spent a couple of hours searching the empty sky, joking with one another and munching snacks.

Red-dot sights speed handgun aiming and aid accuracy.

As the sun dipped toward the horizon, ducks finally began to fly. None wanted to land in our decoys, but we scratched down three fat mallards as they passed overhead.

"This sight really works!" Scott said, folding a drake at extreme range. "I just moved the dot ahead of the bird and fired. This makes hitting easy!"

Disappointed at the light action, we met early the following morning and drove to the Duchesne River. Warm springs keep part of this river flowing after nearby ponds and streams have frozen over. That makes the Duchesne a late-season hot spot for jumpshooting ducks and geese.

The red-dot sights again proved their worth. Shooting at startled waterfowl as they flushed from the water was—if you will pardon the expression—duck soup. In this kind of gunning, little or no lead was required. I have become a big fan of shotgunning with red-dot sights. They may look strange on a scattergun, but they really work!

Whether you are using them on a rifle, handgun, or shotgun, red-dot sights have a lot to offer. There is no magnification, so you can use them with both eyes open. This gives you a wide open field of view. It doesn't matter how well a gun fits you or where your eye is positioned behind the sight. If you can see the reticle, you can hit game. You don't have to line up both front and rear sights with the target. Simply dab the red dot on what you want to shoot and pull the trigger.

Laser Sights

A variety of laser-sighting systems is available, primarily for use on handguns. Laser sights are designed primarily for short-range defensive use in low-light-level situations and are not intended for hunting. Because the subject of this book is hunting optics, laser sights are described in the catalog section, but are not addressed here.

Sections of this chapter were excerpted from articles the author wrote for *Shooting Illustrated* magazine and appear here with the editor's permission.

Red-Dot, Holosight, and Laser Sights

BSA
RD30/22SIL 30mm 5MOA Silver

BSA
PD30SIL 30mm w/25mm obj. lens, 5MOA

Bushnell
Holosight

Manufacturer	Model	Tube Dia (mm)	Water-proof	Magni-fication	Dot	Brightness Adjust (y/n)	Long guns or Handguns	Length (in)	Weight (oz)	Price (MSRP)
Aimpoint	7000L	30	Yes	1X	4MOA	Y	Long guns	7.9	7.9	$319 [1]
Aimpoint	7000 SC	30	Yes	1X	4MOA	Y	Long guns, Handguns	6.3	7.1	$319 [2]
Aimpoint	7000 SM	30	Yes	1X	4MOA	Y	Long guns, Handguns	6.3	7.1	$319 [3]
Aimpoint	Comp C	30	Yes	1X	4MOA	Y	Scout-style Rifles, Handguns	4.8	6.5	$347 [4]
Aimpoint	Comp C SM	30	Yes	1X	4MOA	Y	Scout-style Rifles, Handguns	4.8	6.5	$347 [3]
Aimpoint	Comp M2	30	Yes	1X	4MOA	Y	Scout-style Rifles, Handguns	4.8	7.1	$439 [5]
Aimpoint	7000L 2X	30	Yes	2X	4MOA	Y	Long guns	7.9	10.3	$416
Aimpoint	7000 SC 2X	30	Yes	2X	4MOA	Y	Long guns, Handguns	6.3	10.3	$416
Burris	SpeedDot 135	1.36"	Yes	1X	3MOA or 11MOA	Y	Long guns, Handguns	4.9	5	$291 [6]
Bushnell	Trophy Red Dot	28	Yes	1X	4 choices available	Y	Long guns, Handguns	5.5	6	$120 [7]
Bushnell	Holosight	-	Yes	1X	1MOA dot in 65MOA ring	Y	Long guns, Handguns	4.1	6.5	$390 [8]

[1] 38mm ring can be used for mounting the sight via the objective bell.

[2] Semi-matte carbon black finish.

[3] Silver metallic finish.

[4] Black.

[5] Heavy-duty variant of the Comp C, built for extreme conditions.

[6] Includes Weaver-style mounting rings.

[7] 4 dial-up electronic reticles. Weaver-style mounting rings supplied.

[8] Holographic sight. Available with either N-cell or AA batteries.

Note: Many optical gear retailers offer 10 to 25 percent discounts below MSRP (Manufacturer's Suggested Retail Price).

Red-Dot, Holosight, and Laser Sights

Manufacturer	Model	Tube Dia (mm)	Water-proof	Magni-fication	Dot	Brightness Adjust (y/n)	Long guns or Handguns	Length (in)	Weight (oz)	Price (MSRP)
C-More	Serendipity SL	-	Yes	1X	8MOA Standard 6 sizes available	Y	Handguns	5.4	3.8	$239 [1]
C-More	Serendipity SL	-	Yes	1X	8MOA Standard 6 sizes available	Y	Handguns	5.4	3.8	$299 [2]
C-More	Railway CRW	-	Yes	1X	8MOA Standard 6 sizes available	Y	Long guns, Handguns	4.8	5	$299 [3]
C-More	Railway RW	-	Yes	1X	8MOA Standard 6 sizes available	Y	Long guns, Handguns	4.8	5	$249 [4]
C-More	Slide Ride CRW	-	Yes	1X	8MOA Standard 6 sizes available	Y	Long guns, Handguns	4.8	3	$299 [5]
C-More	Slide Ride SR	-	Yes	1X	8MOA Standard 6 sizes available	Y	Long guns, Handguns	4.8	3	$249 [6]
C-More	Scout	-	Yes	1X	6MOA	Y	Long guns	10	7	$368 [7]
C-More	Tactical	-	Yes	1X	6MOA	Y	Long guns	7	12	$444 [8]

[1] Standard switch. Heads-up display. Integral mount.
[2] Click switch. Heads-up display. Integral mount.
[3] Click switch. Fits all Weaver and Picatinny-style rail mounts.
[4] Standard switch. Fits all Weaver and Picatinny-style rail mounts.
[5] Click switch. Mounts to any flat surface.
[6] Standard switch. Mounts to any flat surface.
[7] For Colt M-16, AR 15 and Match Target Rifles and Carbines. Mounts in rifle's carry handle.
[8] For Colt M-16, AR 15 and Match Target Rifles and Carbines. Mounts on flat-top receiver, replacing rifle's carry handle.

Osprey
Mini Osprey 3.5X42mm

Millett
AK47 MAK-90

Trijicon
CA01

Simmons
30mm & 42mm

Red-Dot, Holosight, and Laser Sights

Manufacturer	Model	Tube Dia (mm)	Water-proof	Magni-fication	Dot	Brightness Adjust (y/n)	Long guns or Handguns	Length (in)	Weight (oz)	Price (MSRP)
Millett	Red-dot SP1	1"	Yes	1X	3MOA	Y	Long guns, Handguns	5	4.5	$138 [1]
Millett	Red-dot SP1	1"	Yes	1X	3MOA	Y	Long guns, Handguns	5	4.5	$138 [2]
Millett	Red-dot SP2	30	Yes	1X	5MOA	Y	Long guns, Handguns	5	4.6	$139 [1]
Millett	Red-dot SP2	30	Yes	1X	5MOA	Y	Long guns, Handguns	5	4.6	$139 [2]
Millett	MultiDot SP	30	Yes	1X	3,5,8,10MOA	Y	Long guns, Handguns	5	4.6	$206 [1]
Millett	MultiDot SP	30	Yes	1X	3,5,8,10MOA	Y	Long guns, Handguns	5	4.6	$206 [2]
Nikon	Monarch Dot	30	Yes	1X	6MOA	Y	Long guns, Handguns	3.1	6.4	$401 [1]
Nikon	Monarch Dot	30	Yes	1X	6MOA	Y	Long guns, Handguns	3.1	6.4	$401 [2]
Nikon	Monarch DOT VSD	30	Yes	1X	1,4,6,10MOA	Y	Long guns, Handguns	3.6	6.7	$461 [1]
Nikon	Monarch DOT VSD	30	Yes	1X	1,4,6,10MOA	Y	Long guns, Handguns	3.6	6.7	$461 [1]
Nikon	Monarch DOT VSD	30	Yes	1X	1,4,6,10MOA	Y	Long guns, Handguns	3.6	6.7	$491 [3]

[1.] Black matte finish.
[2.] Silver finish.
[3.] Team finish.

Millett
RD00006 & RD00906, MultiDot SP 30mm 3, 5, 8,10MOA, Matte/Silver
RD00004 & RD00904, SP1 1in. Compact 3MOA, Matte/Silver
RD00005 & RD00905, SP2 30mm 5MOA, Matte/Silver

Red-Dot, Holosight, and Laser Sights

Manufacturer	Model	Tube dia (mm)	Water-proof	Magni-fication	Dot	Brightness Adjust (y/n)	Long guns or Handguns	Length (in)	Weight (oz)	Price (MSRP)
Sightron	S33-4R	33	Yes	1X	2,4,8MOA	Y	Long guns, Handguns	4.2	5.4	$297 [1]
Sightron	S33-4RST	33	Yes	1X	2,4,8MOA	Y	Long guns, Handguns	4.2	5.4	$297 [2]
Tasco	Propoint PDP2	30	Yes	1X	5MOA	Y	Long guns, Handguns	5	5.5	$118 [1]
Tasco	Propoint PDP2	30	Yes	1X	5MOA	Y	Long guns, Handguns	5	5.5	$138 [3]
Tasco	Propoint PDP3CMP	33	Yes	1X	10MOA	Y	Long guns, Handguns	4.8	5.4	$158 [3]
Tasco	Propoint PDP3ST	30	Yes	1X	5MOA	Y	Long guns, Handguns	5	5.5	$144 [4]
Trijicon	Reflex I	-	Yes	1X	Various dot sizes, plus triangle reticle	Y	Long guns, Handguns	4.3	4.2	$350-$645 [5]
Trijicon	Reflex II	-	Yes	1X	Various dot sizes, plus triangle reticle	Y	Long guns, Handguns	4.3	4.2	$425-$645 [5]
Ultradot	Ultradot 30	30	Yes	1X	4MOA	Y	Long guns, Handguns	5.1	3.9	$149
Ultradot	Ultradot 24	NA	Yes	1X	4MOA	Y	Long guns, Handguns	5.1	3.9	$129
Ultradot	Ultradot 4 Dot	NA	Yes	1X	4 dot choices	Y	Long guns, Handguns	5.1	3.9	$179
Zeiss	2-point	NA	Yes	1X	Variable dot	Y	Long guns, Handguns	2.5	3.5	$450

[1] Black matte finish.
[2] Two-tone stainless finish.
[3] Black matte finish. Includes rings for dovetail bases, mirage hoods.
[4] Stainless finish. Includes rings for dovetail bases, mirage hoods.
[5] Price dependent on mount chosen.

Sightron
S33-4RST

Sightron
S33-4R

Zeiss
2-point on revolver

Zeiss
2-point on pistol

Trijicon
TX 30mm

Zeiss
2-point

Chapter 15
Lens Care and Maintenance

Most hunters pay little attention to caring for the lenses of their optical equipment. I am embarrassed to admit that my first binocular and riflescope were subjected to shameful treatment. When lenses were smudged, dirty, or obscured by rain, I would casually wipe them off with a handkerchief. If I had somehow ignored my mother's advice to "always carry a clean handkerchief," I would use my shirttail or anything else that was handy. I seldom worried about damaging the fragile coating found on the surfaces of the quality lenses.

When water, dirt, dust, or other debris obscure binocular or riflescope lenses, you will have a hard time seeing through them. A dirty lens makes for a foggy image, while cleaning its surface dramatically increases clarity. The trick is removing the debris without scratching the fragile coatings of the lens—or even the lens itself.

During manufacture, binocular and riflescope lenses are ground and polished to precise dimensions. Quality lenses are then coated with multiple, microscopically thin layers of magnesium fluoride or some similar substance. Applied to both outer and inner lens surfaces, this coating reduces unwanted reflections and greatly improves optical performance. A clean lens dramatically improves image clarity.

Lens coatings are made to be as durable as possible, but these coatings are still relatively fragile. (There is one exception to this, which I will mention later.) The microscopic film can be easily damaged through improper care. Rubbing a dirty lens—even gently—with an apparently clean cloth will grind tiny particles of debris into its surface. This can permanently damage the thin coating, and it may even scratch that costly, precisely ground glass lens. Even if your eye doesn't detect tiny scratches, they will reflect light away from the lens, which will diminish optical performance.

First, the brush end of the lens pen is used to brush away dust, dirt, or other debris carefully . . .

Note I said an *apparently* clean cloth. If you think that the handkerchief you have been carrying in your hip pocket the last several days is *clean*, think again. The minute your hand touches a handkerchief, it transmits oil to the cloth. Oil is a magnet for pocket debris. For the same reason, you should never touch the surface of any lens with your finger. A finger leaves a dab of oil that can smear and attract stray particles of dirt and other debris. When cleaning your rifle, take care to avoid getting gun oil on scope the other hand, do not use Windex or some other commercial window cleaner. These products contain chemicals that can damage lens coatings."

Commercial lens tissues—available at optical shops, drugstores, and some sporting-goods retailers—are best for removing cleaning fluid applied to the lens. When you lift the tissue from the lens, the tissue leaves a tiny bit of residue on the surface. The best way to remove this residue is to fog the lens surface with your breath and lightly wipe with another lens tissue or a cotton cloth that you *know* is clean.

Zeiss has recently introduced a lens care kit that includes spray bottles of specially formulated lens cleaner, lens cloths pre-moistened with this same cleaner, micro-fiber lens cloths, and special brushes designed for removing dirt and debris from lens surfaces. The pre-moistened cloths are available in individual, sealed-foil packs. I now carry a couple of these handy packs along whenever I am in the hunting field. The pre-moistened lens cloths and the spray solution are produced for Zeiss by a company called NanoFilm of Cleveland, Ohio.

Leupold, Nikon, and Burris offer special pen-size cleaning tools designed specifically for use on coated lenses. These compact "pens" feature a retractable, soft-hair brush at one end and a flexible cleaning pad at the other. The pad contains a nonliquid cleaning compound that isn't supposed to damage lens surfaces.

. . . then the lens pen is reversed. This end of the pen features a cleaning pad containing a nonliquid cleaning compound that's not supposed to damage lens surfaces.

lenses. The spray from aerosol cans can leave a thin, oily deposit you won't even know is there.

"When cleaning any scope or binocular lens, first blow on it," advises Burris's expert Pat Beckett. "Canned or compressed air is ideal for blowing away small particles, but your breath works, too. (Compressed air is readily available at photography shops.) Then use a clean brush designed specifically for this task to brush away dust and debris gently.

"Next, apply a suitable cleaning fluid. Pharmaceutical-grade acetone works very well, while rubbing alcohol is a good second choice," Beckett says. "Plain water is another option. On

Use the brush to gently clear dust, debris, or any foreign matter from the lens before touching it with the cleaning pad. Apply gentle pressure when you use the pad. Begin at the center of the lens, and, with a circular motion, work your way to the outer edge. This should remove fingerprints and smudges. Because the pads themselves may eventually acquire their own layer of grime, I would suggest replacing them after a season or so of use. They are inexpensive, so I usually keep several on hand. If a lens is particularly grimy, I prefer tackling the job with acetone or the special lens-cleaning liquid Zeiss offers.

Once a riflescope lens is clean, a see-through cover can protect it; however, you should make a

First use the brush to wipe away dust.

The other end of the pen has a cleaning pad containing a nonliquid cleaning compound.

Scope covers are a good idea during transport, but Rees doesn't bother using them when he's actually hunting.

note that the lower-quality glass in these covers will most definitely degrade the viewing image. I prefer good, quickly removable covers to keep lens surfaces clean during transport. When I am actually hunting, I almost never keep the lenses of my scope or binocular covered. When game is in sight, I don't want to bother with removing protective covers.

To keep your binoculars, scope sights, spotting scopes, and other optical gear in top shape and to protect those valuable investments, you need to treat their lenses with tender, loving care. Burris is currently the only company that offers riflescopes with lenses that happily withstand careless treatment.

A few years ago Burris developed a truly revolutionary T-Plate lens coating that creates an ultra-hard, supersmooth surface that resists—no, absolutely *defies*—scratching under any normal

circumstance. When Burris sent me one of these scopes to test, I was told to do my best to screw up the lens. I took Burris up on this challenge by scrubbing the lens with a gritty rag—then finally scratching it—*hard*—with the tip of a hunting knife. After giving the scope this kind of abuse, I could see no visible marks on the lens surface. T-Plate coating apparently shrugs off treatment that would permanently damage expensive lenses lacking this ultratough film. While no one should purposely abuse the lens of *any* sporting optic, Burris's T-Plate coating allows you to wipe oily smudges, grime, and even mud from the lens with a less-than-pristine cloth, the tail of your shirt, or anything that is handy!

T-Plate coating was first offered only on Burris's top-of-the-line Mr. T. Black Diamond 2.5–10X50 and 4–16X50 riflescopes. The bodies of these scopes are made of solid titanium that is molecularly bonded to an outer coating of ultratough, corrosion-proof aluminum titanium nitride. These 30mm tubes contain true, 30mm internal lenses that maximize light transmission, which is not always the case when you buy a 30mm riflescope. Combining a titanium body with costly T-Plate coated lenses is expensive, so these scopes are not cheap. Burris now offers this ultratough coating on two Black Diamond models with less costly aluminum tubes. At last look, the Mr. T Black Diamond scopes listed for around $1,800, while the aluminum-bodied Black Diamond scopes with T-Plating retailed for some $500 less. As I have noted throughout this book, a manufacturer's suggested retail price can be misleading because most retailers offer substantial discounts.

A good riflescope, binocular, or spotting scope represents a serious investment. With proper care and cleaning, these optical hunting tools can offer a lifetime of quality viewing.

Chapter 16
List of Manufacturers

Aimpoint, Inc.
3989 Hwy 62 West
Berryville, AR 72616
877-Aimpoint
www.aimpoint.com

AimShot
Osprey International Inc.
1575 Highway 411, Suite 107
Cartersville, GA 30121
770-387-2751
www.miniosprey.com

Aimtech Mount Systems
P.O. Box 223
Thomasville, GA 31799-0223
229-226-4313
www.aimtech-mounts.com

Alpen Spotting Scopes
10329 Dorset Street
Rancho Cucamonga, CA 91730
909-987-8370
www.alpenoutdoor.com

B-Square (An Armor Holdings Co.)
P.O. Box 11281
2708 St. Louis Avenue
Fort Worth, TX 76110
800-433-2909
www.b-square.com

BSA Spotting Scopes
3911 SW 47th Avenue, Suite 914
Fort Lauderdale, FL 33314
954-581-2144
www.bsaoptics.com

Brunton
620 East Monroe Avenue
Riverton, WY 82501 USA
307-856-6559
www.brunton.com

Burris Company, Inc.
331 East 8th Street
Greeley, CO 80631-9559
888-228-7747
www.burrisoptics.com

Bushnell Performance Optics
9200 Cody
Overland Park, KS 66214
800-423-3537
www.bushnell.com

C-More Systems
Shipping Address
7553 Gary Road
Manassas, VA 20109
888-265-8266
www.cmore.com

Conetrol
10225 Highway 123 South
Seguin, TX 78155
800-CONETROL
www.conetrol.com

Crimson Trace Lasers
8089 Southwest Cirrus Drive
Beaverton, OR 97008
800-442-2406
www.crimsontrace.com

Ironsighter Company
P.O. Box 85070
Westland, MI 48185
734-326-8731
www.ironsighter.com

Kahles
2 Slater Road
Cranston, RI 02920
866-606-8779
www.kahlesoptik.com

Laser Devices, Inc.
2 Harris Court, A-4
Monterey, CA 93940
800-235-2162
www.laserdevices.com

LaserLyte Sights
101 Airpark Road
Cottonwood, AZ 86326
928-649-3201
www.laserlytesights.com

LaserMax, Inc.
3495 Winton Place, Building B
Rochester, NY 14623
800-LASER-03
www.lasermax-inc.com

Leica
156 Ludlow Avenue
Northvale, NJ 07647
800-222-0118
www.leica-camera.com/usa

Leupold & Stevens, Inc.
P.O. Box 688
Beaverton, OR 97075
503-526-1400
www.leupold.com

Millett Sights
16131-K Gothard Street
Huntington Beach, CA 92647
800-MILLETT
www.millettsights.com

Minox
Minox Processing Laboratories
250 Meacham Ave.
Elmont, NY 11003-3208
516-437-5750
www.minoxlab.com

Nikon
1300 Walt Whitman Road
Melville, NY 11747-3064
800-645-6687
www.nikonusa.com

Pentax
16163 West 45th Drive, Unit H
Golden, CO 80403
800-877-0155
www.pentaxusa.com

Redfield Mounts
P.O. Box 39
Onalaska, WI 54650
800-635-7656, Tech Support 800-285-0689
www.atk.com

Remington
3300 W. 71st Avenue
Westminster, CO 80030
800-676-4868
www.remingtonoptics.com

S & K Scope Mounts
RD 2, Box 72 E
Sugar Grove, PA 16350-9201
800-578-9862
www.scopemounts.com

Shepherd
P.O. Box 189
Waterloo, NE 68069
402-779-2424
www.shepherdscopes.com

Simmons Outdoor Corporation
201 Plantation Oak Drive
Thomasville, GA 31792
800-285-0689
www.simmonsoptics.com

Steiner
Pioneer Research
97 Foster Road, Suite 5
Moorestown, NJ 08057
800-257-7742
www.steiner-binoculars.com

Swarovski
2 Slater Road
Cranston, RI 02920
401-734-1800
www.swarovskioptik.at

Swift Instruments, Inc.
952 Dorchester Avenue
Boston, MA 02125
800-446-1116
www.swift-optics.com

Talley Manufacturing, Inc.
P.O. Box 369
Santee, SC 29142
803-854-5700
www.talleyrings.com

Tasco
9200 Cody
Overland Park, KS 66214
800-423-3537
www.tasco.com

Thompson/Center
P.O. Box 5002
Rochester, NH 03866-5002
603-332-2333
www.tcams.com

Trijicon, Inc.
49385 Shafer Ave.
P.O. Box 930059
Wixom, MI 48393
248-960-7700
www.trijicon.com

Ultra Dot Distribution
6304 Riverside Drive
Yankeetown, FL 34498-0362
352-447-2255
www.ultradotusa.com

Warne Scope Mounts
9057 Southeast Jannsen Road
Clackamas, OR 97015
800-683-5590
www.warnescopemounts.com

Weaver (part of ATK)
201 Plantation Oak Drive
Thomasville, GA 31792
800-285-0689
www.weaveroptics.com

Wideview Scope Mounts
13535 South Highway 16
Rapid City, SD 57702-7401
605-341-3220
www.wideview.com

Carl Zeiss, Inc.
One Zeiss Drive
Thornwood, NY 10594
914-747-1800
www.zeiss.com

Optics Digest

Telescopic Sights

BSA
Burris
Bushnell
Docter
Kahles
Leupold
Millett
Nightforce
Nikon
Pentax
Redfield
Schmidt & Bender
Sightron
Simmons
Springfield Armory
Swarovski
Tasco
Thompson/Center
Weaver
Zeiss

Mounting Systems and Rings

Aimtech Mount Systems
B-Square (An Armor Holdings Co.)
Burris Company, Inc.
Conetrol
Ironsighter Company
Leupold & Stevens, Inc. (Leupold Mounting Systems)
Millett Sights
Redfield Mounts
S & K Scope Mounts
Talley Manufacturing, Inc.
Warne Scope Mounts
Weaver
Wideview Scope Mounts

Binoculars

Alpen Outdoor
BSA
Bausch & Lomb
Brunton
Burris

Bushnell
Kahles
Leica
Leupold
Minox
Nikon
Pentax
Redfield
Remington
Shepherd
Sightron
Simmons
Steiner
Swarovski
Tasco
Weaver
Zeiss

Spotting Scopes

Alpen
BSA
Burris
Bushnell/Bausch & Lomb
Leica
Leupold
Nikon
Pentax
Redfield
Remington
Shepherd
Sightron
Simmons
Swarovski
Tasco
Weaver
Zeiss

Laser Rangefinders

AimShot Osprey International Inc.
Bushnell Performance Optics
Leica
Leupold & Stevens, Inc.
Nikon

Red-Dot Sights, Holosights, and Laser Sights

Aimpoint, Inc.

AimShot, Osprey International, Inc.

Burris Company

Bushnell Performance Optics

C-More Systems

Crimson Trace Lasers

Laser Devices, Inc.

LaserLyte

LaserMax, Inc.

Millett Sights

Nikon

Sightron, Inc.

Tasco

Trijicon, Inc.

Ultra Dot Distribution